Fathers and Adolescents

1999

The understanding and ... as traditionally assumed that fathers, compared to ... ... involved with their children. *Fathers and Adolescents* ... a different approach that focuses on the distinctive role of fathers in the lives of their adolescents, especially their role in adolescents' ... ... ent of developmental tasks.

Drawing on a variety of theories, Shmuel Shulman and Inge Seiffge-Krenke examine the relationship of fathers to their adolescents in the context of a changing society. They find that fathers interact in ways that are different from those of mothers, but that are important for both normal and disturbed adolescent development. Psychopathological, aggressive and incestuous behaviour is considered as well as the role of the father in more ideal circumstances.

Drawing on the authors' wealth of clinical experience, *Fathers and Adolescents* is an important resource for all professionals working with adolescents, as well as those in research.

Shmuel Shulman is Associate Professor of Psychology and Head of Program in Clinical Psychology at Bar-Ilan University, Israel. Professor **Inge Seiffge-Krenke** is Senior Lecturer in Developmental Psychology at the University of Bonn, Germany. Her previous publications include *Stress, Coping and Relationships in Adolescence* (1995).

Adolescence and Society

Series editor: John C. Coleman
The Trust for the Study of Adolescence

The general aim of the series is to make accessible to a wide readership the growing evidence relating to adolescent development. Much of this material is published in relatively inaccessible professional journals, and the goals of the books in this series will be to summarize, review and place in context current work in the field so as to interest and engage both an undergraduate and a professional audience.

The intention of the authors is to raise the profile of adolescent studies among professionals and in institutions of higher education. By publishing relatively short, readable books on interesting topics to do with youth and society, the series will make people more aware of the relevance of the subject of adolescence to a wide range of social concerns.

The books will not put forward any one theoretical viewpoint. The authors will outline the most prominent theories in the field and will include a balanced and critical assessment of each of these. Whilst some of the books may have a clinical or applied slant, the majority will concentrate on normal development.

The readership will rest primarily in two major areas: the undergraduate market, particularly in the fields of psychology, sociology and education; and the professional training market, with particular emphasis on social work, clinical and educational psychology, counselling, youth work, nursing and teacher training.

Also available in this series

Fathers and Adolescents

Developmental and clinical perspectives

Shmuel Shulman and
Inge Seiffge-Krenke

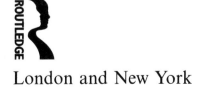

London and New York

First published 1997
by Routledge
11 New Fetter Lane, London EC4P 4EE

Simultaneously published in the USA and Canada
by Routledge
29 West 35th Street, New York, NY 10001

© 1997 Shmuel Shulman and Inge Seiffge-Krenke

Typeset in Times by Routledge
Printed and bound in Great Britain by
T. J. Press (Padstow) Ltd., Padstow, Cornwall.

British Library Cataloguing in Publication Data
A catalogue record for this book is available from the British Library

Library of Congress Cataloguing in Publication Data
Shulman, Shmuel.
Fathers and adolescents: developmental and clinical perspectives/Shmuel
Shulman and Inge Seiffge-Krenke.
(Adolescence and society)
Includes bibliographical references and index.
1. Parent and teenager. 2. Father and child. 3. Adolescence. 4. Adolescent
psychology. 5. Fathers. I. Seiffge-Krenke, Inge. II. Title. III. Series.
HQ799.15.S57   1996
306.874'2–dc20   96–16341
                                                                           CIP

ISBN 0–415–11791–7 (hbk)
ISBN 0–415–11792–5 (pbk)

To Chava and Dirk, and to
Leetal and Osnat, adolescents in the past
Shani and David, adolescents in the present
and our adolescent in the coming years – Moritz

Contents

Illustrations

Preface

In the past two decades a growing interest in the role of fathers in the development of their children has become evident. A majority of the studies on the topic were conducted on younger children, and originated from a deficit model which claims that fathers as compared to mothers are less likely to be involved in the lives of their children. However, father–adolescent relationships unexpectedly remained a rather "neglected" area of research, and were not dealt with until very recently.

Historically, adolescence has been portrayed as a period of turmoil. Adolescents were described as striving towards separation from the family, and establishing their independence. Terms such as "storm and stress" and "the generation gap" reflected the negative effect of the growing distance between parents and adolescents. More recently, research has demonstrated that parent–adolescent relationships do not necessarily have to be tumultuous and negative. On the contrary, parents continue to be an important source of support in the process of their children establishing a separate identity. Following the growing interest in the role of fathers in child development, we felt the necessity of a comprehensive exploration of the father–adolescent relationship. It is not only the concept of adolescence that is evolving and being transformed. The functions and roles of fathers have also changed dramatically over recent years and across cultures, as the roles of women evolve towards greater economic independence. These growing major changes offer the possibility of a new quality of relationship between fathers and their adolescents.

The unavoidable link between these two changes has not yet been acknowledged. Our own experience as researchers in adolescent development, as illustrated in several studies, indicates that fathers contribute significantly to adolescent adaptation. In addition, as clinicians working with troubled adolescents we realized, both in cases of psychopathology and in the course of therapy, that fathers are not peripheral figures. We felt that, taken together the nature of relations between fathers and their adolescents deserves a more elaborate exploration than has been undertaken in the past.

In this book we have tried to delineate the different approaches and conceptualizations regarding father–adolescent relationships in psychology and psychoanalysis. In addition, approaches from sociology, anthropology and ethology were incorporated, and together they serve as a framework for this book. Our goal was to highlight the distinctive role that fathers play in the various domains of adolescent development and adaptation, covering various aspects of the father–adolescent relationship.

In the first chapter we explore both the historical and the changing role of fathers in the development of their children, with a review of the role of fathers among mammals and its evolution in human society. The reflections of these trends in psychoanalytic thought and psychological research are further presented, and the question of the role fathers can fill in modern society is discussed. The next two chapters deal with the relationship between fathers and their adolescent offspring. The role of the father in the separation–individuation process of the adolescent is discussed in Chapter 2, whereas Chapter 3 deals more specifically with the role fathers play in the attainment of developmental tasks. Chapters 4 and 5 address the distinctive nature of the relationships that fathers have with their maturing sons and daughters. In these two chapters, paternal attitudes towards their male and female children are integrated with broader perceptions of sons and daughters, as evident in historical and cultural contexts. Overall, fathers are described as interacting with their adolescents in a different mode from mothers. Fathers are generally less engaged, but it is suggested that they serve both as models and support for adolescent individuation.

Chapters 6 and 7 deal with issues related to the major changes that families are undergoing in our era. Chapter 6 discusses the relationships of custodial and non-custodial fathers with their adolescents, emphasizing the potential risk of a too close or too distant father. Chapter 7 addresses the issue of stepfathers and their adolescent stepchildren. The additional four chapters address relationships under non-optimal conditions. Chapter 8 discusses the specific conditions of fathers whose adolescents are chronically ill. Chapter 9 focuses on the role of fathers in adolescent psychopathology, as reflected in research and as understood from dynamic and systemic perspectives. Chapter 10 deals with issues of aggression, both the aggression of fathers towards their children and the role of fathers in the development of their children's aggressive behavior. Chapter 11 deals more specifically with the issue of incest, pointing to the dynamics related to father–daughter and father–son incest, and to the longstanding effects of incest on subsequent development.

Throughout the book, the distinctive role of the father in adolescent development and adaptation is discussed and emphasized. However, the majority of fathers are in fact less involved than mothers with their children. The concluding chapter discusses the psychological and family-systemic reasons why fathers' parenting behavior continues to be different from that of mothers. In addition, the chapter explores the lifelong dialectic of fathers concerning how close or how distant they should be towards their adolescents and families, and its possible developmental adaptive function.

Acknowledgments

The seeds of the ideas expressed in this book were planted by our research and sometimes more importantly by our patients, both in Israel and in Germany, to whom we are grateful. Discussions with several colleagues helped us to deliberate these ideas. We are particularly grateful to Andy Collins, with whom a research volume was edited. John Coleman, editor of the Adolescence and Society Series, was kind enough to offer an outlet for this conceptualization of adolescents and their fathers. Vivien Ward, senior psychology editor at Routledge, was helpful, encouraging and more than kind: for this we are very grateful. The DAAD (Deutsche Akademische Austausch-dienst) supported Shmuel Shulman's visit to Germany which allowed us to work together during the summer of 1993. The DFG (Deutsche Forschungsgemeinschaft), together with the Israeli Ministry for Sciences and Art, supported Inge Seiffge-Krenke's trip to Israel in May 1994. Additional support was received from Research Authority of Bar-llan University. Special thanks are due to Jane Janser who competently typed the various versions of this manuscript, and to Linda Lewis and Avi Pankover who did a great job editing some of the chapters. Finally, we are grateful to our families who supported this work, and who enrich our understanding of parents and adolescents.

1   Fatherhood

As recently as 1975, fathers were labeled the "forgotten contributors to child development" (Lamb, 1975), but that appellation is no longer true. Starting with ethological, historical and psychoanalytic perspectives this chapter presents a variety of ideas and studies that focus on fathers; their roles, their thoughts, their behaviors and contributions to child development. Psychological researchers are increasingly concerned with processes of development beyond those of the mother–child dyad. As a result, research on fathers, which in the past was limited to the study of father absence, now includes many direct investigations of fathers' attitudes and behaviors. The proposition addressed in this chapter is that the father, as well as the mother, is a significant figure in the child's social world, and adds a distinctive quality to child development. This approach, however, can only be supported by recent research because until very recently several barriers hindered the investigation of father–child relationships.

According to Pederson (1980) several factors interfered with the consideration of fathers as significant figures in the child's world. First, stereotypical perceptions of family roles led to an extreme differentiation in parental roles and a sharp division between the home and the workplace (Aries, 1962). The traditional nuclear family, as it evolved in Western industrialized societies, assigned the primacy of the economic provider role to the husband/father and the childcare and homemaker role to the wife/mother. This differentiation is embraced most explicitly in Parsons and Bales' (1955) theory, which characterizes the male role as primarily instrumental in nature, oriented to the external world and responsible for the social and economic position of the family. The female role, in contrast, is oriented towards the home and is primarily expressive in nature. The wife/mother is responsible for the emotional and affective climate in the home, and for the raising of children. The father was perceived as peripheral to his children's upbringing. The role of the father as portrayed by sociologists resonated in the type of research conducted in developmental psychology. Accordingly, most research focused on the study of the mother–child dyad. The focus on the mother is also reflected by psychoanalytic thinkers such as Melanie Klein and Margaret Mahler. Even in Freudian theory the father was perceived as peripheral up until the oedipal period.

This chapter will thus review and explore the role of fathers as found in ethology, as described throughout history, and as presented in various psychoanalytic approaches. In addition, more recent conceptions of fatherhood portrayed in psychological research will be presented. Finally, the chapter will discuss possible roles for fathers to play in the development of their children.

THE FATHER'S ROLE AMONG MAMMALS

In a recent provocative paper Kraemer (1991) raised the possibility that fatherhood is a human invention. Based on anthropological studies, Kraemer suggests that while living as nomads, female humans could fill all their needs without male help. While living on food that can be easily gathered such as fruits, eggs or honey, the male's presence could be advantageous, but it was not critical for the survival of females and infants. Observation of animals, and especially of mammals who most resemble humans in the prolonged caretaking of their offspring, suggests that males are not active partners in family life. Only 3 per cent of mammals live together as permanent couples; among them only a small percentage is monogamous (Bischof, 1985). In these few instances fathers may share responsibilities with mothers in regular caretaking activities. Only among the marmosets, tiny monkeys, who usually deliver twins, does the male parent take more than half of the share of infant care. In captivity, marmoset males were observed to be the preferred parent when the infant was frightened (Vogt, 1984). In the other cases where males were observed to be actively involved in caretaking of the young, the major share of the task was usually performed by the female, and the male's primary function was to protect the mother and offspring.

In her seminal work Goodall (1984) described chimpanzee males as not involved with the younger generation. Chimpanzees tend to live in bands consisting of mothers and children only. Males express interest in the females only when they are in estrus, the rest of the time males tend to live separately in bands of their own. A female may mate with a few males, and therefore the father's identity is unknown.

A third model is found among wolves, where the mother is the primary caretaking figure. She licks, snoops, cleans the excrement, and carries the young cubs. The males rarely carry the young and are minimally engaged with them (Zimen, 1971). The male role is rather to be close to the mother and offspring to protect them from unexpected predators. Among the savanna baboons and black howler monkeys, infants do develop close relationships with males. The adult males may hold, cuddle and groom infants (Whitten, 1986). However, even in these few examples where male mammals were observed to be involved in the caretaking of the young, their role was secondary to that of the mother, with the mother having the primary responsibility for the welfare of the offspring. The more common interaction between female–children groups and male groups is restricted to the reproductive process and to the transfer of younger males to the adult male group.

Though mammals are different from humans, Goodall (1986) claimed that "a better understanding of the adaptation of chimpanzee behavior... can provide insights into the shaping of our own behavior during evolution" (ibid.: 3). For example, among the Aka pygmies – still hunter-gatherer societies – the father's position in relation to the offspring is very peripheral to that of the mother (Hewlett, 1987). A similar pattern of fatherhood can still be seen in many societies. Until very recently, fathers were not supposed to attend to their wives during labor. The newborn and the mother stayed apart from male society, and fathers could observe their newborns through a window. In some cultures the mother and infant stay close to one another for as long as the infant is breastfed, and the father sleeps in a separate room. This sleeping arrangement can last until the child reaches the age of 3 or 4. Thus, the prevalent pattern among mammals and in so-called "primitive" societies is mother–children groups, with fathers either living separately or filling a very peripheral role. At most the father is considered a "secondary attachment figure" (Bowlby, 1969).

DEVELOPMENT OF THE FATHER ROLE IN HUMAN SOCIETIES

Kraemer (1991) claims that the transition to agricultural life patterns and the domestication of animals required a more organized societal life. Food acquisition required more labor in the fields and in herding of animals. More labor meant more working hands, and therefore women were more in demand to produce babies. However, the men who gained control perceived the agricultural products, livestock, women and their offspring as their property. At that stage the husband owned his wife's and children's services, and had the sole right to collect wages for their work outside the home. He owned his wife's personal property outright, and had the right to manage and control all of his wife's real property during marriage, which included to use or lease property, and to keep any rents and profits from it.

(Babcock *et al.*, 1975)

As a result of this process, men not only gained control, but the concept of patriarchy emerged. Millennia later, the seventeenth-century social, economic and religious reformations strengthened the father's control over his household. Several powers that were formerly in the hands of religious leaders or royal rulers were transferred to the nuclear family headed by the father. Fathers were not only responsible for providing for and protecting their families, they also gained moral and religious authority. Fathers read the Bible and preached to their family members (Schorsch, 1979). They were perceived as responsible for the education of their children, especially their sons. According to the Jewish Halachic law, it is the father's responsibility to educate his son from the time the child can speak. If the father is uneducated, he is responsible for hiring a teacher. Rousseau emphasized men's roles as the educators of the next generation, while mothers were responsible for taking care of their children.

Thus, historical changes that reduced the power of kings and priests, increased the father's power as protector of his family, and his legal supremacy was consolidated. Moreover, the father was the head of the household, although the wife, who worked with her husband on the farm, also helped provide for the family. The industrial revolution strengthened the dichotomy of roles that husband and wife held in the family. Men were expected to be the breadwinners, and "good provider" became a synonym for masculinity (Bernard, 1981). Men stayed for long hours at the workplace and rarely saw their children, let alone took care of them. Women, in contrast, usually stayed at home and were responsible for childcare. A woman's value was based on her success as homemaker and as a mother caring for her children.

World War II, followed by technological and economic development, has led a growing number of women to join the workforce. More mothers are employed and are unable to take care of their children to the same extent as in the past. Moreover, in recent years, growing numbers of dual-career marriages can be found. The father cannot be considered the sole provider, when family income is dependent on the wife's earning as well. However, in the majority of households the historical division of male–female responsibilities for taking care of children has not undergone a major change. Analysis of division of time and activities of working mothers and fathers in the communist, supposedly egalitarian, societies in East Germany and the Soviet Union showed impressively that although wives were not dependent on their husbands for their livelihood, they continued to perform the traditional mother role exclusively. Mothers spent more than four times as much time with their children as the fathers did. Even unemployed fathers did not invest in their children more of the free time that was available to them (Jahoda, 1982).

In very recent years there have been some changes in this pattern and fathers are described as more involved in the household, and in childrearing behavior. An indication of this change can be found in childbirth practices (Fine, 1976). Labor and delivery now occur more frequently in the presence of the father. It is interesting to note that many fathers who participated in the delivery of their child recalled it as a positive experience. However, although men have been described as expressing a greater interest in the lives of their children, even in dual-earning and unemployed families fathers and mothers tend to stick to the distinctive historical roles; mothers are highly involved and fathers tend to be less engaged. Usually the mother is the primary caretaker of the children, and the father, less engaged with them, is perceived as a distant yet important figure in the family. It may be suggested that fathers have not yet learned the new egalitarian role, or that mothers, although they work outside of home, are unwilling to give up their traditional role (Berman and Pederson, 1987). It is interesting to see that the dichotomous parenting behavior found in mammals, and throughout the history of mankind, is still extant at the end of this century. Only when mothers are absent do fathers turn into the primary caregiver, as vividly portrayed by Dustin Hoffman in the film *Kramer vs. Kramer.*

THE FATHER ROLE AS PORTRAYED IN PSYCHOANALYTIC THEORIES

Interestingly, similar concepts of fatherhood can be traced both in the development of psychoanalytic approaches and in psychological research. Perception of the father as a distant figure, yet a powerful one, in the development of his children is found in the major streams of psychoanalytic and neoanalytic thought. According to the Freudian theory the father is introduced only when the child is around the age of 3, when the oedipal issues arise. Until then, the mother and the infant were described as one unit, as we see among mammals, less developed societies, and sometimes in the lower classes. Mother and infant sleep together, separated from the father. When the time for reproduction of a new offspring is ripe, the infant is supposed to be weaned from its dependence on the mother. Goodall (1984) describes how chimpanzee infants try to interfere with the male who mates with their mother. Males on such occasions can be aggressive toward the young ones. The father is then the figure whose overtures toward the mother are perceived as a threat to the affectionate close relationship that exists between mother and infant.

The frightening encounter between the child and the male "stranger" who is sexually interested in the mother recalls the constellation that Freud describes to be symbolically experienced by the 3-year-old in relation to the father. It also recalls the fantasies children have of an attacking father – the burglar under the bed – described by Melanie Klein. After birth the child is embedded in a harmonious and symbiotic relationship with the mother. Absence of the mother or disfulfillment of needs is compensated for short periods of time through hallucinatory wish fulfillment. At the early stage of life, as Freud describes, a dyadic relationship between mother and infant is consolidated. At this stage Freud did not explicitly mention the father. The first introduction of the father brings with it the transition into a triadic relationship. In addition, a qualitative change is also experienced: from a harmony and reciprocity in relation to the mother, to rivalry and competition in relation to the father. However, although the father is a powerful figure to whom the child has to submit, this constellation brings with it a change in the structure of internal representations. Through this process the male child is forced to identify with the father and use him as a model for superego development. The classical Freudian approach had delineated mainly the development of the boy. However, though it is more acceptable for the girl to be like her mother, as recent feminist approaches claim, development for the girl is nevertheless no less complex than for the boy (Smith, 1994). At the pre-oedipal stage there is a strong sense of preliminary wholeness – represented by the bonding to the mother. The introduction of the father into the relationship induces a greater separation between mother and child (ibid.: 110).

Margaret Mahler and Melanie Klein introduce the father at an earlier stage than Freud does, but both point to the distinctive role of the father in the development of the child. According to Mahler (Mahler *et al.*, 1975) the father becomes more central for his child at the rapproachment stage. At this stage the toddler is torn between striving for independence and exploration, and realization of the need for parental help. Accepting help from the mother at this stage may arouse sensations of being engulfed by the mother and driven back to symbiosis. Resenting the mother's help is reflected in the rapprochment crisis. The toddler does not have any fear that the father will lead the child into a symbiotic relationship, since a symbiosis never existed between father and child. Furthermore, fathers are more tolerant of children's explorations. For this reason, Mahler claims, during the rapproachment stage, toddlers prefer their fathers to their mothers.

Although Melanie Klein (1946) does not emphasize the role of the father, she also points to the father's distinctive role. From the early stages of life, in the depressive position, the infant becomes aware that someone else occasionally takes away the "good object." The father-object comes between the infant and the breast. In addition, the father-object interferes with the illusion of mother–child unity and completeness. For the first time the infant is exposed to a triadic relationship and learns that its relationship with the mother cannot be exclusive. In addition, in his behavior the father shows that aggression and firmness toward an object do not necessarily lead to destruction of that object, and can coexist with love and tenderness. Klein suggests that by being exposed to a close and caring relationship between father and mother, despite the fact that the mother invests more time in the infant than in the father, the child can introject a positive attitude toward the mother and the wish to destroy the mother is subdued.

A more elaborated role of the father is described by the French psychoanalyst, Lacan (1977). According to Lacan, in the beginning the infant has an imaginary sense of completeness with the mother. From the mother's perspective, bearing the child is significant since it serves as a substitute for the penis of which she is deprived. Later on the total union between infant and mother is ruptured and a new quality of relationship is developed. For example, in the peek-a-boo game of disappearance and return, the absent mother is experienced as present through the phonemes of inchoate speech (Richardson, 1983). The wish for the mother is no longer a "bodily need" but rather a represented "human desire" similar to the adult's experience of "want." In the experience of "want" the infant wishes to recapture lost paradise by being the desired of its mother, her fullness. In Lacan's terms the infant wishes yet again to be the mother's symbol of omnipotence, by being the phallus for its mother. However, at this stage the father is already there, representing the world and its rules. The "law of the father" (intellect, social order, speech) represents the symbolic structure of societal relationships and hence the father regulates the infant's relation to its mother. It is then that the father and what he represents – the "Name of the Father" – transfers the infant from an innate relationship with the mother to a relationship shaped by cultural limits and norms.

It should be noted that the division between the close and involved yet less powerful mother, versus the remote and powerful father, presented in Freudian and neo-Freudian theories, rather reflects the distinctive perception of males and females developed in society throughout the centuries. Nevertheless, we also find images of the powerful mother (Moorjani, 1994). From the child's perspective the mother is powerful and sexually complete. Moreover, fantasies about the lost breast could be as strong as fantasies about the missing penis. Examples from culture show that "Phallic goddesses are only one instance of a recurrent iconography of the mother" (ibid.: 23). Therefore it would probably be more accurate to claim, in line with psychoanalytic thought, that mothers and fathers carry with them a distinctive contribution to the process of development.

Each of the psychoanalytic schools, however, emphasizes a different component in the father's contribution to the development of his child. The English school mainly perceives the father as a non-symbiotic figure thus facilitating the separation process between mother and infant. Freudian theory rather emphasizes the father's contribution to development of appropriate sexual identity, and as a model for identification with societal rules. The French school more specifically sees the father as the figure who emphasizes and supports the development of non-emotional aspects such as language and intellect. In addition, the different theories introduce the father into the life of his child at different stages. Melanie Klein describes the father as coming between the infant and the breast, which can be assumed to take place at a quite early phase of development. Mahler introduces the father around the practicing and rapprochment sub-stages, at about the age of 18 months. It is Freud who introduces the father at a later stage, when the child is sufficiently mature to perceive the father as a sexual rival.

Taken together, these three psychoanalytic approaches suggest that though the father may seem distant, he provides a distinctive contribution to the development of the child. Being part of a triadic relationship, fathers come between the breast/mother and the child. The father thus breaks the illusionary fusion between mother and infant. On the one hand, the father may be perceived as a threat and a source of frustration, but for the sake of optimal development he keeps the mother and child from becoming too close. By identifying with the father, the child imitates and later incorporates adult roles. The child also learns how sexual partners deal with one another, cope with disappointments, and share attention and affection in triadic and family constellations.

In contrast to psychoanalytic thinkers, scholars inclined towards ethological approaches not point to a specific role for the father. As suggested above, Bowlby (1969) refers to the father as a possible additional attachment figure. Usually the mother is described as the primary attachment figure, and no specific role for the father is outlined in this approach. Moreover, research originating from attachment theories tends to use the term "caregiver," thus omitting a conceptual discussion of the distinctiveness of fathers and mothers. Winnicott (1965), unlike Mahler and Klein, does not emphasize the father's contribution to a healthy separation between mother and child. Winnicott instead emphasizes the role of the inanimate transitional object (a blanket) which is under the child's control, as an important factor in the separation process between mother and child. However, although these more recent theories do not suggest a distinctive role for fathers and mothers in the development of their children, research originating from these theories may carry a different message. A review of a number of studies on father–child attachment patterns, though relatively few, suggests first that there is a tendency for mothers more than fathers to establish a secure attachment with their children (Belsky and Rovine, 1988; Chase-Lansdale and Owen, 1987). In addition, fathers' relationships with their children, not mothers' relationships, were a better predictor for later child relationships with friends (Youngsblade and Belsky, 1995).

FATHERHOOD IN PSYCHOLOGICAL RESEARCH

Psychological research also has not dealt widely with the role of the father in child development until the last two decades. A turning point might be the paper in which Lamb (1975) claimed that fathers are the "forgotten contributors to child development." Since then a growing interest in the roles fathers play in the development of their children can be seen in both research and theoretical articles (Lamb and Oppenheim, 1989).

Since the 1980s an increasing number of articles and publications describing the new emergent father can be found (R. A. Lewis, 1986). Men were described as breaking out of traditional socialization, and becoming more sensitive husbands and fathers. For example, in a study reported in a women's magazine on the responses of some 74,000 women readers, men were clearly portrayed as undergoing a major change in their attitudes towards their families (Enos and Enos, 1985). Sixty-two per cent of women over 40, and 84 per cent of women under 40, thought that men are just as good at childcare as women are. Enos and Enos concluded that "Indeed, in the last twenty years, men and women have crossed once impenetrable boundaries into each other's territory" (ibid.: 183). Moreover, R. A. Lewis (1986) observed in his clinical practice a number of men who were thrilled with their personal developments in nurturing their children. These fathers were as skillful and loving as mothers were. Lewis even suggested that those men were learning how sweet the taste of "generativity" is as described by Erickson, as they learned to give more of their time and resources to others (ibid.: 3). With such attention being paid to the changing role of fathers, researchers began to quantify the new concept of fatherhood. Studies on father–child and mother–child relationships dealt with the frequency and content of interactions. Pleck (1983) found in a study conducted on a US sample that the degree of paternal involvement in two-parent families in which mothers are not employed was about 20 per cent to 25 per cent of the time mothers were engaged with their children. Australian mothers reported that they were available to their children 54.7 hours per week, compared to 34.6 hours per week for fathers. In a Swedish sample of families where the mother was employed, paternal level of involvement was not significantly higher (Lamb *et al.*, 1988). Similarly, when information was collected from the children, 15- to 16-year-olds reported that they spent more than twice as much time with the mother alone as with the father alone each day (Montemayor, 1982). Furthermore, when fathers are present as well, they spend less time engaged in actual interaction with their offspring than mothers do. Observation of mothers and fathers interacting with their infants showed that mothers tended to respond, stimulate, express positive affection and provide basic care, more than fathers do (Belsky *et al.*, 1984). In Israel, Greenbaum and Landau (1982) found that mothers greatly exceeded fathers in the number of verbal interactions they had with their infants. Thus, findings from different cultures consistently show that fathers spend less time and are less engaged with their children as compared to mothers.

Regarding the content of parent–child relationships, there are two components of relationships relevant to our discussion: *interactions*: nature and structure; and *affect*: degree of positive affect during interaction and feelings of closeness (Collins and Russell, 1991).

Inspection of parent–child interactions showed that fathers were observed to engage in different types of interaction with their young children compared to mothers (Lamb, 1981; Yogman, 1982). Mothers' interactions with their children were dominated by caregiving activities like feeding. Fathers acted more as playmates with their children. Even when engaged in a clear caretaking activity such as feeding, fathers might perform it in a playful manner. Parke and Sawin (1980) noticed the difference between mother–child and father–child interaction from the first days of the infant's life. In their study they observed the way mothers and fathers interact with their infant during early post-partum days in the hospital, at the age of 3 weeks at home, and at the age of 3 months at home. Both parents were observed to show similar levels of affection in the forms of kissing and smiling. As reported in other studies mothers spent more time in routine caregiving tasks such as feeding and changing diapers, whereas fathers more frequently showed visual stimulation in the form of mimicking the infant's facial expression, reflecting some form of social stimulation. These differences between fathers and mothers were consistent over the three points of observation. Fathers more frequently than mothers also jiggled or rattled a toy for their infants to hear, although this difference decreased over time. At the age of 3 months mothers and fathers provided almost similar amounts of auditory stimulation.

The distinctions between mother–child and father–child interactions were found also with older children. Fathers of 6- to 7-year-olds were more involved in physical/outdoor activities with their children, where mothers' interaction with their children mainly involved caregiving and household tasks (Russell and Russell, 1987). Moreover, even when mothers played with their children, the nature of their play was different from that of fathers. Lamb (1980) compared play behavior of mothers and fathers with their infants. In the study, various forms of play such as conventional play, physical play such as rough-and-tumble or tickling games, and toy-mediated games between fathers, mothers and their children were observed, as well as who had initiated the game. Comparisons showed that mothers were more involved in conventional play and in toy-mediated play. Fathers were more involved in physical play, and their play was more idiosyncratic. In addition, infants' responses to father-initiated play were more positive than to that initiated by mothers.

Additional differences between mothers and fathers emerged when child-rearing practices relating to achievement and mastery were compared. Mothers showed a greater tendency to direct and supervise their child in daily behaviors such as having a bath or eating a meal. Fathers were found to be less directive than mothers (Russell and Russell, 1987). However, when mothers' and fathers' involvement in cognitive and achievement-oriented interactions were compared during middle childhood, no consistent differences emerged. Russell and Russell (1987) did not find differences in maternal and paternal initiations of competitiveness or in their support of the child's competitive and achievement-oriented activities. Both parents were also found to be similarly involved in the child's school-related activities (Roberts *et al.*, 1984).

The degree of perceived and experienced positive or negative effect in an interaction is an indicator of the quality of the relationship between parent and child (Doane, 1978). Russell and Russell (1987) found that mother–child interactions compared to those between father and child were characterized by more positive parental reactions. However, when together, father–child dyads showed more physical affection, friendly affect, and more playful behavior than mother–child dyads. In addition, fathers were found to display warmer and more egalitarian behavior when with their children (Youniss and Smollar, 1985). Nevertheless, in Mexican-American culture, the father may be affectionate to his young children, but later on the mother is the partner who is loved and adored, where the father is feared and obeyed (Bronstein and Cowan, 1988). Children do not even feel comfortable enough to laugh and joke in front of their fathers.

Overall, in interactions involving social issues, issues of achievement or performance, fathers are not likely to act differently from mothers. Fathers also have close and warm relationships with their children (Collins and Russell, 1991). However, fathers' interactions with their offspring are shorter in duration and are more exclusively associated with specific tasks like play and leisure activities. Furthermore, when fathers were engaged with their children, the responsibility for the caretaking of the child remained the mother's (Lamb, 1987). In sum, fathers are consistently less involved with their children in comparison to mothers. In addition, when fathers interact with their children, the nature and type of interaction differs from that of mothers' interactions.

WHAT ROLE SHOULD FATHERS PLAY IN THEIR CHILDREN'S LIVES?

The following dialectic in the nature of father–child relationships has probably contributed to the stereotypical conception of fathers. On the one hand, fathers are perceived to possess the skills that will enable them to be "good mothers," on the other hand they are observed to interact more with their children in enjoyable tasks and to shed responsibility. In a review of the father image in the American popular media, Mackey (1985) found the image to range from neutrality to a negative connotation: unavailable, aloof, inadequate, incompetent and fumbling. Komarovsky (1976) accused men of cultivating incompetence in the home sphere. Hochchild (1979) implied that men are conducting a deliberate scam in order to encourage their wives to do most of the work with their children. Interestingly, such an image exists even though fathers provide normative contact time with their children. This conception of fathers probably led to the following exhortation:

> Rather than sit by the sidelines or serve as mothers' helpers, men are being urged to participate in the lives of their children, from conception on. And, apparently, increasing numbers of men are reaching out for more sustaining relationships with the young in their lives....
>
> What I am calling the *emergent* perspective on fathering proceeds from the notion that men are psychologically able to participate in a full range of parenting behaviors and, furthermore, that it may be good both for parents and children if men take active roles in child care and child-rearing.
>
> (Fein, 1978: 122, 127)

The conception underlining this call reflects the emphasis on and expectation for *similarity* between mothers and fathers. Therefore, it was reasonable to suggest and expect that fathers be educated to act as competent caregivers similar to mothers. Furthermore, it has been shown that in the neonatal period, there are no differences in level of competence between mothers and fathers (Parke and Tinsley, 1981). Belsky *et al.* (1984) showed that over the course of the child's first year *both* mothers and fathers adapted to their infant's development and demonstrated competence and sensitivity. However, as cited above (Yogman, 1982), when fathers were observed to interact in obvious caretaking activities such as feeding, they did so in a different mode from mothers. The interaction was of a more playful nature, even though it was aimed at a clear task such as feeding.

In sum, in the studies of father–child relationships two major trends can be detected. One trend of research deals mainly with the similarities or expected similarities between maternal and paternal behaviors. The second points to the distinctive nature of father–child as opposed to mother–child interactions.

It is interesting to find that this dialectic of the nature of father–child relationships can be found in less developed societies, and has probably been carried over into current thought. Broude (1988) examined the meaning of couvade in anthropological literature. The term "couvade" is used to refer to a variety of customs applying to the behavior of fathers during their wife's pregnancy, during labor, and shortly after the birth of the child. In the classical form of couvade the father is taken to bed during or after the confinement of his wife and is expected to exhibit pain, exhaustion, and other symptoms typical of women during labor and the post-partum period. In addition, sets of prohibitions and activities are prescribed to the expectant or new father. For example, the new father may not hunt certain animals, eat certain foods, cut any objects, or engage in extramarital sex, and so on. Munroe *et al.* (1973) speculate that the couvade behavior represents an impulse on the part of men to imitate birth-related practices of women. They suggest that when children are raised exclusively by their mothers, boys might also identify with the female role, and identification is allowed an outlet through couvade behavior. A similar dynamic is found in male matric fetishism where a male wishes for a matrix-womb in order to be able to bear a child (Moorjani, 1994). Further inspection of the frequency of couvade across various societies reveals an interesting finding. Broude classified 34 societies into two groups according to level of "masculine protest." Masculine protest refers to indices of hypermasculinity such as boasting, pugnacity, pursuit of military glory, and narcissism. In all of the 14 societies low on masculine protest, couvade was present. In 16 out of 20 societies high on masculine protest couvade was absent. Thus, two approaches to fatherhood are exemplified in the presence or absence of couvade behavior. Fathers are either hypermasculine and less engaged in child-related matters, or they are also identified with the female, and active in matters related to the birth and well-being of their children.

The plenary addresses of the American Association of Marital and Family Therapy Annual Conference in 1989 also dealt with this dichotomy. Augustus Napier (1991) suggested that combining men and marriage is not at all simple. Archetypical men "after all defy dragons, raise the flag on Iwo Jima, scale Mt Everest, walk the moon, hit a home run for the Mets one week and score a touchdown for the Falcons the next." These "conquests are in the great Out There, far from the humdrum concerns of marriage and of the family" (Napier, 1991: 9). In addition, Napier claimed, since men are being raised by unavailable fathers, it is difficult for them to be emotionally giving and nurturant, and they are therefore self-focused. Napier concluded that "Overcoming our narcissism may be the primary challenge for the new male ideal" (ibid.: 14), and by cultivating traditional feminine traits, fathers will be able to make deeper commitments to their families and become more involved with their children.

Doherty (1991) criticized this dualistic approach to fatherhood as a deficit model, which "sees primarily the dark side of manhood and masculinity, our propensity for aggression, our emotional distancing, our overcompetitiveness" (Doherty 1991: 30). Doherty claims that men care for their family and their children in a different way than women do. On the basis of Gilmore's (1990) work, he suggested that protecting, providing, and propagating are the main forms of male nurturing, often accompanied by self-sacrifice (in almost all cultures). The more dangerous the environment, the more men are expected to be invulnerable, competitive and aggressive. Thus, men also demonstrate selfless generosity for others, yet of a different type. "Men nurture their society by shedding their blood, their sweat...and by dying if necessary in faraway places to provide a safe haven for their people" (Gilmore, 1990: 229–30). In a world where the roles of women and men, mothers and fathers, are changing, it is important to understand the new emergent role of fatherhood not just as a motherhood deficit but rather as another form of parenthood.

The approach pursued in this book points to the distinctiveness between mother–child and father–child relationships. The question is not whether fathers are capable of acting as "good mothers." Fathers can probably acquire the skills required for the caretaking of their children, as mothers do. Almeida and Galambos (1991) showed that fathers who are more involved with their adolescents, relative to more traditional fathers, behave more like mothers in expressing acceptance toward the adolescents. However, most fathers do not behave like mothers, either for historical reasons as outlined in this chapter (see Kraemer, 1991) or for sociological reasons reflected in fathers' perception of their sex-role (Russell, 1978). Combined with the psychoanalytic approaches it would then be more important to understand what fathers *do* with their children and to explore the distinctive role of fathers in the development of their children. The focus of this book is on fathers and adolescents, and the following two chapters will explore and discuss the role fathers play in the life of their adolescent children and the extent to which they support their children's development in the second decade of their lives.

2 Adolescent development and fathers

Adolescence is a transitory period during which the individual moves from childhood to adulthood. In this process the adolescent is supposed to renegotiate the nature of his or her relationship with parents, and to become capable of acting independently. This chapter will explore the role fathers may play in relation to adolescents' penchant for growing autonomy.

SEPARATION AND AUTONOMY PROCESSES

A basic and first premise of independence is *separation* – namely the youngster's ability to manage apartness or separation from parents, in the physical sense of distance, but also in the psychological and emotional capacity for sustained separateness. The ability to function separately, that is, apart from parents, is more important than the physical separateness per se (Constantine, 1987). Both psychological research and psychoanalytic thinkers have examined the separation processes that characterize this stage.

Approaching adolescence, children are more content to be by themselves and spend longer periods of time away from their parents even when both parties are at home (Larson and Richards, 1991). Not only do adolescents spend longer periods of time with peers, at home they tend to stay in their rooms and lock the door. However, growing separateness between parents and adolescents is not restricted to "physical" togetherness. Following the onset of pubertal maturation adolescents described their parents as being less close to them in comparison to prepubertal stages. Similarly, parents (with the exception of the father–son relationship) reported feeling less close to their pubertal sons or daughters (Steinberg, 1987a). Steinberg contended that these phenomena reflect the growing "distancing" between parents and their maturing adolescents.

Moreover, the "distancing" is also evident in the nature of interactions which take place between parents and adolescents. Flannery *et al.* (1992) studied children's and adolescents' prosocial behavior toward parents. Parents were asked to complete a questionnaire that was developed to measure adolescent helping behavior. In addition, adolescents' actual helping was observed. Adolescents were given an opportunity to help their parent move 24 books. Parents were asked by an examiner to move books from one location to another and were told not to ask adolescents for help. Results showed that the parents' reports of adolescent help (in the father–son, father–daughter, mother–son but not mother–daughter dyads), and adolescents' helpfulness toward parents in the laboratory, were negatively related to age.

Collins and Laursen (1992) asked parents and children to rate the level of conflict across various domains such as home chores, appearance or interpersonal relations. These researchers documented that conflicts occur more frequently between parents and children in adolescence in comparison to childhood or young adulthood. A conflict signifies that two parties, in our case parents and adolescents, have different views, and thus reflects the growing separation between them. Smetana (1989) interviewed parents and children about self-generated issues of conflicts and asked them to bring the justifications and counter-arguments for each conflict. Findings showed that whereas at younger ages children tend to adhere to and respect parental authority, adolescents tended to question or reject parental authority, which resulted in more conflicts over rule-governed issues such as who has to do some chores, and when. Adolescents tended to perceive and interpret their acts as contingent on personal jurisdiction regardless of parents' preferences.

In another study, Steinberg (1981) engaged father–mother–adolescent son triads in a discussion and asked them to come to a "family decision" on one issue. Observations showed that adolescents at the stage of pubertal maturation tended to interrupt each other with an increasing frequency. In addition, adolescents tried to assert their power over their mothers. Taken together, it can be suggested that a growing distancing between adolescents and their parents is evidenced following the phase of pubertal development. In addition, these processes probably lead adolescents to change their views of their parents (Steinberg and Silverberg, 1986). Adolescents were found to perceive their parents as ordinary people and stopped idealizing them, as younger children tended to.

Taken together, the growing "apartness" between adolescents and their parents is evidenced in three domains. First, adolescents spend increasing amounts of time apart from their parents. Second, adolescents feel that parents are not as close to them as they were in the past. Third, when together, conflicts and disagreements between parents and adolescents are more common. It should be noted, however, that the separation from parents takes place within the context of closeness. As studies have shown, parents remain important sources of support for their adolescents though the salience of peers increases (Youniss and Smollar, 1985).

Where psychological research investigated mainly the changes in the behavioral and cognitive spectrum, psychoanalytic thinkers referred to these changes from the intrapsychic level and perceived them as resulting from physiological/sexual maturation. Anna Freud (1958) claimed that the ego is overwhelmed by the emergence of the sexual instincts and has to struggle again to achieve its supremacy over the id. The inner turmoil requires changes and readaptation in the construction of the personality. Former established attachments to parents can reawaken incestuous fixations and therefore cathexis from parents takes place. However, as in cases of a given-up love affair or mourning the process cannot be gradual. "Adolescents withdraw their libido from them [their parents] suddenly and altogether" (A. Freud, 1958: 269). Consequently, acting against parents and experiencing negative emotions against parents can be evidenced. In contrast to Anna Freud who emphasized the disruptive nature of change, Blos (1962) described several phases during adolescence. First, starting from the later stages of latency, a growing sense of self-esteem is derived from achievements and mastery in academic and social matters. The inner sense of mastery leads to a shift in cathexis from outer subjects (like parents) to the inner object. Subsequently, the emergence of drives leads to changes in relations to self, parents and peers. Instinct gratification is not still ego syntonic and meets a disapproving ego. It leads pre-adolescents to behave in a distant and hostile manner (especially evident among boys) toward the opposite gender, and to be defensive against a regressive pull toward the pre-oedipal parent. The growing investment in same-sex friends may replace, according to Blos, the love for the parent and search for oneself in the face of still unintegrated emergent drives. The close friend becomes an important source of support that enables the adolescent to move into the phase of "adolescence proper" (ibid.: 87) and regain the sense of worth and strength. Moreover, an elevated self perception and self centeredness, sometimes at the expense of reality testing, is witnessed. Altogether, these processes lead to withdrawal of cathexis from parents and from their object representations. The "adolescence proper" phase hence leads to the relinquishment of infantile dependencies upon parents and an over-evaluation of the self. Blos elaborated on these processes:

> While previously the parent was overvalued, considered with awe, and not realistically assessed, he now becomes undervalued and is seen to have the shabby proportions of a fallen idol. The narcissistic self-inflation shows up in the adolescent's arrogance and rebellious-ness, in his defiance of rules, and in his flouting of the parent's authority.
>
> (Blos, 1962: 91)

Through these processes adolescents free themselves from dependen-cies on parents and dissolve childish libidinal attachments to them (Lidz, 1980). The disengagement from dependency upon parents enables adolescents to move to later stages where libido is directed toward non-familial, non-incestuous objects of the opposite sex. In sum, the changes in relationships during adolescence are associated with increased distance between parents and the adolescent (Steinberg, 1988). Distance is evident both in increased physical and emotional separation, and in some sort of felt emancipation from parental authority.

Adolescent disengagement from parents is only one facet of a broader and more comprehensive process termed by Blos (1967) as the second individuation process. "Once the source of the narcissistic gratification derived from parental love ceases to flow, the ego becomes invested with narcissistic libido which is withdrawn from the internalized parent" (Blos, 1962: 91). Thus, according to Blos, as well as developing the ability to be away from parents the adolescent is supposed to "become an individual" and to develop a sense of a distinct identity, clearly differentiated from parents and the family. In the more recent psychological literature various treatments of autonomy are found. Autonomy is understood as the acquisition of self-governance (Hill and Holmbeck, 1986). In their view autonomy is defined in terms of behaviors and attitudes that reflect growing self regulation. For example, Feldman and Quatman (1988) assessed adolescent behavioral autonomy across a variety of everyday life management domains such as choosing what books to read, what TV programs to watch, how to spend money, and whether to stay at home alone or to go on family trips. Yet autonomy is not expressed only in who performs an activity. Collins and Luebker (1991) talk about transfer of responsibilities to the adolescent and Holmbeck (1992) talks about who the person is who makes the decisions. In addition to behavioral regulation of daily life, common activities and responsibilities, autonomy is also perceived as positive emotions about one's own competence. Blatt and Blass (1990) pointed to the positive feelings such as pride, esteem and confidence which one has about oneself. Positive internalized feelings about oneself allow an individual to maintain a positive and active orientation when having to accomplish a goal or when facing stress.

THE FAMILY AND THE SEPARATION-INDIVIDUATION PROCESS

In the preceding paragraphs, the adolescent's role in the separation-individuation process was described. It is now recognized that the family also plays a role in its offspring's burgeoning autonomy (Constantine, 1987). Moreover, it now appears that adolescent autonomy develops within a context of "connectedness" to the family. In fact, autonomy depends upon parental support, and the gradual transfer of regulation of children's behaviors from parents to children themselves (Hill and Holmbeck, 1986; Collins and Russell, 1991). Relationships with parents are not replaced by relationships with peers, but rather they are transformed into mature relationships. Two dynamics are described in the literature concerning parents' impact on the development of their children (Parke *et al.*, 1989). The first assumes that children internalize basic expectations and attitudes concerning and significant others, through participation in salient relationships with parents and family. Assuming a coherent organizational perspective, an individual projects his/her representation of the self and of others onto future contexts, and the expectations consolidated within the family are enacted. The second dynamic refers to active parental management of children's activities and social life by their parents. As children approach adolescence, parents' ability to actively control their lives undoubtedly decreases (Steinberg and Silverberg, 1986). It is reasonable to assume that parents play a less direct and active role in organizing the life of their adolescents. Parents may rather serve as models, or construct the atmosphere that allows adolescents to assert their individuality.

The study of Grotevant and Cooper (1985) demonstrates how parents "indirectly" support their adolescents' penchant for independence. Grotevant and Cooper recorded discussions between parents and adolescents and analyzed them in terms reflecting four characteristics of family communication and relationships:

1 *self-assertion*, or the awareness of one's point of view and responsibility for communicating it clearly;
2 *separateness*, or expressions of difference in views between self and the other;
3 *permeability*, or responsiveness and openness to others' ideas; and
4 *mutuality*, or sensitivity and respect in relating to others.

The interplay between the four characteristics presents possible family interactions. The following vignette may demonstrate how a family responds to its adolescent's suggestions during a family discussion. The vignette, taken from a larger study on adolescence and family process in normal and diabetic adolescents conducted by Seiffge-Krenke, describes a discussion between two parents and a well-functioning, 14-year-old adolescent girl. The family was instructed to plan a three-week holiday, given an unlimited spending allowance (a task taken from the Grotevant and Cooper study).

MOTHER   Of course, I can make a suggestion right away. If we could go away for three weeks then I would suggest renting a camping van and fulfill a wish we have had for a long time. Hm, we'd for example go to Italy or Greece or maybe over to the Balkans. What do you think of it? (Mother turns to others, asking for their opinion.)

KATHERINA   Well, the idea of a camping van is not bad, but I would also like, for example, to go to America for three weeks. Just drive through and stop where we feel like it. (Katherina is sensitive to her mother's suggestion but also allows herself to express her own point of view.)

MOTHER   I also think it is a good idea. (Mother respects Katherina's point of view.)

FATHER   Great, I could imagine it.

KATHERINA   Yes.

FATHER   Yes, so if the money is unlimited, then most of all I would like to take a trip around the world.

MOTHER   Wow!

KATHERINA   Yeah, right. (Family members respond to and respect each other's suggestions.)

The discussion continued and family members raised several destinations like America, China or Japan and Africa.

KATHERINA   Hm, like I said. I'd like to fly to three different countries and stay in each for a week.

FATHER   Yes, then tell us which one again.

MOTHER   And how do you think it would be in Africa? What would we do there? (Parents do not accept Katherina's suggestion automatically. They ask for clarifications which lead Katherina to develop her own ideas.)

KATHERINA   I'd like to...something unusual. Well, something new. Something we do not have here, like safari. I think that would be very interesting. (Parental respect allows Katherina to raise ideas that still have to be developed and she feels confident to discuss them with her parents.)

This suggestion raised again the question: what country or countries should the family go to since it was still not clear where to go:

FATHER   I can understand the dilemmas, but I have another completely different suggestion. I would like to go to the Allgau area [a region in Germany].

MOTHER   (laughs)

KATHERINA   (laughs) I thought so! I thought it would happen!

MOTHER   Aha! To go hunting and stay in a nice hotel!

KATHERINA   You two go to Allgau, and I'll go to Kenya. (Katherina feels confident enough to assert herself.)

FATHER   Or we do both. (And the father is flexible enough to listen to and consider Katherina's reflection and to integrate it within a joint family interest.)

KATHERINA   Yeah.

MOTHER   Exactly.

FATHER   Yes, good. So one week in Kenya, and we will do something together. And the second week?

MOTHER   One could...

KATHERINA   America! I think we have three weeks, and so we have one and a half weeks in Kenya and one and a half weeks in America.

FATHER   Yes.

MOTHER   Yes, I think so too.

FATHER   Good. Let's do it like that.

MOTHER   Yes, good.

KATHERINA   Yes.

The importance of the described interaction in this vignette is not the fact the family reached an agreement. From Katherina's perspective she was allowed to express her personal preferences. Her preferences were attended to, responded to and incorporated into the joint family decision. Through such a mundane discussion parents are actually able to support or suppress adolescents' own ideas and assertions. Grotevant and Cooper found that in families where members respond to each other and show mutual sensitivity and respect, adolescents are more individuated both in relation to other family members and in relation to themselves. Similar findings were reported by Hauser *et al.* (1984). Hauser and colleagues differentiated between parents who "enable" or "constrain" their adolescents when facing a joint family task. Enabling pertains to parental respect and support of adolescent ideas, whereas constraining refers to parents being either indifferent or judgemental toward their adolescents. Adolescents whose parents exhibited a higher level of enabling behavior reported a higher level of ego development and reflected a higher level of independence.

The Grotevant and Cooper, and the Hauser *et al.* studies emphasized parents' actual though "implicit" support of adolescent individuation. Shulman and Klein (1983) arrived at a similar conclusion while addressing family interactions from a systemic perspective. Parents and their adolescents were given a similar task and were allowed to consult one another. In line with Reiss model, several family paradigms could be observed. In the optimal family paradigm, family members were supportive of individual views, and were capable of balancing between those views and the family's needs to co-ordinate actions and to feel close to one another. During the final stage of solution of the task, family members' negotiations reflected a delicate balance between individual needs and preferences, and family cohesion. In the less optimal family paradigms, members tended to criticize distinctive views, and solutions reflected either an over-emphasis on consensus, or family members acting apart from each other and lacking any co-operation. Results showed that adolescents from families that were unable to balance individual and family needs, and adolescents from families which overemphasized consensus, revealed lower levels of differentiation and self assertion. Overall, when the family is sensitive and supportive of the developmental needs of their offspring, it may serve as a "facilitating environment" for adolescent attainment of developmental tasks such as differentiation from the family and the establishment of a consolidated identity.

Studies on the association between adolescent development and family/parents relationships have not explicitly dealt with the distinctive role of fathers versus mothers in this process. In line with the scope of this book, our question is: what is the distinctive contribution of each parent, and more specifically the father, to adolescent development? First we will review the existing research on the father–adolescent relationship, and second we will discuss the possible distinctive contribution of this relationship to adolescent development. Results from a study we have conducted on adolescents' relationships with their mothers and fathers will be incorporated.

FATHER–ADOLESCENT RELATIONSHIPS: DISTINCTIVE FEATURES

Studies have shown that fathers spend less time with their infants and preschool children than do mothers (Lamb, 1987). In adolescence findings are similar. Fathers are reported to spend a third (Russell, 1983) or half (Montemayor and Brownlee, 1987) the amount of time that mothers spend with their children. Fathers were described by adolescents as the least preferred targets for disclosure (Seiffge-Krenke, 1986). Adolescents reported that fathers as compared to mothers had less knowledge of them (Youniss and Ketterlinus, 1987). When together, adolescents are engaged in different activities with mothers and fathers (Montemayor and Brownlee, 1987). Adolescents reported that fathers exhibited less affection toward them (Youniss and Smollar, 1985), were perceived to be less understanding (Richardson *et al.*, 1984) and less involved (Steinberg, 1987a). Mothers were found to share a greater degree of intimacy than did fathers with both male and female adolescents (LeCroy, 1988). When together, a greater proportion of adolescents' time with fathers is spent in leisure activities or in play, similar to the trends found in early childhood when fathers were more playful with infants, whereas mothers were more engaged in caregiving activities (Belsky, 1979). The general trend of the findings indicates that fathers are more distant and less sensitive, and are perceived as such by their adolescents (Collins and Russell, 1991).

In a study we conducted, 12-, 14- and 16-year-old Israeli high school students (Shulman and Posen, 1992) were interviewed regarding their relationships with their fathers and their mothers. Results showed that in the afternoon hours mothers spend three and a half more hours at home per day than fathers do. However, adolescents do not need caretaking by parents as they do at younger ages and may spend hours locked in their rooms. Thus, no significant difference was found in the frequency of caretaking behavior performed by mothers and fathers. Nevertheless, mothers were found to be more involved in discussions with their adolescents, and in outdoor activities such as shopping. Fathers were found to be more involved in playful activities both at home and outdoors. It was interesting to note that playful activities were reported to be more frequently performed by fathers with their sons, whereas mothers had more discussions and shopping experiences with their daughters. Adolescents were also asked to rate the level of paternal and maternal involvement regarding seven mundane issues. As can be seen in Figure 2.1 mothers were more involved in day-to-day issues such as what to wear and with whom to go out. On issues that are of greater importance, such as studies and discipline, fathers were involved at a similar level as mothers. In a study conducted by Dravoj (1983) on 224 German adolescents, aged 12 to 16, a similar pattern reflecting lower levels of closeness between fathers and their adolescents as compared to mothers was found. An overall decrease in levels of self-disclosure toward parents was evident, yet the level of disclosure toward fathers was consistently half the amount of disclosure toward mothers throughout adolescence. However, when the frequency of discussing various issues with fathers and mothers was compared, adolescents discussed more mundane issues with their mothers. Issues such as the future, and professional preferences, were more frequently discussed with fathers. Emotions, family issues and mundane topics were more the territory of the mother, whereas future development and extrafamilial issues were considered by adolescents as a paternal territory.

Functions of fathers' "distance"

In general, the results of our study are similar to results of other studies pointing to the lower involvement of fathers with their children. Our suggestion is that fathers' being less engaged with their adolescents may serve a developmental function. It is well established that fathers spend less time than mothers with their children and adolescents. However, a distinction should be made between "distance" and "detachment." Although fathers spend less time with their offspring and are less familiar with their children's daily activities this does not mean they are uninterested in their children. When it comes to issues such as studies, fathers are as much involved as mothers. Being distant allows a "bigger space" between father and adolescent; it also enables the adolescent to exert individuality and leads to less friction (Steinberg, 1987a). What may appear to be fathers' indifference, aloofness or judgmental attitudes, may in fact serve as an incentive for adolescent separation. It is the mother's closeness that may interfere with the tendency to separate and therefore lead to conflicts (ibid.). As suggested above, an important task during adolescence is to experience and establish separateness. Fathers, by their non-intrusive attitudes, allow the adolescents a wider space of their own: for example, fathers

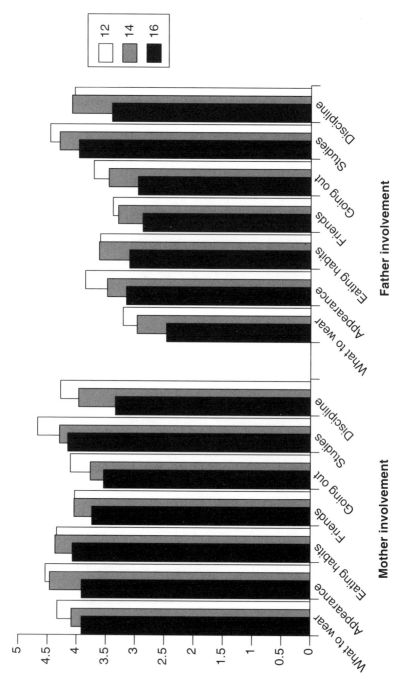

Figure 2.1 Level of mother and father involvement in seven daily matters across ages 12, 14, 16

are less bothered when their adolescents are in their own rooms, separated from the rest of the family. By acting in a manner that seems indifferent, fathers enable their adolescents to better experience separateness. Thus, the "distant" relationship that fathers have with their adolescents serves a function in the developmental process. Fathers serve as models for relationships where separateness is allowed and respected. Fathers understand that being distant does not mean being detached, rather it reflects the search for more personal space within a close relationship.

Men have different models of close relationships than do women, with men placing more emphasis on the importance of separateness within a close or intimate relationship (Gilligan, 1982; Grossman, 1989). Fathers are therefore not offended when they are not their adolescents' partners for disclosure, as fathers themselves do not emphasize intimacy and disclosure. Nevertheless, as findings show, when it comes to crucial issues such as scholastic studies or discipline, fathers are involved on a level similar to mothers. This suggests that although fathers' immediate presence is low, what counts, especially during adolescence, is the strength of inner confidence in the availability of the parent. Attachment theories have already shown that secure attachment is based on confidence in the caregiver's availability rather than on immediate and continuous presence (Ainsworth *et al.*, 1978).

In sum, it is suggested that by their natural inclination to be distant, fathers are more capable of acceptance and respect for the adolescent's wish to be separate. In addition, since fathers' being distant does not reflect disinterest or detachment, fathers can serve as an alternative model for separateness within a close relationship. We speculate then that fathers indirectly support adolescents' penchant for separateness. A similar process is described in children's acquisition of gender roles, whereby fathers (as well as mothers), by exhibiting gender-appropriate behavior, serve as sex-role models for their children.

Fathers' support for adolescent independence

It would be incorrect to claim that fathers foster adolescent development only by default. As presented, in our own and other studies, fathers were observed to be more involved in playful activities with their adolescents compared to mothers. The nature of a playful activity suggests that both players have a similar status in the interaction. Youniss and Smollar (1985) described parent–child relationships as asymmetrical, compared to peer relationships, which are symmetrical in nature. Being involved in a symmetrical interaction enables the individual to assert his/her own preferences/individuality. As Youniss and Smollar have suggested, peer relationships are an important arena for the attainment of individuality. It may be suggested that something similar can occur in father–adolescent relationships, especially during playful encounters. In our study, adolescents were asked if there was an activity they would like to do with either parent. As could be expected for this developmental stage, adolescents did not seek additional activities together with parents. However, younger adolescents said they would like to have more playful activities with their fathers. During early adolescence there is an increase in parent–child conflict (Steinberg, 1987a), and children may prefer not to be too close to their parents. Yet our results showed that this is not the case regarding joint activities with fathers, especially when joint play is involved.

In our study, adolescents were interviewed and asked to answer: "What is a good father?" "What is a good mother?" "What is the difference between a good father and a good mother?" Vignettes from adolescents' responses reveal the distinctive nature of fathers and mothers:

> A father is more preoccupied with work, a mother has more free time for her children and therefore they run to her. A mother loves her child as a father does but she really does it. A father is more like a friend with whom you can do things together.
>
> (Male, 12)

> A good father is more strict and more peer-like; a good mother cares, is more at home.
>
> (Male, 12)

> A good mother is more at home and therefore is more aware of what's going on. A good father is less at home, cannot be aware of everything that happens. Whatever he does see, he sees from a different perspective.
>
> (Female, 13)

> A good mother is more spoiling, helps me, teaches me to cook. A good father helps mainly in learning new things, building things.
>
> (Male, 14)

Adolescents drew on the traditional distinctions between fathers and mothers, emphasizing the fact that fathers, because of their work, spend less time at home. However, when they are at home fathers add an additional perspective to relationships. In their behavior fathers combine a "parental" and "peer-like" role. This combination probably allows fathers, especially with adolescents, to care for and to guide their children in a flexible manner that leads to fewer conflict situations. In addition, the father is perceived as the parent who is more familiar with the world outside the family, and therefore he can be a greater source of information on such matters than the mother.

In our study, adolescents were also asked specifically whether parents foster dependence or whether they feel that parents rely on their independence. A clear difference emerged between perception of fathers and mothers on this issue (see Figure 2.2). Fathers perceive their growing adolescents as less dependent than their mothers do. The older the adolescents, the more fathers perceive them as less

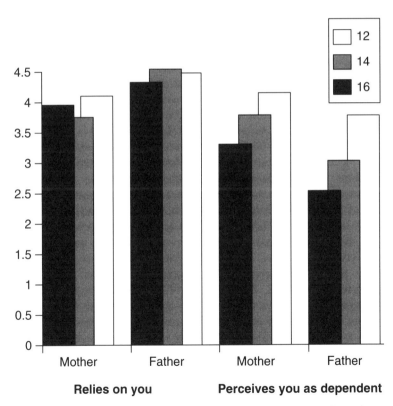

Figure 2.2 Level of parental emphasis on adolescent reliance or dependence across ages 12, 14, 16

dependent. Even in early adolescence, the father transmits messages that the young people can be relied upon. Mothers, on the other hand, continue to perceive their children as dependent well into adolescence, and rely on them less. Comparisons of correlations between level of parental reliance on adolescents' independence, and a variety of interaction measures with both fathers and mothers, further highlighted this point. For fathers, the more they were involved with their adolescents the more they relied on them. Fathers' involvement did not interfere with their support of their offspring's independence. Maternal involvement, however, was not related to a tendency to rely on their adolescent offspring.

In adolescence actual closeness to parents is not required for development. On the contrary, Greenberg *et al.* (1983) found that the frequency of parent utilization and proximity-seeking was not related to adolescent well-being. Rather, a balanced closeness was a better predictor of adjustment. A similar conclusion can be drawn from the findings of LeCroy's (1988) study. Although mothers were perceived to have a more intimate relationship with their adolescents compared to fathers, the level of maternal intimacy did not predict positive adolescent functioning. However, paternal intimacy, even though it was less than maternal intimacy, did predict adolescent functioning.

Yet it would be inaccurate to describe father–adolescent relationship only as peer-like, or to perceive as solely benevolent a father as the parent who expresses his support for adolescent independence. Fathers were reported to use more forceful techniques in interactions with their children. Fathers more than mothers tended to punish their adolescents, while encouraging independence. Traditionally, the concept of the strict and disciplinarian father has been widely described. In some cultures the father is described as a detached and strict figure. This depiction is found among Mexican fathers, who are affectionate with younger children, but become distant as children enter puberty, when the fathers become stern disciplinarians who expect to be respected and feared. As Madsen (1973) explains, it is the fathers' mechanism to transmit societal values and to transform the adolescent into an adult member of society. The combination of both flexible and strict approaches by fathers in relating to their adolescents is reflected in the words of a 12-year-old boy in our sample, when asked to compare a good father and a good mother. The boy responded: "A good father is more strict and more peer-like; a good mother cares, is more at home."

In a study by Stocker and McHale (1992), pre-adolescents were asked to describe their relationships with their fathers and mothers, and to rate their behavior toward siblings on dimensions of affection, rivalry and hostility. Pre-adolescents whose relationships with their fathers were characterized by high levels of warmth, reported less hostility and rivalry and more affection toward their siblings. Maternal warmth was negatively related to siblings' rivalry. Brownfield (1987) found that adolescents who identified with their father or with a father figure exhibited lower levels of violent behavior. It is suggested then that fathers, either by active monitoring of their adolescents or by serving as models, enhance self-control in their offspring within the family and in society. This suggestion recalls Lacan's (1977) contention that the father's role is to introduce structure and societal rules to the child. In one of our clinical cases of an acting-out adolescent girl, her behavior became more and more provocative. In the first session with the family, it became clear that the father was very weak, and unable to exert his authority over the family. When referring to her mode of behavior, this 16-year-old girl reflected: "I want him to change, to set limits, he is the father. And if he is unable to do it then he should call the police. We as a family cannot proceed anymore."

In sum, our suggestion is then that fathers interact with their adolescents in different ways than mothers do. Regarding their traditional roles, fathers are less engaged with their adolescents. When they are together, they prefer to engage in play-like activities. This apparently "distant" model is what adolescents need at this period of separation – a model of a "close enough" parent that allows and respects separation. Fathers in their natural attitude are more capable of balancing closeness and separateness than are mothers. In addition, fathers also actively support individuation of their adolescents more than mothers do. This support may be expressed in a benevolent mode, yet there are fathers who may also employ more strict methods to achieve adolescent independence and movement toward society. It is interesting that adolescents do not perceive their fathers as distant; on the contrary, although they spend less time together, adolescents perceive their fathers as supportive of their independence and even expect their fathers to set goals and limits for them.

FATHER–ADOLESCENT RELATIONSHIPS AND MID-LIFE ISSUES

Historically, fathers did not grant autonomy to the younger generation until their own death (Roberts and Zuengler, 1985), reflecting values of commitment to continuity and stability. In such cases the father allowed individuation under his control. A profession was chosen for the youngster and the youngster's social relationships were primarily family bound. However, more recent research has shown that the interface of fathers' mid-life issues and their offspring's adolescence is more complex.

Freud designated two major spheres of adult functioning: "to love and to work," yet the combination of the two was described as a source of strain for fathers. Greenberger and O'Neil (1990) showed that fathers' concerns about their children were related to their stress at work, and were associated with a less positive attitude toward work. Bailyn (1978) found that family-oriented males held lower-status positions in organizations in comparison to career-oriented males. It can then be understood why fathers, who are in many cases the main breadwinners, were found to be less engaged with their children. Mid-life issues may also arouse questions of family continuity. Is the family falling apart? Is the adolescent trying to outmanoeuver his/her parents? In such cases the family's needs may be emphasized at the expense of the adolescent's needs. Lavee *et al.* (1987) measured family satisfaction at different stages of the family life cycle. The early years of marriage start with high levels of satisfaction. When children reach adolescence or when they leave home both fathers' and mothers' satisfaction reach their lowest level.

This possible conflict of interests between parents and adolescents recalls the psychoanalytic approach to father/mother–adolescent relationships. Psychoanalytic thought, starting with Freud, and later elaborated upon by Anna Freud (1958) and Blos (1967), emphasized the "storm and stress" qualities of adolescence. While adolescents are separating from their parents, and the oedipal conflict is reactivated, relationships between parents and children can be stressful. Rivalry between father and son, and between mother and daughter, is re-experienced. Following the psychoanalytic approach, father–adolescent relationships are thus also colored by competition, as well as by a "distant" yet supportive attitude. Esman (1985) adds that the father's conflict with his adolescent may reactivate the father's old, unresolved adolescent conflicts: "I couldn't get away with this stuff when I was his age – why should I let him do it now?" (Esman, 1985: 147).

More recent approaches, on the other hand, point to the possible complementarity between fatherhood and male mid-life issues. Examination of men in their mid-forties showed a better balance between family and work, reflecting a higher level of psychological maturity (Heath and Heath, 1991). This raised the possibility that success in one role may be predictive of success in others. Snarey (1993), addressing this issue from an Eriksonian perspective, claimed that at the seventh stage in the life cycle – generativity – mature love (caring for others) is correlated with mature work (creativity, productivity). Thus the care of children becomes an integral part of fathers' functioning.

Snarey followed fathers for four decades, looking for the mid-life consequences of what he termed "paternal generativity" – namely fathers' experience of rearing a child. First, he found that a father's caring for his teenager's social-emotional development made a significant contribution to the father's upward mobility at work. Second, fathers who cared for their children's social-emotional development during the first decade of the child's life, and also cared for social-emotional and intellectual-academic development during the second decade, were, at mid-life, considerably more likely to have become generative beyond the family sphere. The association between adjustment and parenting in mid-life was also supported in a study by Montemayor *et al.* (1993). In this study, the relationship between fathers' mid-life stress and the quality of their interaction with their adolescents was assessed. Fathers were asked to report on their levels of stress related to mid-life issues such as their expectations of themselves and of their marriages. They were asked to rate statements such as "I find myself thinking about what kind of person I am and what I really want out of life," or "Marriage is as rewarding and enjoyable after 15 or 20 years as it is in the earlier years." In addition, the quality of interaction between father and adolescent was measured. Results showed that fathers' mid-life stress was negatively correlated ($r = -0.59$) with the quality of communication with their adolescents. A study by Silverberg and Steinberg (1990) indicates that parents' perceptions of well-being were correlated with reported characteristics of parent–child relationships. For example, both fathers' and mothers' mid-life identity concerns were greater when their adolescent children reported a higher degree of detachment from parents.

The interrelatedness of personal and parenting issues can be explained using the family life cycle model suggested by Combrinck-Graham (1985). According to this model, the family system oscillates between periods of family closeness, and periods of family distance. At adolescence, which coincides with the parents' "40s evaluation," there is an emphasis in the family on drawing apart and allowing individuals to work on issues of personal identity. However, as Combrinck-Graham states, the ability of the family to draw apart is related to their inner confidence that relationships are maintained, though in a different form. At this stage of life, the parent is not expected to provide the physical care and close supervision characteristic of earlier years. The parent is rather supposed "to be there," complementing the needs of the developing adolescent penchant for individuation. Similar ideas are expressed by Duvall (1977), who was among the first to describe several developmental tasks through the family life cycle, regarding parents with teenage children. Parents prefer to become less responsible as their adolescents become emancipated and establish personal interests, relations and careers. Thus the needs of the maturing adolescent fit the needs and expectations of the maturing parent (and probably the father). A close inspection of Snarey's (1993) findings reveals that paternal generativity (associated with positive outcomes for the father) consisted mainly of activities such as taking the adolescent to a cultural event or encouraging social activities. It would therefore be reasonable to assume that fathers' parenting of their adolescents fits their mid-life issues. On the one hand, it allows some space, and on the other hand it contributes to the father's sense of closeness and generativity for his offspring.

Although fatherhood and men's individual issues may be in conflict, adolescent developmental needs and the personal tendencies of fathers complement each other fairly well. Men's model for close relationships is different from women's, and involves caring in a manner that allows more for "personal space." This approach, when built on foundations of intimacy and sincere care, enables fathers to arrive at a higher level of personal adjustment (Snarey, 1993). The following chapter will elaborate on how fathers support and enhance the attainment of various developmental tasks that adolescents are expected to achieve.

3 Fathers and adolescents' developmental tasks

In the preceding chapter, fathers were described as showing greater respect and support for their developing adolescents. Fathers, in comparison to mothers, have a greater tendency to perceive their adolescents as independent, to express support and to show interest in their suggestions (Hauser *et al.*, 1987). In their behavior, fathers also reveal a greater sensitivity to the physical changes that their offspring undergo (Salt, 1991). Together, these findings suggest that fathers are sensitive to what Hill (1980) defined as the primary changes in adolescence: cognitive, physical and social definition – namely the expectations that others form of the adolescent. In addition to the changes experienced in the family arena, changes also occur within the contexts of both peer relationships and school. The interacting influences of the primary changes and the contexts produce a set of changes that introduce many psychological issues to the adolescent. Hill refers especially to an increase in adolescent autonomy, an emerging sense of identity or self, an altered view of achievement including new goals for the future and views about how such goals might be achieved, and a transformation in personal and social outlook on close relationships and on life. The fact that fathers are both more aware and more supportive of the changes that adolescents are trying to cope with, may help fathers serve as models with whom it is easy to identify. This chapter will review the major developmental tasks adolescents face, and will explore the father's role in these processes.

DEVELOPMENTAL TASKS DURING ADOLESCENCE

Havinghurst (1972) was among the first to describe the changes in adolescence in terms of developmental tasks. He suggested a list of demands that an adolescent encounters:

- Achieving emotional independence of parents and other adults.
- Accepting one's physique and using the body effectively.
- Developing intellectual skills and concepts.
- Desiring and achieving socially responsible behavior.
- Achieving a new and more mature relation with peers.
- Achieving a masculine or feminine social role.
- Preparing for marriage and family life.
- Selecting and preparing for an occupation.
- Acquiring a set of values and an ethical system as a guide to behavior.

These tasks reflect the fundamental dilemmas the developing individual has to deal with in relation to self and to significant others. This approach carries with it a more flexible view of development and underlines the adolescent's actions as central in solving relevant developmental tasks. The adolescent can be somewhat responsible for his or her actions and determine the pace of development. It is understood that the various tasks are not achieved at a similar pace, and their attainment reflects the continuous negotiations and struggles with self and with others. The process of adaptation covers a span of years, attempting to resolve first one issue, and then the next (Coleman, 1992: 3). Conceptually, we may speak of three main categories that compose the developmental task. First, prior to coping with the developmental tasks, the growing adolescent is supposed to develop a sense of separateness from parents. This sense should incorporate awareness of the maturing body and sexuality. The second category involves the acceptance and enactment of normative expectations, for example taking more responsibility for one's own actions or establishment of peer relations. The third category refers to the development of values and aspirations that guide future actions and is reflected by the attainment of a consolidated identity.

Similar approaches are found in more recent discussions and studies of the process of adolescent attainment of autonomy (Hill and Holmbeck, 1986), and were elaborated in the preceding chapter. Feldman and Quatman (1988) assessed adolescent behavioral autonomy across a variety of everyday activities. Collins and Luebker (1991) talked about transfer of responsibilities to the adolescent and Holmbeck (1992) described autonomy in terms of capability of decision making and regulation of daily life. In addition, autonomy is also perceived as positive emotions about one's own competence. Blatt and Blass (1990) point to positive feelings about oneself, such as pride, esteem and confidence. Positive internalized feelings about oneself allow an individual to maintain a positive and active orientation when having to accomplish a goal or when facing stress. Fend (1990) also suggested assessing the attainment of developmental tasks with regard to two aspects. On the one hand, success can be measured via indices such as school performance or social acceptance. In addition, individuals develop a universe of meanings: how to relate to others, what goals and ideals are central for developing competence and responsibility. According to Silbereisen and Noack (1990), during the process of development individuals form and revise orientations with regard to goals and steps in their future development. These developmental orientations function as a frame of reference for future action.

The theories and models of identity development present an additional perspective on the tasks adolescents are supposed to cope with. According to Erickson (1968), the major task of adolescence is to integrate earlier identifications of childhood and one's own aptitudes with socially approved roles. In this process the adolescent is expected to become committed to some ideological view, while remaining sensitive to his/her own needs and talents. Grotevant and Adams (1984) expanded the concept of identity to include both ideological and interpersonal domains. The ideological identity status is evaluated in domains such as political views, religious beliefs, philosophical lifestyle and choice of occupation. Interpersonal identity is evaluated in domains such as friendship, dating and sex-role.

However, age-appropriate autonomy as suggested by Erikson is not only the adoption of socially acceptable behavior and norms in the various domains. On the contrary, the individual is also supposed to be sensitive to his or her own preferences and inclinations, and to arrive at a synthesis of self and others. Similar ideas are found in the discussions of the ego ideal and ideal self by Blos (1974) and Sandler (1987). Two main aspects are described in the content of the ideal self. The first aspect refers to a narcissistic core based on former achievements and on the increased drive for mastery experienced as a result of to the acquired capacities in adolescence. The second aspect refers to positive identification with features of loved, admired or feared objects such as parents or other significant persons in the individual's environment. The balance between these two poles "reduces self and object idealizations to the level of more realistic self and others appraisals" (Blos, 1974: 57).

In the preceding chapter the unique role of the father as a model for and facilitator of an optimal balance between self and other was outlined. As delineated by Havinghurst (1972), developmental processes may also be defined as tasks the adolescent is supposed to cope with. As we have discussed, we identify three major tasks: the development of a sense of separateness and body self, taking more responsibility for the individual's own behavior, and developing an outlook toward life. In the following section we will review studies that point to the role fathers may play in the attainment of various developmental tasks. Specifically we will present theories and studies dealing with domains related to the development of a sense of a separate body, of behavioral autonomy such as social competence, and of domains pertaining to emotional autonomy reflecting attitudes toward self and life.

FATHERS AND ADOLESCENTS' ATTAINMENT OF DEVELOPMENTAL TASKS

The father and the adolescent body

Psychologically, the body of the child belongs to the mother, and the fusion between mother and child is a cornerstone in several developmental theories. According to Melanie Klein (1975), as we have described in Chapter 1, the child fantasizes at a very early stage that the mother's breast is part of its own body. The frustration of physical needs, or "good enough mothering" (Winnicott, 1965), is necessary to differentiate between the two bodies. Fathers are supposed to come between the infant and the breast, thus separating the two bodies and destroying fantasies of fusion, and thus dissolving the fusion between mother and child. By doing so, the father enhances the sense of physical separation and distinctive identity of the child. It is not easy for the child to accomplish this task, since it is through the mother that the infant perceives itself. The mother's empathy and mirroring enhance the infant's sense of oneness. As described in the previous chapters, fathers are more engaged in play and physical activities with their children than mothers are (Siegal, 1987; Lytton and Romney, 1991). Although the joint activities of father and child bring their bodies together, this sense of togetherness is experienced via activities which involve their bodies being separate. Thus, the father, whose separateness is emphasized through his activities with the infant, contributes further to the infant's sense of separateness.

The growing sense of the separate body carries with it a growing awareness of sexual differences. Freudian theory has attributed the consolidation of sexual identity to the resolution of the oedipal complex. Notwithstanding the criticism of Freud's differential description of male and female development (Chasseguet-Smirgel,

1979a), in reality, infants as young as 15 months are aware of sex differences. For example, Shopper (1989) described how differential toilet training may contribute to the awareness of sexual identity. Girls are taught to sit down for elimination, to wipe after elimination, with minimal distinction found between bladder and bowel control training. Boys must learn to urinate differently from girls. The differential training of boys is usually done with the active participation of the father. The boy is taught urinary control in an upright position, with emphasis on skill, mastery and fun. The father is of course proud when his daughter is dry, but her feminine identity is also conveyed simultaneously. With boys, upright urination can be a joint activity with the father that enhances the boy's sexual identity.

Physical maturation and pubertal changes reintroduce the issues of body self and sexual identity to the developing adolescent. As a result of pubertal changes, adolescents are faced with sexually mature bodies. They feel that they are different from their own perceptions, with which they were familiar, and are required to integrate the physically mature body into the representation of self. According to Laufer and Laufer (1984), this process evokes incestuous wishes latent during childhood, and increases anxiety, owing to the need to choose between consolidating a mature male or female body. If the adolescent is not able to integrate the physically mature genitals into the body concept a "developmental breakdown" may result (Laufer and Laufer, 1984: 23). Consequently, such individuals cannot progress and incorporate the major physical changes in relation to self and significant others.

Numerous studies confirm certain aspects of the psychoanalytic theory on the stress associated with physical and sexual development. Evaluation of physical development marked by breast development and menarche in girls consisted mainly of ambivalent and negative statements (Brooks-Gunn and Ruble, 1980; Schulz, 1991; Alsaker, 1992). In contrast, boys tended to report on a positive evaluation of their bodily changes and were proud of their first ejaculation (Gaddis and Brooks-Gunn, 1985). Marked gender differences were also found in the evaluation of the body image. For example, twice as many girls as boys in high school want to change their appearance (Musa and Roach, 1973). Furthermore, adolescent girls consider themselves less attractive than their female peers, and tend not to be satisfied with their body weight (Rauste-von-Right, 1989; Freedman, 1989).

Tensions between adolescents and their parents during the pubertal changes were described by psychoanalytic writers (A. Freud, 1958; Blos, 1967) and substantiated in recent studies (see Steinberg, 1987a). The transformation in parent–child relationships, and more specifically father–child relationships, during adolescence was discussed in Chapter 2, but there is a lack of research concerning the father's role with regard to the maturing body of the adolescent. Clinical material has shown that body image disturbances in adolescents were related to less than accepting attitudes expressed by parents (Sarigiani, 1987), particularly in regard to fathers and daughters.

We must address the dearth of research concerning the father's relationship with the developing body of the adolescent. Daily experience seems to suggest that the adolescent's physical maturation is a secret which cannot be shared with the father. Evidence from two studies on body contact between parent and adolescent tells us something about the father's role following the beginning of physical changes.

Schulz (1991) investigated 15-year-old girls and the changes in their physical relationships with their parents. She discovered that shortly before the onset of menarche, the nature and amount of physical contact with both parents changed dramatically. The previous close physical contact (sitting on the lap, embracing and kissing) with the father was drastically reduced, and replaced by ritualized physical contact, e.g. hugging him before departure or upon returning home after traveling. Such behavior was typically justified with the explanation: "That's just what one does." Forty-seven per cent of the girls refused to have any physical contact with the father, and 30 per cent reduced it to levels which were unavoidable or absolutely necessary. Frequent physical contact with fathers, as it has occurred during childhood, was reported by only 23 per cent of the girls. Physical contact with the mother decreased as well but was "tolerated" more than with the father. The majority of the girls also reported that they withdrew from physical contact initiated by the father. Over 75 per cent of the girls refused to be seen by the parents, under any circumstances, while undressed. In addition, girls avoided any type of physical contact in the bathroom, and a substantial number of girls locked the bathroom door as a rule. We can see that the changes resulting from maturational processes led girls to become more sensitive about their bodies and to reduce physical contact with the father.

Interestingly, very similar trends are found in a study on physical contact between fathers and adolescent sons. Salt (1991) asked fathers and sons to rate the acceptability of affectionate touching between father and son. In addition, fathers' and sons' joint play in various physical and cognitive games was videotaped, and their incidental and non-incidental touches were counted. Results showed that although father and son enjoyed affectionate touching, as the son grows older and approaches adolescence both demonstrate a decrease in the acceptance of touch between themselves. In sum, we can see that physical changes bring with them a decrease in body contact between father and adolescent daughter or son. Moreover, fathers are expected by the adolescent not only to acknowledge but also to respect the "new" body. The respectful distance fathers keep from the developing bodies of their adolescents may, paradoxically, signify the father's acknowledgement of the physical changes that are happening.

The awareness and acceptance of the "new" body cannot be disconnected from the consolidation of sexual identity. As Laufer and Laufer have written: "Although the precursors of male–female differentiation are established during the oedipal period and are tested throughout latency, only by the end of adolescence is the image of oneself as being either male or female finally established" (Laufer and Laufer, 1984: 25). Adolescents use relationships, autoerotic activities, fantasies and various forms of trial to establish their body image, which includes the sexually mature genitals and the recognition and integration of the genitals of the opposite sex. The achievement of such a state entails the ability to dissolve oedipal incestuous wishes, and to establish mature relations with parents of either sex. When relations with parents are free from guilt and hate, parents can become models for sex-roles.

In a study now in process, we investigated the association of parent and adolescent marital expectations. Both adolescents and parents were asked to rate their expectations regarding issues of closeness and individuality in marital relationships as well as expected sex-role division. Boys' sex-role expectations were highly correlated with those of their fathers and mothers. Interestingly, mothers' expectations for closeness in marital relations predicted their sons' expectations for closeness. Fathers' expectations were better predictors for their sons' expectations regarding individuality and sex-role divisions. Parents' marital expectations were poor predictors of daughters' marital expectations. The association of fathers' and sons' sex-role attitudes are further supported in a study by Emihovich *et al.* (1984) which addressed two questions. First, they studied the extent to which fathers' sex-role beliefs influence their attitudes towards the sex-roles they would like their sons to hold. Second, they asked whether fathers' desires regarding the sex-role attitudes they would like their sons to hold, influence the attitudes their sons actually hold. Results of the study showed a highly significant relationship between fathers' own sex-role beliefs and their expectations for their sons. In addition, both fathers' sex-role beliefs and their expectations for their sons were significantly related to the responses of the sons. Similar trends pointing to the impact of fathers on sex-roles were reported in the literature (see Snarey, 1993). Traditional fathers tend to promote their daughters' conformity to traditional sex-roles, but when fathers were highly involved with their children, daughters were exposed to more egalitarian models. Furthermore, Sagi (1982) contrasted traditional and non-traditional families, and found that involved fathers did not eliminate the feminine tendencies of their daughters, but added a masculine perspective to the daughters' sex-role orientation. As can be seen, both psychoanalytic writings and psychological research point to the role of the father in children's and adolescents' consolidation of sexual identity.

In summary, fathers are perceived and described as being more aware of the separateness of their children than mothers are. During childhood, when parents and children are supposed to be close and attached, fathers and children are involved in activities where the child's and father's bodies are separated. During adolescence, when separation is the rule, fathers decrease physical contact with their adolescents. When the sense of being a separate body is enhanced, adolescents probably feel more confident about perceiving their fathers as models for adult life.

The father and the development of adolescent behavioral autonomy

Discussion of the father's role was originated in many cases from a deficiency model, whereby fathers compared to mothers were less involved with their children. However, this concept of deficiency is not supported by children's perceptions. Although adolescents reported that the amount of time their fathers spend with them is less than the amount of time spent with their mothers, adolescents were nevertheless satisfied with the role fathers play in their lives (Hanson, 1988; Montemayor and Brownlee, 1987). A functional perspective would then suggest evaluating the role of fathers in relation to their contribution to the development of their adolescents. We assume that fathers employ different modes of supporting and encouraging the development of their children and adolescents in comparison to mothers. This understanding is supported when the father's contribution to attainment of behavioral autonomy is under discussion. This approach is further supported by Lee (1991), who suggested that effective parenting can be understood as an interactional process of adjusting to the child's different levels of competence. Thus, it is important to ask to what extent does a parent address a child's or an adolescent's needs.

Fathers have been described as the parent who places a greater emphasis on the behavioral autonomy of their adolescents. Power and Shanks (1988) interviewed fathers and mothers of adolescents regarding the behaviors that they encouraged and discouraged in each of seven areas: self-care behavior, household responsibilities, household rules, prosocial behavior, problem behavior, other behavior with peers, and independence. Parents were also asked what they do to encourage or discourage a certain behavior, and what they would do if a certain technique did not work. Results showed that fathers saw themselves as more actively involved in encouraging instrumental behaviors such as assertiveness and independence. Mothers, on the other hand, were more likely to report encouraging interpersonal behaviors such as manners and politeness, and adolescent involvement in domestic chores.

Similarly, Hauser *et al.* (1987) analyzed verbal interactions between parents and adolescents while working on a joint task. Fathers expressed more support and showed more interest in their adolescents' suggestions. Mothers, on the other hand, expressed more constraining speech that did not support the adolescents' own suggestions. The role of paternal encouragement for adolescent development is also found in a study that predicted children's educational expectations, aspirations and actual school grades. Smith (1989) found that adolescents' educational expectations were accounted for by their personal characteristics, their father's level of education, and the degree to which the father recognized the child's achievements by complimenting, expressing pleasure or praising. Adolescents' educational aspirations and school grades were explained by their fathers' recognition of achievement.

A more elaborate understanding of how fathers support the developmental tasks of their adolescents can be seen in Snarey's (1993) longitudinal study. Men were interviewed at ages 25, 31 and 47, and asked to describe their participation in childrearing. The frequency with which each father reported participating in rearing his first-born child was tabulated for the child's first decade – childhood – and second decade – adolescence. Each childrearing participation was classified according to six varieties as follows:

1 Support of childhood social-emotional development.
2 Support of childhood intellectual-academic development.
3 Support of childhood physical-athletic development.

4   Support of adolescent social-emotional development.
5   Support of adolescent intellectual-academic development.
6   Support of adolescent physical-athletic development.

The novelty of Snarey's approach is that an activity is classified

> according to the father's intent, in terms of an activity's *primary function* rather than simply according to content. Teaching a child how to pitch a baseball counted as a form of parental generativity that primarily promoted the child's physical development, for instance, but teaching a child how to understand baseball strategy or baseball statistics counted as promoting intellectual development, and accompanying a child to a baseball game for the sake of companionship counted as promoting social-emotional development.
>
> (Snarey, 1993: 37)

Examples of the actual childrearing activities that were assigned to each of the six varieties are shown in Table 3.1. On average, fathers were involved in 9.3 childrearing activities during childhood and adolescence. During both periods fathers provided more support for their children's social-emotional development, relative to other types of childrearing participation, although the level of this support decreased from childhood to adolescence. The second most common paternal caretaking behavior during childhood was support of physical-athletic development, which subsequently decreased, and was ranked third during the adolescent period. Fathers provided the least support for intellectual-academic development during childhood but this type of support increased during adolescence, and became the second most common form of fathers' childrearing participation. Further analyses indicated that whereas social-emotional and physical-athletic support were greater during childhood than adolescence, support of intellectual-academic development was greater during adolescence than childhood. Two important conclusions can be drawn from Snarey's findings. First, fathers' involvement with their adolescents should not be considered solely on a quantitative level, namely the extent to which a father is involved with his child or adolescent, but rather for its function in fostering the development of the child. Second, fathers are sensitive to the changing needs of their children. During childhood, fathers provide emotional and physical support. During adolescence, they focus more on the promotion of the child's age-appropriate tasks. Former physical support of a child is transformed into support of intellectual tasks.

Table 3.1 Childrearing rating categories: examples of fathers' parental generativity

Support of social-emotional development	Support of intellectual-academic development	Support of physical-athletic development

During the childhood decade

Support of social-emotional development	Support of intellectual-academic development	Support of physical-athletic development
Rocks to sleep	Provides educational toys	Takes to doctor
Comforts child when afraid of the dark	Plays with and responds to baby's sounds	Gives bottle, feeds
Takes to visit relatives	Reads to child	Plays exercise games
Plays social games like peek-a-boo	Plays word games	Changes diaper
Takes trick-or-treating	Takes to children's museum	Teaches how to swim
Gives birthday party	Takes to library, bookstore	Takes shopping for first baseball glove
Spends special time with child before bedtime	Consults with teacher	Makes child's breakfast
Takes around with him during evening routine	Monitors homework	Monitors immunizations
Accompanies to church	Changes residence so child will be in better school	Demonstrates and encourages use of an erector set
Takes on Sunday drives	Provides music lessons	Takes to skating lessons, gymnastic lessons, others
Encourages child to invite friends home	Gives child a magazine subscription	Teaches how to ride a bike
Supports joining Scouts	Teaches how to identify different bird species, star constellations, and so on	Teaches how to dribble a basketball

During the adolescent decade

Support of social-emotional development	Support of intellectual-academic development	Support of physical-athletic development
Takes on duo camping trip	Takes to science museum	Monitors personal hygiene
Monitors character of children's friends	Teaches baseball statistics	Teaches how to pitch a curve ball
Accompanies to church	Enrolls child in a nature study field trip	Provides sex education
Buys new house to provide non-delinquent peers	Takes to art gallery	Gives boxing lessons
Accompanies to ball game	Enrolls child in special courses	Teaches how to fish
Spends special time with child on weekends	Provides religious education	Takes shopping to buy new corrective shoes
Talks about emotionally charged issues	Takes on trip to visit other cultural groups	Takes to dentist
Chaperons a dance	Takes to library, bookstore	Monitors nutrition
Allows slumber party	Discusses school courses	Teaches how to improve hockey game
Provides guidance on dating problems	Discusses books or newspaper articles with child	Teaches how to drive an automobile
Gives advice on resolving a social conflict	Gives feedback on term paper	Takes for physical exam
Encourages to invite friends to the house	Solicits and discusses political opinions	

Source: Snarey, 1993

We can therefore suggest that fathers are aware of, and actively support, their adolescents' normative behavioral expectations. This is done in a variety of ways, and is not contingent upon the exact amount of time a father spends with his adolescent. The importance of the paternal role in adolescent development and adaptation is also supported by findings based on adolescents' perspectives. Forehead and Nousiainen (1993) studied the perceptions adolescents have of each parent, and their own functioning in school. As in other studies, fathers were perceived to be less involved, but parenting by fathers, and not by mothers, was a significant predictor of adolescent functioning in school. The mother's score on parenting level of acceptance/rejection accounted for 25 per cent of adolescent cognitive functioning as rated by teachers. Perceived paternal acceptance/rejection, however, accounted for 44 per cent of the variance. Forehead and Nousiainen give two explanations for the finding that the father's contribution is important even though his involvement is lower. The first explanation suggests that adolescents are more eager to obtain the approval of the father than of the mother, since the father's acceptance is less available. The second explanation for fathers' impact on their children is that their acceptance is more conditional than mothers'. That is, fathers may be more likely to be approving or accepting when their adolescent children perform well outside the home, and disapproving when such behavior does not occur. The role of paternal conditional acceptance is further supported in a study by Deb and Gulati (1989), who found that positive father–child relationships, combined with high expectation of intellectual and career success, were related to adolescent daughters' academic achievement.

Fathers are also perceived by adolescents as the intermediary between the family and the external world, and as such contribute to behavioral competence. A study by Oliveri and Reiss (1987) points to the centrality of the father in adolescent social interactions with the outside world. In their study, mothers, fathers and adolescents were asked to describe the composition of their personal network, by listing all individuals outside the nuclear family whom they felt were important or significant in some way. In addition each family member was asked to describe the frequency of contact, help given, and feelings about each respondent. A comparison of father–adolescent and mother–adolescent associations, in characteristics of personal networks, revealed them to be distinctive. For kin networks, mother–adolescent associations were stronger and more numerous than those involving the father. For example, the number of adolescent contacts with kin was better predicted by the level of the mother's contacts with kin than the father's. However, regarding friendship networks, fathers' contacts with extra-family figures were a better predictor of adolescent contacts with peers. Adolescents' density of peer networks and frequency of contact, for example, were related to those of their fathers. Oliveri and Reiss speculate that parental behaviors serve as cues for their children on how to interact with others, with fathers in particular serving as models for contacts with peers.

Harris and Howard (1984) suggest an additional mechanism to assess the way fathers impact their children's interaction with the world. In their study, they measured the perceived psychological and physical resemblance of adolescents to each of their parents. Boys more often claimed psychological and physical resemblance to their fathers, yet a similar percentage of girls reported a resemblance to their father or mother. Harris and Howard claimed that the more frequent selection of the father as resemblance object was not based on a negative emotional reaction to the mother. The father, they suggested, "represents the figure more familiar with, and more successful in, the outside world – the world that the adolescent is preparing to enter. Identification with such a knowledgeable figure would lessen the anxiety about leaving the security of the family" (Harris and Howard, 1984: 131).

Together, these studies suggest that fathers may influence adolescents' attainment of behavioral autonomy tasks in various ways. Fathers may either encourage certain behaviors, or serve as models for competency and interaction with the external world. Yet, as suggested above, parental impact on children is not limited to the behavioral sphere, as parents also shape children's self perceptions and moderate the philosophy children develop toward life.

Fathers' consolidation of adolescent values, and philosophy of life

Fathers have been found to play a role in shaping the attitudes adolescents develop toward self, and their philosophy of life. Gecas and Schwalbe (1986) examined the relationship between perceived parental behavior and adolescent perceptions of self worth and self efficacy. Both parents and adolescents were asked to rate parental behavior on measures of control/autonomy, support and participation. Self worth referred to the moral aspect of self evaluation in such terms as "good," "worthy," "virtuous," and living up to standards of moral conduct. Self efficacy referred to one's sense of competence or effectiveness in dealing with the social and physical world. Adolescents' perceptions of parental behavior were found to be related to adolescent self esteem as follows: boys' self worth was most strongly affected by paternal control, i.e. the more the father was perceived to exert control, the higher level of self efficacy the adolescent reported. Girls' self esteem (both self worth and self efficacy) was most strongly related to parental support and degree of participation. Although for girls the influence of fathers and mothers was similar, fathers had a slight edge. Thus, fathers who were more supportive and participatory with their daughters had daughters with higher self esteem and self efficacy.

As with behavioral autonomy, parents also influence the attitudes and values of their children indirectly, by serving as models. Lapsley *et al.* (1984) studied adolescent attitudes toward parents' authority and impersonal authority such as police and government. Although a distinction was found in connection with adolescents' attitudes towards personal and impersonal public authority, their attitudes toward their fathers were significantly correlated with attitudes toward the police and government. Lapsley *et al.* suggest that "the authority of the Father is seen as a representative of 'official' sources of authority more often than is the case with the authority of the mother" (ibid.: 535).

Similar trends emphasizing the role of the father were found when adolescents' religious beliefs were studied. Krol (1983) tested the interdependence between the image of one's father and the image of God among Polish adolescents. Adolescents were divided into two groups: those having a "good" functioning father, and those having a "bad" father (addicted to alcohol). Results indicated that adolescents with a "good" father had a significantly more positive image of God than did adolescents with a "bad" father. In addition (among those with a "good" father) the evaluation of the image of God and the image of the father were highly correlated. Clark *et al.* (1988) studied the transmission of religious beliefs and practices among Protestant families. Mothers mostly influenced sons' practical applications of religion, but regarding religious beliefs, it was the father's theological and mythological orientation that was related to the beliefs of the son. In a study on Jewish adolescents (Herzbrun, 1993), it was shown that adolescents' religious beliefs were in consensus with their fathers', once the fathers provided emotional support for their adolescents.

In sum, results of various studies point to the special role fathers play in the development of their adolescent children. Fathers were found to be more aware and respectful of the adolescent's developing and changing body. The support and encouragement of fathers was also found to contribute to the attainment of academic and social competencies. In addition, adolescents perceived fathers as better models for interaction with the extra-family environment and societal values.

Fathers' support and children's early adulthood consequences

The studies presented so far have pointed to the father's role in the attainment of developmental tasks during adolescence. A stronger indication for the attainment of a developmental task would be the level of functioning at a later stage of life. Heath and Heath (1991) interviewed college-aged men who had succeeded vocationally and were mentally healthy. These young men tended to remember their fathers as available and affectionate. Their descriptions portrayed fathers who helped the boys with homework, and encouraged their physical-athletic growth. Snarey (1993) approached this topic in a more elaborate manner. Children whose fathers' behavior was evaluated during their childhood and adolescence were evaluated during early adulthood with respect to their educational and occupational mobility outcomes. Mobility reflected the extent to which an individual's educational or occupational achievement was higher than that of his/her father. In general, children's educational and vocational levels were related to those of their fathers. Mobility was differently accounted for by fathers' behavior regarding girls versus boys.

Sixteen per cent of the daughters' educational mobility was explained by their fathers' childrearing behavior. Fathers who gave their daughters a combination of more support for physical-athletic development during childhood and adolescence, a lower level of social-emotional support during childhood and a higher level during adolescence, made a positive contribution to their daughter's educational upward mobility. In addition, 8 per cent of girls' occupational mobility was explained by fathers' support of physical-athletic and social-emotional development during adolescence. Fathers' contribution toward their sons' mobility was somewhat different. Fathers who provided higher levels of intellectual-academic support during both childhood and adolescence, as well as social-emotional support during adolescence, had sons who achieved greater educational mobility. Sons' occupational mobility was predicted exclusively by fathers' support for physical development during childhood. Snarey's longitudinal data show that father–adolescent interaction has a longstanding impact on adaptation in later stages in life. The differential impact that fathers' support has on their sons' and daughters' developmental outcome will be discussed in the following section, and elaborated upon in Chapters 4 and 5.

FATHERS' DIFFERENTIAL IMPACT ON ADOLESCENT BOYS' AND GIRLS' ATTAINMENT OF DEVELOPMENTAL TASKS

As we have seen, boys and girls were found to cope differently with the developmental tasks of adolescence (Seiffge-Krenke, 1990). Girls have greater difficulty incorporating the image of their new bodies, and throughout most phases of adolescence girls report a poorer body self concept. A comparison of over 1,000 12- to 19-year-old adolescents on the Offer self concept scale showed that boys had higher confidence in their own abilities, while girls reported more positive relations with peers.

The question we would like to ask is, to what extent are such sex differences related to a possible distinctive relationship that adolescent males and females have with their fathers? Seginer (1985) examined the contributions of father–adolescent and mother–adolescent relationships to scholastic achievement, using two relationship measures: perceived similarity to parent and emotional closeness to parent. Results showed that perceived similarity to the father related to females' academic performance, whereas emotional closeness to the father was negatively related to males' academic performance. Relationship with the mother was not found to be related to academic performance of the adolescents.

A study by Benson *et al.* (1990) investigated the identity consequences of attachment to mothers and fathers. Identity status was measured within interpersonal and ideological domains and was assessed with regard to four statuses: diffusion, moratorium, foreclosure and achievement. A status of diffusion refers to a state in which the individual has few commitments to any set of beliefs, and seems directionless and wandering. In the status of moratorium there is a genuine search for alternatives, and a testing of oneself in a variety of experiences. The main theme in foreclosure is the avoidance of autonomous choice, with the adolescent accepting and identifying with values or attitudes of significant others. Identity achievement is the final phase of identity formation and is characterized by inner confidence in one's ability. Benson *et al.* found that for both females and males, attachment to one's mother predicted higher levels of identity achievement and less diffusion. However, attachment to one's father had differential effects on males and females. For males, attachment to their fathers predicted lower diffusion, whereas for females, attachment to their fathers predicted higher foreclosure.

The findings of these two studies point to the possible nature and subsequent effect of being close to one's father. Closeness to the father may provide a secure base for adolescents. For example, it may serve as a protective factor against diffusion. However, closeness may also carry with it certain obstacles for adolescent development, which are differently expressed for males and females. For females, closeness to the father supports the daughter's academic achievement. Yet, as Benson *et al.* suggest, when a female is strongly attached to her father she may idealize him. This idealization may lead her to conform to her father and to commit herself to his values. Boys are probably less pressured to conform to their father's values. Yet such closeness may to some extent interfere with males' movement towards autonomy and, as found in the study by Seginer, can be related to a lower level of academic achievement.

This speculation assumes that males have a greater need for some sort of push toward independence from their fathers; this is supported by the findings of the study by Gecas and Schwalbe (1986) presented above. Boys' self esteem was found to be more affected by paternal control, while girls' self esteem was more strongly affected by paternal and maternal support and participation. Boys' self esteem may depend more heavily on self attribution related to action and consequence, and this is probably enhanced by paternal control and paternal models for action. Boys are more encouraged to emphasize mastery, agency instrumentality and exploratory behavior (Block, 1973). Girls' self esteem, on the other hand, is more embedded in interpersonal relationships, and sensitivity to others, which may make them more dependent on reflected appraisals for their self definitions.

Taken together, support and acceptance by parents is a protective factor for children. However, for adolescents, continuous parental support may turn into some form of binding (Stierlin, 1974) and thus interfere with the developmental tasks of separation and independence. Studies presented in the preceding chapter and in this one show that paternal acceptance is more often combined with paternal support of adolescents' striving for independence. Fathers' more balanced acceptance may be attributed to three factors: fathers are less involved, they actively support independent behavior, and finally they are models for independence through their greater interaction with the extra-family milieu. Yet it is interesting to note that fathers act differently toward their male and female adolescents. While males' penchant for separation and independence is encouraged, females are expected to individuate within the realm of the family. In addition, paternal closeness carries with it a different meaning for boys and girls. The next two chapters will explore and elaborate further upon the historical, sociological and psychological bases of the differential attitudes that fathers have and enact toward their male and female offspring.

4   The father–son relationship

Maccoby and Jacklin's seminal review of the literature on sex differences found limited evidence of differential socialization of boys and girls. Their review lacked extant information about fathers, and they suggested that "it may be that fathers differentiate between the sexes to a much greater degree than do mothers" (Maccoby and Jacklin, 1974: 348). Using a meta-analysis, Siegal (1987) reviewed 39 independent published studies on parent–child differential socialization processes, and found little evidence for mother-specific differences in the treatment of boys and girls. In contrast,

> a modest degree of support exists for father-specific differences from results that are significant. In 20 studies, the father's ratings of behavior or treatment of boys and girls differed significantly and the differences for mothers, if present at all, were comparatively few.
>
> (Siegal, 1987: 190)

In general, fathers gave more evidence of belief in sex-role stereotypes, which were reflected in their different attitudes and behaviors toward boys and girls. In a study conducted by Rubin *et al.* (1974), fathers were asked to rate their newborns within 24 hours after birth. Fathers tended to describe their newborn sons as big, firm, strong and hardy. Fathers vocalized less than mothers to their 5-month-old sons (Palkovitz, 1984), and showed less affection toward their toddler sons during separation in a day care setting (Noller, 1978). Fathers responded more negatively to boys' doll play (Fagot, 1978), and Noller (1980) observed more negative statements among the 5- to 8-year-old father–son dyads than in father–daughter dyads. Bronstein (1984), in a sample of Mexican fathers, found that fathers more frequently reprimanded their sons and were more restrictive toward them than toward daughters.

Brody and Axelrad (1978) conducted a longitudinal study of the relationship between forms of parental caregiving and the psychological development of children. In the study they followed the development of children for seven years and interviewed parents regarding their childrearing attitudes and practices. Results showed that fathers behaved differently toward their male and female children. As found in other studies, male children received firmer discipline and were exposed to more strict demands by their fathers. However, fathers also favored their male children, as was apparent in their efforts to spend more time with their sons and in their higher aspirations for boys. More favorable attitudes of fathers toward their sons were also reported in additional studies. Kotelchuk (1981) found that fathers played longer with their first-born sons. Fathers tended to touch their sons more, to encourage physical play and exploration, and responded more positively toward them (Jacklin *et al.*, 1984).

Taken together, past research suggests that fathers' attitudes and behaviors toward their sons are complex, if not contradictory. The father–son relationship is characterized by strictness combined with engagement. We can therefore understand the unique vulnerability of sons who may be generously fostered by their fathers and yet at the same time be dramatically restricted. We would like to explore the historical and social aspects of this duality in the father–son relationship, as observed almost from the beginning of life (Rubin *et al.*, 1974), and to understand its possible implications for father–son relationships during adolescence.

THE DIALECTIC OF THE FATHER–SON RELATIONSHIP

The oedipal drama as a symbol of the aggression in father–son relationships

Apparently, one of the unique characteristics of father–son relationships pertains to the mode in which aggressive feelings are dealt with. It interesting to note that the father–son relationship exemplifies basic societal issues such as power sharing, intergenerational conflicts and rivalry. Perhaps for this reason this issue is raised in mythology, and subsequently became a prominent topic in psychoanalytic theory.

A central issue in psychoanalytic thought refers to Oedipus' relationship with his father. In this well-known Greek tragedy, Oedipus slew his father Laius and married his mother Jocasta; this family drama reflects the ambivalent desire of a son to displace his father and possess his mother. It is interesting that the name of Laius is not as well known as that of Oedipus, nor are Laius' motives and behaviors widely discussed in psychological literature. A relationship exemplifies sustained interaction between partners (Hinde, 1976). We suggest, therefore, that a closer inspection of both partners, father and son, will allow us a better understanding of the father–son relationship.

In this Greek drama, Laius is informed that he will bear a son who will one day slay him. When Oedipus is born, Laius orders that his son be left on a mountaintop to die. Thus, the drama starts with the father who perceives his son as a threat, and later on it is Oedipus who wants to replace his father. As Kaplan *et al.* (1984) have suggested, the myth typifies the underlying conflict between father and son, and the mutual fears of destruction. Nature and reality show that this fear may be justified. As a result of principles of territoriality and dominance adult male animals may in some cases act aggressively toward the juvenile males of the troop (Fox, 1982). Suomi (1990) described the maturation processes of the male macaque primates. Following pubescence, adolescent males are expelled from their maternal troops. In search for company and support the younger male may approach a troop of adult males. However, adult males are not too sympathetic toward these youngsters. The attempts at approach are perceived by adult macaques as aggressive, and they react accordingly. Statistics have shown that as many as 50 per cent of the younger generation of macaque males perish, either following direct aggression by adult males, or through inability to live on their own in the wilderness. Although human fathers and sons do not fight for territory, at least 700 children are killed each year in the United States, far greater numbers are battered or abused, and the perpetrators are mainly fathers (Ross, 1985).

The question we must ask is: why would a father want to destroy his son, and why would a son want to destroy his father? When reading the story of Laius and Oedipus, a few ideas emerge. On the one hand, Laius' abandonment of his infant son is motivated by self-preservation, an act that can be understood though not condoned. Yet as Ross (1982) points out, during the encounter with his grown-up son – Oedipus – at the crossroads, Laius does not refrain from a direct confrontation, he humiliates and strikes out against the stranger-son. Greek mythology is depicting Laius' (and men's) inability to perceive of a son as an heir rather than a rival. Laius could have accepted the Oracle's prophecy not as destiny's curse but as a symbolic promise that his throne would be continued by his own son. However, through narcissism and hubris, Laius wants to provide his own continuity. The destructive behavior toward offspring is exemplified by the rite of sacrificing sons, especially the firstborn, that existed in the cultures of the Ancient East, perhaps reflecting the universality of the father–son conflict.

While in former times the father's role required him to provide and to discipline, fathers today, as portrayed in Chapters 1 and 2, are also found to be engaged in playful and recreational activities with their children. Nevertheless, remnants of fathers' aggressive attitudes toward their children can still be detected in the way fathers interact with their infants (Ross, 1985). In a tape that portrays a father interacting with his 2-month-old baby, the father is observed to stare at his son and to refer to him as "young man." The father then asks the son whether he has been good to his mother and whether he has eaten his beef for dinner. The father then taps the infant's abdomen vigorously as his animated face dives repeatedly toward that of his first-born son – wide-eyed, alert, high-keyed and excited. According to Yogman (1982) this pattern – the intrusion, the tapping, the high-keyed stimulation – is typical of fathers' interactions with their babies. This type of interaction is distinctly different from the more tender dialogues between mothers and infants (Ross, 1985: 118). Herzog (1982a) termed it a "kamikaze mode" of play between fathers and sons. In these interactions, for example, fathers may throw the baby up into the air like a plaything.

It is interesting that on the one hand fathers are described as over-stimulating their sons, yet on the other hand, as described in the previous chapters, fathers are less intensively engaged with their children and are more distant. Esman (1985) suggests that these contradictory attitudes of fathers toward their sons may constitute a defense against fathers' aggressive impulses. Moreover, Esman claims that the destructive wishes of fathers are unconscious, and, except in pathological states, are expressed only in dreams, and can be derived only indirectly.

The son as the mirror of his father

Aggressive or destructive tendencies of fathers are but one aspect of fatherhood, and have been transformed from overt expression to more subtle cues. Overt aggression has perhaps been replaced by intensive joint motor activities, especially between father and son. A further characteristic of the father–son relationship involves the perceived similarity between them, an aspect that can be found throughout history and is best reflected in Kierkegaard's conceptualization of the father–son relationship as a mirror.

Kierkegaard ([1847] 1954) wrote that a son is like a mirror in which a father sees himself, and a son looks up to his father as a mirror of his own future. This contention points to the reciprocal nature of the father–son relationship and identity, and suggests that a unique sense of closeness exists between fathers and sons. Historically, and to some extent today, fathers perceived their sons as their heirs, and tended to shape them in their own image. This description of the father–son relationship also fits Lidz's (1980) description of firm affectional ties between parents and children that characterize the nuclear family.

These additional facets of fatherhood are revealed in various cultures. For example,

> A young father was chasing his son, a little toddler, who was playfully running away from him, in a park: "Careful, Papi," he said in Spanish, "You get hurt. Careful, Papi." Why would a father call his own son Papi (or Papito), the Spanish equivalent of Daddy?
>
> (Palmeri, 1989: 385)

Palmeri suggests that the message to the child is that his very existence gives the father pleasure, gratification, comfort and nurture, just as these feelings once came to the father from his nurturing parents. Through the father's positive experience with his own child, former experiences are relived. Although such messages may serve some narcissistic gratification for the father, nevertheless we cannot overlook the perceived similarity, closeness and tenderness to the child. The close positive father–son relationship recalls the isogender ("negative") oedipal complex (Blos, 1985). During the pre-oedipal stage the boy is attached to his father, asserts himself through him, shares his grandeur and is fascinated by his activity. In response to their infants' growing interest in them, fathers become more interested in their sons, and enjoy seeing their sons as reflections of themselves.

The father's search for his own image in his son recalls the mirroring phenomenon (Kohut, 1977), in this case from the father's perspective. The son's very existence and his following in his father's footsteps, can regulate the father's self esteem. Historical examples can show how important it was for kings to raise their sons as reflections of themselves. Frederick-William I, king of Prussia at the beginning of the eighteenth century, also known as the Soldaten Koenig (soldier king), raised his son Frederick II in a strict military manner. Frederick, however, had different interests, was attracted more to arts and music, resisted his father's dictates and fled the country with his best friend, Katte. Frederick and his friend were captured and imprisoned.

Thus we can see how important it is for a father that his son succeeds to his legacy. However, we can observe two opposing tendencies in fathers' relationships with their sons, when dealing with this issue: on the one hand, aggressive tendencies, and on the other, overtures of closeness and love. It is interesting that these opposing tendencies are exemplified in the nature of play throughout childhood. Fathers and sons can be observed engaging in rough-and-tumble play (Yogman, 1982). A son's wrestling with his father allows an incomparable physical closeness to him. Yet at the same time being too close may be painful and sometimes, though unintentionally, harmful (as may happen in rough-and-tumble play among friends; Smith and Bulton, 1990), and therefore distance is also valued.

This dialectic between aggression and love, closeness and distance, in the father–son relationship, has been mainly referred to on the unconscious level and at most as a derivative of father–son interactions. Yet, as presented at the beginning of this chapter, integration of various studies has also pointed to the dialectic nature of father–son relationships. In addition, this pattern of paternal interaction can serve as a model for individuation (Mahler *et al.*, 1975). The child experiences closeness that is co-ordinated with separate and sometimes opposing needs and wishes. The fact that both father and son have different wishes yet are able to co-operate, may in turn enhance each one's sense of independence, which becomes a major issue during adolescence.

Father–son relations during adolescence

The complexity of father–son relationships is increased once the son reaches adolescence. Holmbeck and Hill (1988) analyzed parent–adolescent interactions during various stages of adolescent pubertal development. He found that mothers' verbal interruptions of sons and daughters, and children's interruptions of mothers, increased as a function of pubertal maturation. In father–child interactions, the degree and type of reciprocity varied with the sex of offspring. Fathers interrupted sons more often as a function of pubertal status, and sons typically yielded. Similar results were reported by Steinberg (1988). Steinberg asked parents and adolescents to complete a conflict checklist indicating the intensity of discussions they had regarding day-to-day issues such as curfew or clothing. Scores revealed the frequency and intensity of conflict in parent–child relations. Results showed that pubertal development of boys was related to more frequent arguments with the mother, and greater distancing from the father.

As presented in Chapter 2, no clear link between pubertal changes and increased adolescent argumentativeness has been established. Nevertheless, some researchers have attributed the increase in conflicts to the change in adolescents' acceptance of parental authority. For example, Smetana (1989) has documented how young adolescents raise questions about the legitimacy and wisdom of parental attitudes. In addition, parents also carry some responsibility for the increase in conflicts, as they sometimes are not sufficiently sensitive to the changes their adolescents undergo. Shulman *et al.* (1993) investigated children's and early adolescents' perceptions of parental behavior. Early adolescents perceived their fathers to be less controlling but also less accepting of them. However, fathers' perceptions of early adolescents were similar to their perception of younger children. The fathers overlooked their young adolescents' penchant for expressing different ideas, and being less close to their parents.

Similar trends are found in a study by Salt (1991), who asked fathers and sons to rate the acceptability of affectionate touching between father and son. In addition, fathers' and sons' joint play in various physical and cognitive games was videotaped, and their incidental and non-incidental touches were counted. Results showed that although father and son enjoyed affectionate touch, as the son approached adolescence both demonstrated a decrease in the acceptability of touch between them. As for actual touch, fathers tended to touch their sons twice as often as their sons touched them. Thus, although fathers perceived that the amount of touch should decrease with the age of their sons, in reality they continued to express their affection physically more than their early adolescents did or wished for.

It seems that in early adolescence, although fathers may understand sons' wishes for distance, these wishes may not always be respected. The gap between fathers' and adolescents' perceptions may lead to conflicts between both parties. However, it would be incorrect to assume that mothers and fathers become less important figures in the lives of their adolescents. Although friends become important partners for intimacy, adolescents rated parents as their most important source of nurture (Hunter and Youniss, 1982). The duality of control versus closeness becomes more complicated during adolescence, when it conflicts with the adolescent's penchant for growth, and the father may be perceived as the person who undermines this process.

It is thus understandable that during adolescence, intergenerational conflict, and often more minor arguments, can become a reality, and perturbations are found even among non-clinical families (Collins, 1990). Going back to mythology, the question is: who will have his way, the father or son? Laius does not offer a compromise, he wants total submission. In response to this provocative challenge, Oedipus kills the king – his father. What is it that causes these two men, father and grown-up son, to be engulfed in such a high level of aggression, ultimately leading to the destruction of father by son? Why could the father and grown-up son not arrive at some sort of compromise or at least distance themselves and stay apart? Developmental changes and sexual maturation lead to changes in patterns of ·parent–child relationships (Collins, 1990), and sons and fathers must renegotiate their relationships. Blos's (1985) description of two distinct patterns of relationships between adolescent sons and their fathers is relevant to this discussion. One pattern is referred to as the "triadic father" – the son's relationship to the father is part of the relationship to both mother and father. The second pattern is referred to as the "dyadic father" – an exclusive relationship between father and son.

The "triadic father" is relevant to the re-emergence of the oedipal conflict, which must be resolved at this stage (Anna Freud, 1958; Laufer and Laufer, 1984). Owing to the arousal of sexual urges, the adolescent boy is afraid of being subjected by the female – the mother. The father can be a source of help and support in preventing maternal engulfment. In early childhood the boy's attraction to the mother is resolved by his perception of the father as punishing and restraining. During adolescence, boys are repulsed by maternal attraction and they turn to the father not as a rival of the triangular oedipal phase (Atkins, 1989), but as savior, and the person who can affirm the boy's manhood. The "dyadic father" refers to the relationship that has developed between father and child prior to the oedipal stage and is desexualized and less mature. The boy's relationship to his father during this early stage oscillates between submission to him, sharing his grandeur, and self assertion vis-à-vis the father. The "dyadic father" seems to follow a generally positive path (though termed the negative oedipal complex), especially in light of the fact that the father has never been a full-fledged symbiotic partner (Blos, 1991). In early childhood the resolution of the oedipus complex is achieved through the boy's identification with the strong father. In adolescence disengagement from the mother is undoubtedly age appropriate, but a too close identification with the "strong" father does not sound appropriate at the stage when independence should be pursued. Furthermore, adoption of paternal attributes would raise the issue of a foreclosed identity (Marcia, 1966; Waterman, 1985), reflecting the absence of autonomous choice. According to Marcia some adolescents are more directed by other people, and tend to accept whatever role figures such as their father or coach prescribe for them. In such a case, although the behavior may seem adult-like, the adolescent is still identifying with the prescribed roles and does not struggle for own preferences. The mature quality of such an identity can be questioned.

Psychoanalytically oriented writers have hence described the role of the father as savior, and as the parent who is supposed to recognize and support the boy's penchant for individuation. However, in reality the nature of father–son relations during adolescence is more dialectic, and is presented as such by researchers.

Perturbations in parent–child relationships were considered and described by developmentalists (Collins, 1990) as part of normal development, when adolescents disengage from infantile attachment to parents. Yet conceptually, the perturbations in father–son relationships reflect their complicated nature. The continued need for parental support combined with criticism of parents shows how a son can be caught between submission to, or at least acknowledgement of, the father's grandeur and power on the one hand and urges for self assertion and individuality on the other (Atkins, 1989). From the intrapsychic perspective, we witness what Blos describes as "the son's struggle between a murderous defense against submission, and a passionate yearning for paternal acknowledgement of his manhood" (Blos, 1991: 9). When combined with fathers' penchant to impose power and authority over their sons (Esman, 1985), it seems that during adolescence father and son are torn between the assertion of a separate legacy on one hand, and cultivation of closeness and continuity on the other. Metaphorically, it can be understood how the meeting at the crossroads between Laius and Oedipus could have deteriorated to bloodshed.

History presents us with examples of unresolved conflicts both when father-kings were unwilling to step down from the throne, or when son-princes revolted against their fathers. In the last year of King David's reign, Abshalom his son revolted against him. He organized an army, and planned an attack on the king in Jerusalem. David was forced to flee the city. When Abshalom entered the city, he went to the palace and abused his father's mistresses. The friction between father and son escalated into a full-scale war, in which Abshalom's army was defeated and more than 20,000 of his men were killed. Abshalom tried to escape, but was captured and executed by one of David's commanders. Although the revolt was contained, the death of his own son was difficult for David, who could not stop mourning him until forced to do so by his adviser – fighting the son cannot be disconnected from loving him.

Resolution of the father–son conflict: cultural models

Different cultures present us with different models for resolving the father–son conflict. A central story in the Bible is Abraham's binding of his son, Isaac. Abraham is commanded by God to bind Isaac and offer him as a sacrifice. Abraham fulfills the command and binds his son to the altar, but when he is ready to slay Isaac, an angel of the Lord calls out to him and prohibits the act; a sacrificial ram is offered instead. The majority of Bible commentators and philosophers, among them Kierkegaard, see this act as a sign of Abraham's ultimate belief in God. However, even among traditional commentators a different view can be found. According to this view, infanticide was common among the cultures of the Ancient East. God's purpose was to teach Abraham to transcend man's innate aggression toward his children and to provide a different model of the father–son relationship. On the basis of the Abraham–Isaac story Wellisch (1954) proposes a three-stage model of the parent–child relationship. The first stage is characterized by intense parental aggression and possessiveness of the child. This aggression is particularly strong in fathers and is directed toward first-born sons. The second stage is characterized both by guilt about the aggressive and possessive tendencies, and by attempts to compromise between aggression and guilt. Laius does not kill his infant son, but tries to suppress the conflict. Wilhelm II did not kill his son Frederick, but did execute Frederick's friend, Katte. The Abraham–Isaac story presents a third stage, abandonment of aggressive and possessive tendencies. Kaplan *et al.* (1984) suggest that in this model fathers are taught that they are not the owners of their sons. Furthermore, as other Biblical stories tell, the father is expected to offer his blessing to the next generation. By offering his blessing, the father affirms his son's manhood (Blos, 1985).

The father's ambivalent role, and the change required in his attitude toward his son, are reflected in initiation rituals. "In all such rituals the father's authoritative, castrating attitudes, symbolically acted out, are balanced by his educative, supporting role in promoting the boy's emergence into adulthood" (Esman, 1985: 147). This dynamic is exemplified in the initiation rites found in Papua New Guinea (Bosse, 1990). At first boys are separated from their mothers in order to sever the symbiotic bond between mother and boy. A "male society" separated from females is established and controlled by male elders. At the first stages of initiation, when boys are separated from their mothers and villages, they are humiliated by initiators (representing fathers), repeatedly beaten, mocked and punished. The violence includes cutting into the boys' penises and letting them bleed. This weaning process is clearly aggressive, as if to wipe out any childish or female characteristic in the boy. However, although such rites are repeated until the young boy is transformed into a man, the rites do not end with the aggressive acts. The boys are subsequently courted by adult men who invest enormous quantities of food, activities, time and fantasy in them, as if to convince the boys that men are better "mothers." In some cases the alliances formed between men and boys are so strong that they may have a homosexual undertone.

It is interesting to note that the importance of both paternal control and affection is also supported by research. Feldman and Wood (1994) examined the nature and correlates of parents' expectations of sons' behavioral autonomy in adolescence. Parents of sons in sixth and tenth grades were asked to indicate at what age they expect to grant their sons privileges (choose what clothes to buy), and require responsibilities of them (keep their rooms clean). Mothers' expectations of their pre-adolescent and adolescent sons showed no relationship with the son's functioning. Yet pre-adolescent boys whose fathers anticipated that they would postpone their sons' privileges until later in adolescence, were significantly more likely to earn higher grades and exert greater efforts in school four years later. In addition, pre-adolescents whose fathers anticipated granting privileges later were less likely as mid-adolescents to engage in social misconduct and early sexual activity with multiple partners. Thus, paternal control contributes to sons' adaptive functioning. It is probable, as Feldman and Wood have suggested, that paternal standards direct the son's movement toward autonomy (Feldman and Wood, 1994: 62). However, it is not only paternal control that is related to sons' later functioning. Millen and Roll (1977) investigated the relationship between psychological well-being of undergraduate male students, and their sense of being understood by their fathers. Results showed that sons who described feeling close to their fathers, and for whom acceptance by their fathers had been an enduring pattern in their relationship, reported higher levels of self concept and fewer somatic complaints. Taken together, these findings suggest although fathers tend to control their sons, control can be combined with an accepting attitude.

A recent study by Weinberger (1994) shows how a pacific father–son relationship during adolescence is an important predictor of the son's later adjustment. In the study, a variety of parents' and sons' personality measures were taken when the sons were 12 years old. Conceptually, the measures dealt with two superordinate dimensions:

the subjective experience of distress (including anxiety, depression, low self esteem and low well-being), and self restraint (including impulse control, suppression of aggression, consideration of others, and responsibility). Adolescents' socio-emotional adjustment was reassessed at the age of 16. Overall, results showed primarily that fathers' adjustment predicted sons' subsequent level of functioning. More specifically, fathers' self restraint predicted sons' lower engagement in at-risk behaviors (antisocial behavior/drug abuse), and enhanced scholastic and social adaptation. Interestingly, fathers' considerate attitudes were not related to their sons' early emancipation. As suggested by Almeida (1991), by being involved and by being capable of acting as a model of restraint, fathers help their sons move through the emerging conflicts of this period toward individuation.

However, it would be overly simplistic to claim that the close, "dyadic" father–son relationship (which may carry with it some sense of friction) is basically functional and targeted to promote the son's development. Paternal aggression is not aimed solely at rooting out childish and female characteristics in boys. Conflict is also about power and authority: who will cross the bridge first, or who will sit in the front seat of the car. The adolescent boy faces a similar conflict: how to renounce the dyadic close relationship with the father and to assert individuality. This conflict is expressed especially at the pubertal apex when change is vividly and strongly experienced. Hauser *et al.* (1985) asked adolescents and their parents individually to complete a Kohlberg moral judgment interview. Subsequently, family members were brought together and their different moral judgment responses were revealed. For each of the differences, family members were asked both to defend their individual position and to attempt to reach a consensus representing both the adolescent and the parents. Both mothers and fathers of adolescents at the time of the pubertal apex tended to control their adolescents, were more judgmental, and more devaluing of the adolescent's suggestions. Adolescents tended more to resist paternal suggestions, explained their suggestions less, and quite often changed their topic of speeech. In contrast to the results in Holmbeck and Hill's (1988) study presented above, where some sort of father–son balance could be detected, Hauser *et al.*'s results resemble more of a struggle.

This "struggle" between generations recalls what Gunsberg (1989) and Loewald (1979) have suggested: that sons need to be able to be aggressive toward their fathers and to feel the fathers' retaliation. Aggression toward the father helps the son give up the image of the powerful father and leads the way toward individuation. Moreover, by attacking the father-object but not destroying him (Winnicott, 1969), the adolescent learns several important realities. First, it is possible to attack the father, as neither the father nor the son are destroyed by the attack. In addition, they can renegotiate their relationship on a more equal footing, with the relationship reality-bound. As reflected even in "innocent" dicussions in the Hauser *et al.* (1985) study, adolescents can be critical of their father's suggestions, and not look upon him with awe, as was the case in the past. Only through deidealization of the father (Steinberg and Silverberg, 1986) is the son able to perceive him realistically, consolidate his own individuality and re-establish a mature and loving relationship with his father. The older generation is required to relinquish control, as the younger generation lessens dependencies and attains control.

This conflict is solved when fathers are able to respect the sons' separation, and nevertheless maintain an ongoing relationship. Subsequently, a close relationship between father and son can develop, whereby the father not only respects and affirms his son's independence but also offers his blessing for the emergent manhood. Blos (1985) elaborates:

> The eloquent and classic pronouncement of this fateful condition we find in James Joyce's 1916 autobiographical work – *A Portrait of the Artist as a Young Man* – when Stephen Dedalus speaks of the terminal exit point of his youth, namely his self-imposed exile from Ireland. The last sentence of the book reads, "Old father, old artificer, stand me now and ever in good stead."
>
> (Blos, 1985: 11)

Thus, the son evokes the good and strong father's spiritual presence whenever in need. Usually the father's ongoing spiritual support is conveyed by a ritual act of blessing. Blos describes the story of Jacob, for whom the father's blessing was vital before moving into adulthood. Jacob, with the conspiratorial help of his mother, tricked his father into bestowing upon him the special blessing of the first-born son. Although Jacob did receive the blessing, he was probably not satisfied, as it could not signify continuous spiritual presence and support. Only after wrestling with the angel, as man to man, did he feel that he was deserving of the blessing, and he did not let the angel leave until he blessed him. Jacob was then ready for the reunion with his brother Esau. This illustrates that the son is expected to pursue independence either by conflict resolution or by actively seeking the blessing of the older generation.

Wrestling with the father and deidealization of the father figure is one aspect of adolescent separation, particularly in the relational domain. Consolidation of individuality is yet another facet that undergoes changes. During adolescence, feelings of omnipotence and grandiosity are experienced (Spruiell, 1975; Blos, 1985), and are reflected in egocentric behavior (Elkind, 1967). According to Blos, this sense of being the center of the world is challenged, and the second individuation should consist also of *deidealization of the self.* Realization of incapabilities and difficulties leads adolescents to experience feelings of sadness, fright, anger and abandonment. It is not uncommon to hear an adolescent claiming that "nothing will ever work out" or that he "will never accomplish anything great the world needs, admires, and loves" (Blos, 1985: 162). The father's ability to understand his son's inner doubts, and to be supportive, can help the son pass through such dysphoric periods when reconstructing his identity. Moreover, the deidealized father can then become a realistic model of manhood, and the son can identify with aspects of his father that complement him, and thus re-establish both the sense of identity and the father–son continuity.

In sum, father–son relationships have several distinctive features. On the one hand, the son is supposed to separate from his father and move toward a growing independence. On the other hand, father and son are supposed to balance separation-individuation and control. In addition, proximity of two mature males may lead to conflict and struggle. Both father and son must also deal with possible competition between them. Only the process of working through these conflicts can lead to the emergence of a new, interdependent relationship between father and son. The father then respects and blesses his grown-up, separated son, while the son learns to perceive his father in a realistic manner. Father and son thus support each other's manhood, both the emergent one and the one that is already in mid-life.

Non-optimal father–son relationships

The previously described father–son conflict does not always end in a peaceful solution. Similar, though less dramatic, conflicts are found in father–son relationships in the modern family. Fathers have been portrayed as the parent who is more likely in his "distant" attitude to allow the adolescent to assert an increasing level of individuality. However, in reality there are fathers who are unable to distinguish between what they want for their adolescents and what their adolescents might want for themselves (Dickerson and Zimmerman, 1992). Stierlin (1974) writes that there are cases where fathers or families interfere with the separation-individuation process. In such a family, the parents may dictate to the son how he should act. In the past, families had a great deal of control over their members, and fathers in particular tended to force their children to act in a certain way. In the well-known Schreber case, the son was forced into complete submission and passive surrender to his father. The father's control of his children was so strong that he even built mechanical devices for coercing them. For example, he used a "straight-keeper" in order to prevent the child from leaning forward while writing (Israels, 1989). In the modern family, where the use of force is sanctioned, parents employ different techniques to enforce their will, for example binding their adolescents on the cognitive level. "The binder (the parent) forces the bindee (the adolescent) to rely on the binder's ego instead of using and developing his own discriminating ego" (Stierlin, 1974: 42).

Blos (1967) emphasizes the importance, in the individuation process, of becoming responsible for one's actions. There are cases of families and fathers who seem to pave the way toward the youngster's independence (Constantine, 1987). Parents, or one of the parents, may be very supportive of their adolescent's independent behavior. However, independence is not only something that is granted, it is also something the individual achieves through struggle in his/her own actions. Stierlin (1974) describes how in some cases parents may use the adolescent as a proxy for their own wish for independence. Mandelbaum (1988) writes of a case when unresolved problems and conflicts from the parents' own adolescent years are projected onto a child who seeks more freedom. In her classic work, Johnson (1949) described how delinquents express the defective superego of their parents. Thus where the adolescent may seemingly act independently, he may actually express the wishes of his parents.

Yet another non-optimal father–son relationship is found in the family constellation of a strong mother and weak father. Under such circumstances the son may feel that he has lost his father. According to Nachmani (1992) this may lead to regressive behavior on the part of the adolescent son, unable to draw strength from his father or to identify with him. It is important for the adolescent son to know that his father is not powerless, and will be available to him in times of need. Stierlin (1974) claims that the achievement of an adaptive separation and identity formation in the son depends on the father's successful resolution of his mid-life crisis, which is related to unresolved issues of the past and present. Only under such circumstances do "annihilating fights" between father and son change into "loving fights" which support mutual liberation, and the adaptive father–son relationship outcome is witnessed.

Another problematic relationship between father and son is witnessed when, following maturation, the son leaves the father and relationships between the two are almost non-existent. Strozier and Cath (1989) describe the estranged relationship between Abraham Lincoln and his father. In 1851 Thomas Lincoln, Abraham's father, lay dying in his home. The older man wished to see his son, but Abraham declined to come, and the father passed away without seeing him. This significant episode clearly reflected the relationship that Lincoln had with his father, whom he perceived as incompetent and uneducated. Examination of Lincoln's early years suggested that the father did not respect his son's love of learning, perceiving this to be a sign of his refusal to work and help on the farm. As Strozier and Cath suggest, Lincoln seemed to have been deeply hurt by his father's attitude and behavior. He distanced himself from his father and some doubts have been raised as to whether Thomas Lincoln was Abraham's biological father. A near-complete disengagement from the father figure may be counter-productive to normal development. The father's blessing and spiritual support are crucial for a son's development. The solution for Lincoln was to identify himself with the fathers of the nation. The need for the father figure probably provided "the psychological basis for Lincoln's enormously significant attachment to the thought and deeds of the founders" (Strozier and Cath, 1989: 298), whom he perceived as the ideal surrogate fathers.

In summary, during the normal course of development, a dialogue between father and son is expected to develop. Their encounters may be argumentative from time to time, but a mutual respect should exist between the two. Lansky (1989) wrote about this process, claiming that the young male sees himself as understudy to his father. The formation of the father as a model for the adolescent is made through dialogue and experience predominantly within the home. The father model termed by Lansky as the paternal imago, then, contains a record of an entire set of attitudes toward the father, which serves as a model for identification. A new conceptualization of the identification process of the adolescent with his father is thus suggested. Identification does not mean carrying out the father's wishes, as found in clinical cases where the youngster does not question whether or not the father's (unconscious) messages are in accord with his own needs, and may idealize his father to unrealistic proportions. Yet neither is the adolescent expected to reject his father and his legacy entirely: he is supposed to become aware of the negative aspects of his father (deidealization of the father) and simultaneously allow the emergence of the father's positive aspects. After this process the father emerges with positive and negative aspects and bound to reality limits, worthy of respect and admiration, and becoming a model for identification (Gunsberg, 1989). Chapters 2 and 3 have focused on the nature of the father–adolescent relationship, and on how issues of closeness and individuation and attainment of developmental tasks are balanced. This chapter has added an intergenerational perspective to our understanding of the balance between father and growing adolescent son, in exploring which aspects of the son's self continue those of the father, and which are developed on his own.

5 The father–daughter relationship

The underlying assumption in our discussion of the father–son relationship was that sons are expected to separate and establish a distinctive identity. Fathers' perceptions of their daughters are fundamentally different. Within 24 hours of birth, fathers were more likely to describe their newborn daughters as little, delicate, cute, weak and beautiful (Rubin *et al.*, 1974). Fathers vocalized more to 5-month-old daughters than to sons (Palkovitz, 1984), and were more affectionate toward their 3- to 5-year-old daughters (Noller, 1978). In contrast with boys, young girls were described as having a closer relationship with their fathers, and fathers revealed a strong social-emotional nurturance during their daughters' childhood years. However, this support was in a mode in which fathers excessively protected their daughters from exposure to the external world and hence inhibited their autonomy (Lamb *et al.*, 1974). This chapter will discuss the possible reasons for fathers' differential and over-protective attitudes toward their daughters. We will later elaborate on the implications of such paternal attitudes on daughters' development during adolescence.

The over-protective attitude of fathers toward daughters is in line with historical trends whereby women were perceived as the property of their fathers (and later their husbands) (Carter, 1989). Even a women whose husband had died was subject to the authority of her oldest son. However, the role of women in modern society is considerably different. Although women still attribute more importance to close relationships than do men (Gilligan, 1982), women now also insist on personal autonomy, and many pursue careers. We will therefore also discuss models of father–daughter relationships in which fathers support and encourage their daughters as they strive for autonomy.

HISTORICAL PERSPECTIVES ON FATHER–DAUGHTER RELATIONSHIPS

The father's perspective

The traditional model reflecting historical male–female relationships perceived the daughter as the property of her father. The daughter's role was to fulfill various functions for her father or for the paternal clan. The mother's role in the nuclear family was to enable the reproductive link between father and son. Similarly, the daughter's role was to connect two groups of males (Boose, 1989). A common practice among kings of Germanic tribes was to marry off daughters into enemy tribes (as was common in European royal families), in the hope that kinship would enhance alliances and preclude hostilities. As Boose elaborates, in many descriptions of such ceremonies the daughter was absent and was referred to as a gift, an object. The daughter's own will was not considered. When a daughter tried to break away from her family without parental consent, the outcome was often death, as exemplified in the myth of Romeo and Juliet. A similar motif is found in the story of Dinah and Shechem, in Genesis 34. Dinah, the daughter of Jacob, was abducted by Shechem, the prince of the city of Shechem. In order to settle the conflict the Shechemites offered a covenant involving mutual exchange of wives. Even today in some Middle Eastern groups, prearranged marriages, aimed to strengthen paternal kinship, can be found. A widow is not allowed to resume an independent life of her own, and her children belong to the deceased husband's family.

Although marrying out the daughter may have been considered an appropriate practice, nevertheless there are additional myths which further reflect the extent to which the daughter is perceived as her father's property. Agamemnon, at the head of the Greek fleet about to sail to war against Troy, agrees to sacrifice his daughter Iphigenia, in order to placate the goddess Artemis' anger and gain her favor. By sacrificing his daughter, he will ensure his success. Agamemnon does not show his daughter affection, but treats her brutally in order to maintain his position as head of the Greek army. A similar phenomenon is found in the story of Jephthah and his daughter. Jephthah leads the war of the Israelites against the Ammonites and vows that if God will grant him victory he will sacrifice whoever comes out first to greet him upon his return home. Returning victorious, he is greeted by his daughter. Jephthah does not annul his vow and his daughter is sacrificed.

A similar attitude can be found in the early psychoanalytic writings.

In his earlier writings Freud presented the "seduction theory" according to which fathers have a tendency to be over-involved with their daughters, even to a stage that may resemble sexual flirtation. In the case studies of hysteria, it is mainly the father or father substitute who is sexually involved with the daughter. Freud's suggestions in the case of Dora show that he himself did not work through these issues, and may have believed that a father has special rights over his daughter (Decker, 1991). In the analysis of Dora, an 18-year-old girl, it was revealed that she was attracted to K., the husband of her father's lover. Freud suggested that K. get divorced and then marry Dora. K. and Dora's father were of the same age, so Freud's proposal was a distinctly oedipal solution given to an adolescent girl, which is supposed to resolve the reactivated oedipal conflict. Furthermore, this solution clearly met the wishes of the father rather than the needs of the adolescent Dora.

It is interesting that similar behavior can be found in the relationship between Freud and his youngest daughter, Anna. In a historical account on Freud and the case of Dora, Decker (1991) writes that Freud psychoanalyzed Anna from 1918 to 1921 and then again in 1924. Moreover, in 1935 Edoardo Weiss, an Italian psychoanalyst, asked Freud for his advice about analyzing his son who had just graduated from school. Freud's reply, quoted by Decker, was frank:

> Concerning the analysis of your hopeful [of becoming a psycho-analyst] son, that is certainly a ticklish business. With a younger promising brother it might be done more easily. With [my] own daughter I succeeded well. There are special difficulties and doubts with a son.
>
> (Decker, 1991: 122)

Decker suggests that the unconscious psychodynamics that are present in a father's analysis of his own daughter probably include the father's desire (and perhaps even his right) to possess his daughter, and to control her separation from the family and establishment of an independent life.

Carter (1989) claims that even in today's middle-class families, similar attitudes can be found. A father might spend a fortune on the education of his daughter, but may not really expect significant personal achievement of her. Instead, the father may pride himself on his strength and accomplishment and reward compliance and dependency on the part of his daughter. Daughters, in more than a few cases, tend to fit into this pattern. They have a strong need for their fathers' approval of their actions and choices, and do not pursue an independent track. At most, they may value achievement in the "new" males in their lives, namely husband and son. It is interesting to observe how the marriage ceremony symbolizes these attitudes. At the wedding, at the moment of severance, the question is presented: "Who giveth this woman to be married to this man?" Only the father is authorized to answer: "I do," thereby affirming the matrimonial unity of his daughter to another man. The bride's mother is "irrelevant" to this act. It is the father who hands over his daughter to another man, and her "belonging" to another man is legalized by adopting the husband's name. Boose (1989) adds that although contemporary women sometimes change the matrimonial ceremony to be more egalitarian and remove the emphasis on the bride's traditional vows of obedience, many independent daughters still choose to be "delivered and given away" by their fathers.

The daughter's perspective

When the daughter was perceived as her father's property to be handed over to her new master-husband or even to be sacrificed in order to accomplish the father's own needs, the issue of daughter individuation was irrelevant. Nevertheless, it is interesting to contemplate daughters' reactions under such circumstances. In the past, as Boose (1989) states, the daughter may actually have been absent from the exchange ceremonies. Instead, a golden cup symbolizing the treasure and legacy of a noble race was handed over to the future husband. Thus, the daughter was not asked whether she was willing to marry her designated husband, as she was supposed to obey the dictates of her father and his clan. As the story of Iphigenia recounts, she at first tried to plead, then to protest and finally accepted her death. When Achilles then offered her his protection she refused, giving herself up to the total idealization of her father and preservation of his honor, and simultaneously to the total self-debasement of her own wishes. Similarly, Jephthah's daughter was willing to accept the consequences of her father's vow, and did not raise any reservations of her own (Kaplan *et al.*, 1984). Only Juliet showed some resentment of the norms, raising the question asked today of why she should not keep her maiden name. She felt that by exchanging her name she would guarantee the extension of her enemy's line – the Montagues – and the simultaneous extinction of her own breed – the Capulets. Thus, in comparison to father–son relationships described in Chapter 4, the traditional attitude of daughter to father is one of unquestioned authority, with submission to "the law" a common mode of the relationship.

Our question now is, what is the source of the daughter's readiness to accept her father's dictates, even to the point of worshipping him? On the one hand this may be attributed to the historically lower social status of women that led them to adhere to male dictates. However, a psychological explanation can be suggested. One of the postulates of classical Freudian theory is an unresolved longing of the daughter for her father. The daughter is disappointed with her mother, who has given her insufficient genital equipment, and unconsciously wishes for a penis. When the daughter turns to the father expecting his love, the mother is perceived as a rival, not infrequently viewed with hostility. Freudian theory did not elaborate clearly on how this female oedipal complex is resolved. Wieland (1991) has suggested that penis envy leads to an identificatory love for the father, which evolves into a strong relationship with him (Willbern, 1989). Dalton (1986) has pointed out that unlike boys, who resolve the oedipal complex by identifying with the father, girls cannot achieve this stage. The resolution of the oedipal complex provides the boy with a balance of masculinity-femininity due to the fact that the boy has experienced a close relation to both mother and father. For the girl who does not get enough from her father, no real balance of masculinity-femininity exists. Therefore, Dalton claims girls/women continue to long for their father (the lost part of themselves). According to Chodorow (1978), who presents a feminist approach, the girl lacks an intense relationship with the father, as compared to the dyadic relationship that the boy has with his mother from an early stage. The more intense relationship the daughter has with her father emerges in the oedipal stage. Therefore, owing to a lack of close knowledge of her father, a girl's relationship with him may be more on the level of fantasy and lead to idealization. The daughter wishes to be recognized, loved and valued by her father, whom she may not know well, but longs for (Monreau, 1989). It is possible that being involved in this flirtatious relationship with her father leads the daughter to be highly identified with the father-male.

Yet another explanation for the daughter's yearning or submission to her father is offered by Gilbert (1989), in line with Lacan's theory. At around the time of the oedipal complex the child enters the language-defined system of culture and learns that he or she cannot remain forever under the mother's embracement. The child acknowledges that his/her social standing is assigned by the father's name (the Law). The father represents the social order, which disrupts the mother–child dyad. For the boy this realization leads to temporary frustration, but also promises a later accession to power, following the father. For the girl, the realization is that submission to her father can be the only source of power. Consequently, daughters may continuously submit to the will of their father and subsequently their husband (Gallop, 1989). The tendency to perceive the father as a source of power and discipline can also be seen in the differential relationship of a mother with a young male versus a female child (McGuire, 1991). Mothers were observed to establish the father as the authority figure for girls, but not for boys. Fathers were used as a threat, as someone – whether present or absent – who would not approve the child's actions. The following, quoted verbatim by McGuire, shows how the father is portrayed by the mother to the girl:

MOTHER   No you're not climbing on there.
CINDY   Just get the tea pot.
MOTHER   No, you know Daddy doesn't like you to, come on, Cindy. Don't sit on the arm [of the sofa].
CINDY   Uh?
MOTHER   Don't sit on the arm. Sit on the seat or go sit on your chair. Do as you are told. [Cindy continues to sit on the sofa arm.]
MOTHER   Please, Cindy, do as you are told!
CINDY   No.
MOTHER   Right! [To father] You tell her. [Father glares at Cindy, and she gets off the arm at once.]

(McGuire, 1991: 153)

The wish and need for the strong father or a male substitute to resolve the female oedipal conflict is also demonstrated in the literature of myths and fairy tales (Kestenbaum, 1983). The main point of such myths presents the ever-present triangle of father, daughter and mother, with mother and daughter vying for the father's love. In the tale of *Snow White*, the young girl is exposed to a strong hostile stepmother. The father is not strong enough to protect his daughter from the malice of his second wife, and the girl is either expelled or flees the unbearable situation. Finding sanctuary with the dwarfs is not enough to protect her from the wicked stepmother, who poisons her. Only a strong male prince is able to free her from confinement in the glass coffin, to destroy the wicked stepmother, and to allow Snow White to move into adult life. The tale ends with the young royal couple living together happily ever after. It does not elaborate on Snow White's interaction with her strong husband-savior. Similar themes are found in the tales of *Cinderella* and *The Taming of the Shrew*, where the girl needs a strong protector in the face of the rival mother. It may even be suggested that whereas the daughter's relationship with her mother stands for confinement and lack of autonomy, the relationship with the father stands for vitality and life (Heilbrun, 1976).

It may be assumed that, under such circumstances, both daughter and father-protector can become strongly attracted to one another. Although the relationship with the father is supposed to be desexualized, an intense relationship may continue to exist. It is beyond the scope of this chapter to answer how and whether this complex is resolved, yet it can be understood that daughters and fathers alike have to learn to manage their closeness. As Willbern (1989) suggests, daughters' sexuality is not always well managed, especially when the relationship is too close and the daughter may be pressured by the incestuous demands of her father (as described in the well known case of Dora and later elaborated in this book). When the father–daughter closeness is managed, only a symbolic expression of incestuous wishes is found. The desire itself is repressed, which is probably the case during the latency period. The question now is: how do fathers and daughters redefine their relationship when the daughter's sexuality and wishes for independence start to surface as she approaches adolescence?

FATHER–DAUGHTER RELATIONSHIPS IN ADOLESCENCE

With the approach of adolescence, changes in physical appearance and pubertal maturation evoke differential expectations and behavioral reactions from significant others (Lerner, 1985). In early adolescence, cues of physical maturity were found to elicit positive responses by both adults and peers as well as by the adolescents' own self evaluations (Tobin-Richards *et al.*, 1983). In addition, maturing and pubertal adolescents become preoccupied with their emerging sexual drives, which may also contribute to changes in their relationships with others. According to Lerner, the differential reactions of others act as feedback and influence further development. The nature of these reactions, including their positive or negative valence, depends on the goodness of fit between an adolescent's characteristics, and the expectations as well as the reactions of significant others. Collins (1990) has suggested that previously established adolescent perceptions and expectations of parents, as well as parental perceptions and expectations of the adolescent, are violated. For example, parents' ongoing perception of their maturing son or daughter as a child is a source of disagreement and conflict. As Collins has elaborated, these processes may lead to perturbations in family relations. So long as parents do not advance toward perception of the adolescent as mature and adult-like, unease in the family can be expected.

Psychoanalytic writings have also emphasized the strife that accompanies the maturation process in adolescence. Anna Freud (1958) referred to adolescence as a stage characterized by the reactivation of the oedipal wishes and conflicts, with these wishes being tested within the context of the person now having physically mature genitals (Laufer and Laufer, 1984). Sarigiani (1987) found that it was especially true among adolescent girls that affective and body image disturbances were associated with the nature of their relationships with their fathers but not with their mothers.

More recent writings have further elaborated upon the complexity of such changes, and proposed the existence of two different oedipal complexes. The first refers to the attraction of the child to the parent of the opposite sex, and is termed the *positive oedipal complex*. The second refers to the child's attachment to the parent of the same sex and is termed the *negative oedipal complex* (Blos, 1985). The girl is required to renounce her attraction to her father, and to identify with her mother. Identification with the female role presents the girl with additional tasks: to change from activity to passivity, to give up the clitoris (as an equivalent of the penis) and discover the vagina, and to change the object from father to mother. Altogether, the girl is required to deal with three tasks that are connected with identification with the mother. The boy, in contrast, is only required to renounce his attraction to his mother. Whereas in childhood the oedipal issues remain primarily dormant, in adolescence not only do pubertal forces lead to more confrontations and conflicts, but adolescents are also expected to loosen their attachment to the same-sex parent (resolution of the negative oedipal complex). Blos (1985: 40) considers the resolution of the negative complex a main task of this developmental stage. The adolescent girl is thus expected to pursue the three tasks mentioned above, while simultaneously renouncing her dependency on her mother. In sum, it may be suggested that pubertal development in girls calls for basic changes in relationships with others and self, and as such can be a source of elevated stress.

Inoff-Germain *et al.* (1988) investigated the association between pubertal changes and family relationships. In the study, boys and girls aged 9 to 14 were given a joint task to complete with their parents. Family members were presented with three problem situations and were instructed to decide how their family would handle each of them. For example, one situation involved deciding who would stay home with an elderly grandparent who could not be left alone. Family interaction was coded to describe the nature of adolescents' relationships with parents. For example, interaction variables included expression of modulated anger, and acting defiantly toward mother or father. In addition, adolescent biological indices measuring various hormonal levels were taken. Results showed that higher levels of the estradiol and androstenedione hormones which affect physical and sexual development were positively associated with female adolescents' behavioral expressions of anger and power, when interacting with parents. No such findings were seen for boys. A study by Smetana (1989) also showed that the period of pubertal development creates more parent–adolescent conflict for girls. In her study, Smetana interviewed adolescents and their parents and asked them to describe family conflicts and to justify their position in each dispute. Her results showed that early adolescent girls were less likely to agree with their parents' perspective than were early adolescent boys. Results of Steinberg's (1988) study presented in Chapter 4 point to changes in girls' relationships with both father and mother, unlike boys, who experience greater perturbations in relationships with their mothers. Pubertal maturation in girls increased the number of arguments they had with their mothers, decreased the number of calm discussions they had with their fathers, and increased the intensity of father–daughter conflicts.

The results of these three studies are very relevant to our contentions. In the case of girls, who are more attached to the family than are boys, pubertal development perturbs the strong relational patterns between daughters and parents. The re-evaluation of relationships which daughters and parents need to undergo isdifferent from processes found in son–parent relationships. First, daughters' sexuality, more than sons', becomes an issue for parents. Second, parents are less willing to grant autonomy to their daughters. In addition, girls are also expected to change perceptions about themselves more than boys are. Bronfenbrenner (1979) has suggested that a possible danger for the development of the daughter is related to "oversocialization" through an overdose of parental affection, which the daughter finds difficult to give up later. Taken together, the separation-individuation process for girls probably has a different connotation than for boys, and is more complex. The most challenging task for maturing girls is to negotiate between the natural inclination to be engulfed in relationships with their parents, and the developmental task of individuation.

Individuation within relationships

Males tend to express themselves in terms of separateness, and to insist on their independence. Females perceive themselves as embedded in relationships, and regard them as important to secure connectedness (Gilligan, 1982). Females have been found to express intimacy and to be open and self disclosing more than males (Clark and Reis, 1988). Similarly, during childhood and adolescence, when asked to point to the important aspects of their friendships, girls raised issues such as disclosure and trust, while boys pointed to joint activities. However, it is not only in early childhood that the girl's development does not emphasize separation. Even during adolescence, parents (and fathers in particular) tend to keep their daughters under their control, and psychologically convey the message that the girl needs her father's protection.

Grotevant and Cooper (1985) videotaped interactions of father–mother–adolescent triads discussing a joint task. Their data revealed that fathers more actively encouraged or at least tolerated their sons' opinions and striving for separateness. In contrast, fathers showed a tendency toward fewer interruptions of their daughters' suggestions within a family discussion, but also showed less encouragement of their daughters' differing views. As Grotevant and Cooper suggest, adolescent females are expected to individuate *within* the relationships they are part of, and not to separate from the relationships. Nydegger and Mitteness (1991) interviewed fathers about their relationships with their adult children. Fathers revealed differential attitudes toward their sons and daughters. Fathers' relations with their sons covered many domains, and some sustained tensions remained unresolved until the sons were in their thirties. Relations with daughters were more relaxed, mutual, affectionate and stable. Fathers tended to guide and advise their sons, on many occasions causing conflict. Daughters on the other hand were protected in their relationships with their fathers, perhaps more at peace with this paternal attitude, thus relationships were predominantly calm.

It may be suggested that fathers are aware of their daughters' need to be involved in close relationships as part of their maturation, and it is this tendency that fathers support. Such an attitude may be perceived to reflect historical attitudes of men toward women. However, its contribution as one of the pathways for adaptive female adolescent development cannot be dismissed. In a study one of us conducted, mothers of toddlers were interviewed about their relationships with their fathers and mothers during childhood and adolescence

(Shulman *et al.*, 1992). A few parent–daughter relationship topologies emerged. One type of relationship germane to our discussion consisted of women who described a detached or conflict-ridden relationship with their mothers in the past, especially during adolescence. The relationships these women had with their fathers were described as close and supportive. They were treated as "women," yet this relationship was not of a "role reversal" nature, and fathers did not involve the daughters in their marital issues. These women's involvement with their own children as well as with other children was appropriate. They were engaged with children, showed affection, and supported the children's independence.

A similar phenomenon, of the father serving as a compensatory figure for the absent mother, is described by Apter (1990) regarding adolescent girls whose mother died. Following the death of the mother, some girls developed a sudden closeness to the father. Apter describes how one girl reported that her relationship with her father changed "overnight," and she started to consider him a confidant.

> I used to get the jitters whenever he tried to talk to me. You know, I'd get so irritated, and start tapping my foot or my finger, showing him how I couldn't wait for him to go away, because whatever he said seemed so stupid and so wide of the mark that there was no point to discussion. And now he seems suddenly to understand me, and care for me, and he isn't asking too much of me. I dreaded seeing him again after my mother died because I thought he'd be sulking and wanting me to comfort him. Because he just seems to be there for me now. He's much more real – well, he loves me more effectively than I ever thought he could.
>
> (Apter, 1990: 218)

Thus, a father can compensate for a dysfunctioning or a deceased mother, and serve as a source of support for the developing female adolescent. Similar findings were reported in a study from Sweden. Uddenberg *et al.* (1979) interviewed women about their relationships with their fathers, partners and first-born sons. A woman's relationship with both her partner and her son was more strongly related with her reported relationship with her father than her relationship with her mother. In short, the paternal support women had during childhood and adolescence was related to "good enough" mothering as observed in their behavior with their partner, own child and other children.

Similarly, Ritvo (1975) states that a father plays a pivotal role in helping solidify the feminine identity of his daughter during adolescence. By giving the girl the feeling that she can be an "object of desire," her sense of femininity can be enhanced. However, this should not be experienced within an atmosphere of over-involvement, where the father undermines the daughter's relationship with the mother. In such a case the over-involvement with the father may lead the girl to identity diffusion (Fullinwider-Bush and Jacobvitz, 1993). Balsam (1989) described the development of college-aged functioning females whose mothers were emotionally disturbed. In these cases the father became the key figure for the adolescent girl, not only the admiring adult who could be trusted, but also the object of oedipal drives. Under such circumstances the father–daughter relationship could carry some sexual fantasies. To some extent, as Balsam elaborated, the father was almost the girl's husband, but this fantasy did not become a reality. The fathers were aware of and at ease with their daughters' neediness, which they perceived as a feminine trait. By setting limits and not allowing the situation to lead to a generational boundary dissolution, on the one hand (Fullinwider-Bush and Jacobvitz, 1993), and by addressing the needs of their daughters on the other hand, the fathers allowed the daughters to pursue developmental tasks and to formulate their attitudes toward their femininity. In sum, within the framework of a close relationship fathers can support their daughters' individuation by acknowledging their independence within an atmosphere of guidance and advice. In addition, fathers may compensate for a disfunctioning mother by establishing a delicate balance between emotional closeness with the daughter and preservation of the generational boundary.

Daughters' individuation and attainment of personal goals

Fathers have been described as supporting their daughters' investment in close relationships and in the consolidation of their sexual identity. However, fathers were less often described as supportive of their daughters' separation or encouraging their personal interests, as found in paternal relationships with sons. Family therapists have begun to question whether this is the appropriate mode of raising daughters today. Papp (1989) claims that women were traditionally expected to stay connected in meaningful ways and fathers today may be encouraging this tendency so that women will retain their traditional roles. Walters (1989) suggests there is an inherent danger for daughters if during the formative years of adolescence fathers are close to them but do not take them seriously. For example, if the father is sympathetic toward his daughter's moods, conflicts, aspirations and ideas, but perceives them as not entirely understandable – "it is difficult to know what a woman really wants" – the daughter will learn how to charm rather than to take charge. Such fathers are warm, protective, sometimes strict, sometimes indulgent, but they rarely deal directly with their daughters' emotional and intellectual issues.

Moreover, fathers may also interfere with their daughters' expressions of separateness, as reflected in a study by Vuchinich (1987). In this study, spontaneous conflicts that occurred in non-distressed families during dinner were videotaped. A conflict was defined as opposition raised by one family member to an idea or suggestion raised by another. Analysis of conflict episodes in 52 different families revealed gender differences in parent-initiated conflict with their children. The interesting finding relevant to our discussion was that fathers initiated conflict with their daughters three times as often as they initiated it with their sons. Fathers also tended to interfere with their daughters' assertion of their own ideas. The following discussion between a father and his son and two daughters (Bronstein, 1988: 116–117) clearly shows that fathers may not support a daughter's pursuit of autonomy, trying rather to guide her into a traditional female role:

FATHER   (to Maria) What do you want to study when you finish elementary school?

MARIA   I'd like to study... that is...

FATHER   How about you, Manuel? Now that you are graduating elementary school, what do you want to study?

MANUEL   To be a lawyer.

FATHER   A lawyer?

MARIA   I want to be a doctor.

FATHER   (to Manuel) And you think you will be able to do that, do you? You think your brain is going to help you do that?

MANUEL   Yes.

MARIA   I'd like to study to be a doctor.

FATHER   A doctor, hmm? And you, Josephina?

JOSEPHINA   Also a doctor.

FATHER   You'd like to study to be a ballerina, because you really like to dance.

JOSEPHINA   Yes, a doctor and a ballerina.

Nevertheless, fathers' interactions with their daughters may also provide experience in exciting joint endeavors aimed at commitment to personal initiative and achievement (Tessman, 1982). Fathers thereby can not only support the consolidation of the traditional female identity, but also encourage the attainment of personal goals reflecting the emerging role of women in our society. Tessman claims that the role of the father is especially crucial when individuation from the mother is under process. During this process the quality of the father's emotional engagement with his daughter shapes her attitudes to the two central issues of life: love and work. As a result of the emotional engagement, two kinds of excitement are experienced and directed toward the father. The first is "erotic excitement," reflecting former oedipal-related themes, and mutual attraction of father and daughter. The second is "endeavor excitement," associated with autonomy and self agency. This pertains to the father's appreciation and respect for the capabilities of his maturing daughter. A child's assertive behavior can be perceived by a parent as aggression, and evoke controlling reactions. Moreover, an opinionated, assertive adolescent girl may be perceived as acting in a manner inappropriate to her gender role. Only if the father is sensitive enough to recognize his daughter's penchant for self assertion, to understand its positive tones, and to support it, will the daughter be more capable of consolidation of her individuality.

Lasser and Snarey (1989) compared older adolescent girls at three different levels of ego development. The most mature girls had fathers who were continuously involved in their lives. Fathers often participated in athletic activities with their daughters, and, in addition, the girls were able to disagree with their fathers openly. Adolescent girls at the conformist level – mid-range – reported having fathers who were critical and who undermined their self-confidence. Adolescents at the lowest level of ego development reported having cold and remote fathers. Lozzof (1974) studied the impact fathers had on three groups of competent college female students. The first group consisted of students who were achieving academically, and were interpersonally effective as well. These women tended to recall their fathers as energetic and ambitious men who encouraged them, even though they frequently disagreed with their fathers' views. Students in the second group were achieving academically but were socially incompetent. These women tended to recall their fathers as aloof, often demanding. The third group consisted of students who were academically incompetent but were described by peers as socially competent. These students tended to have fathers who adhered to rigid sex-role definitions and did not encourage their daughters' academic achievement. Heath and Heath (1991) similarly found that vocationally successful women recalled their fathers as having high expectations for them, and encouraging their academic achievement.

In a more recent paper Tessman (1989) analyzed the life histories of women who have developed independent careers and lead a meaningful family life as well. These women, who graduated from MIT in the 1960s, described the special relationships they developed with their fathers when they were in their teens. The fathers were described as encouraging, stimulating their daughters' curiosity, exploration and independent judgment. Fathers tended to involve their daughters in joint endeavors, showed trust in their growing capacities and did not treat them as the "little girl." It is interesting to note that in some of the cases these paternal attitudes emerged when daughters approached adolescence, whereas earlier these fathers had seemed less involved and less interested. During adolescence, through their increased involvement fathers assisted their daughters to separate from their mothers and pursue their own interests. The differentiated closeness to the fathers enabled the daughters to combine both relatedness and autonomy, and to consolidate this pattern as a model for later life. For some women mutuality and autonomy may seem to be in conflict. They may either fill the traditional role of women, which valued mutuality, or a role that values autonomy regardless of the relational nexus. According to Tessman (1989), a supportive and autonomy-encouraging relationship with the father during adolescence may pave the way for a new role for women that combines mutuality and autonomy.

Snarey (1993) summarizes, on the basis of previous studies, what might be considered a lifelong trajectory of optimal fathering for daughters.

In contrast (to sons) the daughters' primary identification remains with their mother during childhood. Fathers' friendly but not extremely warm or tender childrearing support does not draw them away from this primary identification, while their rigorous physical-athletic interaction also helps them to avoid an extremely traditional sex-role identification. Fathers also provide *secure excitement* during infancy and optimal freedom during toddlerhood which contribute to their daughters' achievement of favorable ratios of trust over mistrust and autonomy over doubt. During early childhood, fathers are also an important resource of a favorable ratio of initiative over guilt. For adolescent daughters, it is fathers' active, energetic involvement on life's physical fields that can promote their ability to achieve a significant degree of separation from their mothers and to establish a bridge to the outside world. It is in adolescence that paternal childrearing participation can function as a possibly crucial conduit or bridge from the mother to the larger society, allowing young women to successfully negotiate the establishment of an autonomous identity and providing opportunities for them to be constructive, in assertive interaction with males.

(Snarey, 1993: 184–185)

NON-OPTIMAL FATHER–DAUGHTER RELATIONSHIPS

The most described example of non-optimal father–daughter relationships refers to cases of incest, comprehensively discussed in Chapter 11. In the case of incest, the father interferes with the daughter's development and establishment of extra-family relationships. A different pathological relationship includes cases in which fathers support daughters' movement away from the family, to the point of becoming over-involved with the launching of their daughters. In the past it was common for a father to arrange the marriage of his daughter, regardless of her wishes and sometimes against her better interests. Today it is less common to find fathers actively arranging the marriage of a child, yet they may indirectly try to push their daughters into the female adult role, and interfere with their striving for personal autonomy.

Such a dynamic is found in a study by Elder *et al.* (1985) that investigated the impact of the drastic changes and economic hardships during the Great Depression on the psychological outcomes of adolescents. Economic hardships increased the risk of paternal rejecting behavior, but did not influence maternal behavior. The causal sequence from economic hardship to the rejecting behavior of fathers then to the social affective behavior of children was found primarily among girls. As Elder *et al.* explain, family hardships increased the peer orientation of boys, therefore fathers' impact on boys' functioning was limited. Girls under the same conditions were expected to assume more domestic responsibilities, which meant greater exposure to tensions within the family. An additional interesting finding of this study was that fathers exhibited more rejecting behavior toward daughters who were less attractive. No clear explanation was offered in the Elder *et al.* study as to why fathers were more rejecting toward less attractive daughters, whose need for paternal support may actually have been greater. It may be suggested that the fathers' fears that their daughters might not be feminine enough, raised anxieties about whether they would be able to assume the role of a woman/wife. Under conditions of elevated stress (such as mid-life issues, or economic hardship), the father may be more critical and rejecting of his less attractive daughter which may in turn lead to a higher level of incompetence in the girl. As we can see in this less than optimal mode of parenting, some fathers tend to over-emphasize sexuality and attractiveness, thus impeding the optimal development of the adolescent daughter.

Yet another non-optimal father–daughter relationship refers to the constellation of a strong mother and weak father. This pattern was described as particularly adverse for the development of boys. It may seem that an adolescent girl in such a case may identify with her mother but (as suggested above) identification with the mother represents a lack of autonomy (Heilbrun, 1976). It is identification with the father that can contribute both to a sense of femininity and to independent endeavors in the adolescent girl.

In sum, the traditional trajectory of the father–daughter relationship was as follows. Throughout childhood and adolescence the father acted as benevolent protector of his daughter, attending to her needs and forgiving her childishness and moodiness. When the daughter matured and married, she was then expected to assume the role of caregiver toward her father. This dynamic is well described in the relationship between Cordelia and her aging father, King Lear (Tessman, 1989). Cordelia, who had been favored by her father in her early years, remained loyal to the tenderness she had experienced in childhood and embraced her father even in his madness. Daughters and women were expected in the past, and are expected to some extent today, to care for the people close to them. According to Gilligan (1982), an individual's behavior on the level of "Goodness as self sacrifice" provides the actor with a strong sense of security. However, emphasis on the care of the other may lead people to disregard their own needs, or be torn between attending to their own needs or those of others. It is through a relationship with the father, consisting both of closeness and of respect for the daughter's own initiatives, that a girl can develop a model integrating self and others: autonomy combined with mutuality.

6 Custodial and non-custodial fathers

Family structure in the Western world is undergoing a metamorphosis. More marriages are being dissolved and as a result, more children are being raised in families whose structures differ greatly from that of the traditional, intact family. In the United States, more than a third of all children are being raised by only one parent or in families with a step-parent (Hanson, 1988). In line with the focus of this book, this chapter will discuss the relationships fathers and adolescents develop in divorced families. In the following chapter, adolescent relations with step-parents, and more specifically stepfathers, will be analyzed. Although divorce is the most frequent reason for a father's absence, structural variation in families in recent years has created a variety of different alternatives for father–child interaction. Before we focus on the relationships that custodial and non-custodial fathers have with their adolescent children, the construct of father absence must be clarified.

FATHER ABSENCE: CLARIFYING A CONSTRUCT

The evidence is unequivocal that the proportion of children being raised to adulthood in a traditional family unit has been decreasing (Glick and Lin, 1986). For a variety of reasons, this less traditional pattern of child-rearing may have potentially far-reaching implications. Clearly, the absence of a father from home can have major economic ramifications for the well-being of the remaining family unit. As discussed in the previous chapters, father absence can also have significant psychological implications for a child's cognitive, physio-logical and socio-emotional development, although such effects are not found uniformly and are certainly related to a variety of characteristics of the child and family unit (see Hetherington *et al.*, 1989 for a review). Research examining the consequences of the presence or absence of a father has frequently considered demographic dimensions such as a child's age at the time of the father's moving out or the duration of the father's absence as critical factors in evaluating potential implications for a child's development (e.g. Hetherington *et al.*, 1982; McLanahan, 1983). In addition, a disproportionate share of the literature has focused on the traumas associated with the father's absence per se (e.g. Hess and Camera, 1979; Hetherington *et al.*, 1976, 1982). However, it should not be forgotten that a great deal of marital conflict may have been present at home for a long period prior to the relationship's formal breakup (Shinn, 1978; Rutter, 1981). Under these circumstances, the complete absence of the father from home may, at least in some cases, be a preferable situation. Also, leaving the family is not necessarily a discrete event. Frequently, there is evidence of the father's coming and going, even within a relatively short time span. Furthermore, this pattern may vary considerably according to race, socio-economic status and culture. At one extreme, the father is hardly ever home, or he may just leave one day and is never seen again. At the other extreme, even though a father may not live in the home, he may maintain extensive and continuing contact with his children. In the case of father absence due to divorce, the effects of fathers' visits cannot easily be generalized, but depend on a variety of factors, including specific traits of the absent father, the duration of his absence from home, the nature of the relationship between the mother and the absent father and any substitute father figure at home. What is more, absent fathers of young children may visit them more often than fathers of older children or adolescents.

Thus, a father's physical presence at home is only one, although an important, manifestation of his centrality in the child's life. The frequency as well as the quality of father–child contact must be examined, too. The influence of potential father substitutes in the child's life may also shape the father–child relationship. In a unique longitudinal study, Mott (1990) has examined not only the nature of the father's presence at home, but also the flow of his presence and absence during the first years of life, the quality of father–child contact in father-absent homes and the child's contact with new father figures. Mott does not explicitly deal with father-absence resulting from divorce but rather examines a variety of reasons for father absence, and his findings help to clarify the construct of "father absence." In 1976 and 1986, Mott interviewed 5,404 fathers and mothers residing in the United States. The participating men and women had various ethnic backgrounds: 70 per cent were white, 20 per cent black, and 10 per cent Hispanic. The children studied were born to mothers in their late teens or early twenties. About one-third of them were born to adolescent mothers, especially in the group of black participants. The father's absence at the time of birth was marked among both Hispanics and blacks but was particularly pronounced in the youngest ages of motherhood/fatherhood. More than 60 per cent of children born to non-black women (i.e. Hispanic and white women) but only about 10 per cent of children born to black women below the age of 18 lived with both parents following birth. With increasing maternal age, e.g. at maternal ages between 20 and 25 years, this statistical trend correspondingly increased to about 90 per cent and 40 per cent respectively.

The gross and net leaving patterns of non-black fathers parallel this overall trend to a considerable extent. Between birth and the fourth timepoint in the survey, the percentage of non-black children whose fathers were living in the home declined from about 87 per cent to 78 per cent. This decline of 9 per cent actually reflects a measured gross outflow of about 17 per cent which was countered by a return flow of about 8 per cent. In contrast, the percentage of black children living with their biological father increased from 32 per cent to 34 per cent over the same interval, masking a gross outflow of 12 per cent and inflow of 14 per cent.

In Table 6.1, several of the dynamic dimensions of family transition have been summarized from a sub-sample of 2,078 participants. Overall, about 60 per cent of all the children's fathers were present from birth to the fourth post-birth survey point; the remaining 40 per cent were divided about equally between children who had never lived with their father and children whose father was present at some but not all survey points. The variation according to race in this regard is considerable. While about 70 per cent of non-black children had always lived with both parents, only 20 per cent of black children had fathers who were always present. Indeed, the majority (about 55 per cent) of the black children in this population group never lived with their father at all, compared with less than 10 per cent for the non-black children.

It should be noted that while the father is certainly more present in white families, a considerable state of flux, marked by fathers returning at some point and then leaving again, is found in the whole population. For example, 27 per cent of non-black and 18 per cent of black fathers returned home at least once among the post-birth survey points. Leaving and re-entering home was closely linked, and the analysis of father–child contact also revealed that the contact between father and child was comparably frequent. There was no difference related to the

Table 6.1 Summary gross and net leaving statistics (per cent) for children for at least four post-birth survey points

Variable	Total n = 2,078	Nonblack n = 1,419	Black n = 659
Father always present			
60.5	70.3	21.5	
Father always absent	18.1	8.6	55.7
Father partially absent	21.4	21.1	22.8
Father absent			
At birth	24.5	13.5	68.5
By first post-birth survey	26.2	15.5	69.0
By second post-birth survey	30.7	20.0	73.4
By third post-birth survey	36.5	26.5	76.2
By fourth post-birth survey	39.5	29.7	78.5
Father always absent			
Until second post-birth survey	19.1	10.2	57.8
Until third post-birth survey	18.6	9.7	56.9
Until fourth post-birth survey	18.1	8.6	55.7
Absent father returning at intervals			
Birth and second post-birth survey	2.5	2.0	5.9
Birth and third post-birth survey	5.5	4.4	10.0
Birth and fourth post-birth survey	6.5	4.8	12.1
All absent fathers returning at least once post-birth	23.2	26.7	18.0
Absent (excluding never present) fathers returning at least once	42.7	37.7	62.1
Absent (excluding never present) fathers with multiple leaves	4.3	2.8	26.6

Source: Mott, 1990

age of the children. The visiting patterns for the older and younger children whose fathers were not present are presented in Table 6.2.

It can be seen that as the children grew older, the frequency of visits decreased. Overall, about 25 per cent of the older children not living with their father at the time visited him at least once a week, with 13 per cent seeing him virtually every day. Interestingly, racial differences

Table 6.2 Pattern of father–child contact and visitation in younger and older children

Variable	Children under 4 (total)	Children older than 4 (total)
No. of times father was visited in past year		
Almost every day	18.6	12.6
1–5 times a week	18.5	12.1
1–3 times a month	9.9	10.3
Once every 2–3 months	15.4	12.9
Once a year	7.3	10.5
Never/deceased	31.3	41.5
Length of last visit	64.3	64.8
Less than 1 day		
1–6 days	33.3	32.1
7 days or more	2.4	3.1

Source: Mott, 1990

were found again. Absent black fathers saw their children much more frequently than non-black ones. This is consistent with the findings that absent black fathers are much more likely to live near their children than are their white counterparts. Thus, it appears that to some extent, the elevated level of black fathers' absence from the home is countered not only by a greater tendency to be occasionally present in the neighborhood area, but also by more frequent visits to children, and perhaps to mothers.

Although the proportion of children living without their biological father yet having had contact with a potential father figure is about the same for black and non-black children, the absolute percentage differs greatly because the percentage of all black children without a biological father at home is much greater. After one considers the various father-substitute possibilities, however, the absolute racial gap appears less extreme. About 28 per cent of the older non-black and 66 per cent of the black children did not live with their biological fathers, and for 11 per cent of the non-black and 27 per cent of the black children, no apparent possibility for significant father-figure contact existed. For the younger children, the father-figure absence statistics are reduced from 16 per cent to 7 per cent and 57 per cent to 22 per cent for the non-black and black children respectively. Thus, while there is a dramatic difference in father-figure presence between black and white children, the frequency of visits as well as various father substitutes seem to indicate that there was a male figure present in the life of these children, at least from time to time.

These findings suggest that new forms of family life are coming into existence and that possibly these forms vary with culture and race as well. In Western industrialized countries, divorce and remarriage appear to be more characteristic among white people, while single-parent families with no parental cohabitation are more frequent among other racial groups. Mott's (1990) study impressively demonstrates that this type of family structure may nevertheless be marked by fairly stable and permanent relationships with the biologicial father or with a father substitute.

DIFFERENT TYPES OF NON-CUSTODIAL FATHERS: THE UNINVOLVED FATHER AND THE "DISNEYLAND DADDY"

After divorce, two different types of father–child relationships develop when the mother has sole custody. We would like to analyze the motives for these behaviors and the consequences for adolescent development.

Fathers who become uninvolved

Most divorces result in the typical situation where the mother has sole custody of the children who see their father according to the visitation schedules determined by mutual agreement or as specified by the courts. In such cases children may meet their fathers for a few hours during the week and for weekends. The literature is relatively inconsistent concerning the regularity and duration of paternal visits and the influence of the mother on both of these aspects. Some studies have reported that a large number of children are not visited by their fathers at all. In one study, Hetherington (1979) reported that 40 per cent of the children of divorced parents in America were not visited by their fathers. Badinter (1993) has reported similar statistics for France. More than the half of all children lose all contact with the parent who is not awarded power of custody for them, and this is usually the father. In this regard, Badinter's (1992) finding that 27 per cent of fathers separated from their wives never see their children again, and just about as many of them do not pay any child support, also points to a marked negative trend in father involvement. Whatever the motives for this behavior may be, such findings bluntly demonstrate that from the father's standpoint, the stability and intensity of the relationship to the child or adolescent does not manifest itself. In contrast, Wallerstein and Blakeslee (1989) showed in their longitudinal study that most of the children and adolescents studied by them were visited by their fathers on a regular basis. Over 10 years after a divorce, a third of the boys and girls saw their fathers at least once a month or more. In light of the fact that teenagers are often very busy with their friends, these authors consider this finding to be an "astonishingly high frequency of visits" (Wallerstein and Blakeslee, 1989: 281). Another 20 percent saw their fathers several times a year. In the Wallerstein and Blakeslee study, only a couple of fathers did not visit their children because they were consistently hindered from doing so by their former wives. A few children were occasionally urged by furious mothers to lie to or to reject their fathers. In one of the 112 families, the children were not allowed to mention their father's name, as if he no longer existed. Almost half of the mothers, however, viewed the father's visits positively and encouraged their former husbands to continue them. In the course of time, the mother's influence decreased and as the children became older, the mother interfered less often. Ten years after the divorce, the visits no longer had anything to do with the mother's feelings and a growing number of adolescents arranged the visits on their own initiative.

It is not apparent to most people how difficult it is to transform the father–child relationship as it once existed into the complicated visitation relationship. A relationship based on visits is not clearly defined and is therefore full of tension. What kind of role does the visiting father play? Since his domain of responsibility and authority is not clearly demarcated, he can easily feel superfluous. The organization of the visitation relationship is extremely difficult as well. Where does one go with the children? What does one do with the child or adolescent every other Sunday? It should be mentioned that the visitation modalities usually become fixed in the course of the first year after the divorce, which is the most difficult phase for all parties involved. All this takes place during a time in which feelings about the divorce are still fresh. Children may possibly be confronted with unknown adults at the father's new home, and general insecurity is the result. Adults and children must take on new social roles for which there are no conventions, and all those involved find themselves caught in a whirlpool of frustration, anxiety and dissatisfaction.

Different reactions of fathers to the visiting arrangements are described in the literature. According to Hetherington (1979), some fathers who had been relatively uninvolved became concerned parents, while others who were attached to their children prior to the divorce withdrew from them. Moreover, their interest in their children continued to decrease over time. Some authors relate the father's decreased interest in his child to the constraints of visitation and the mother's attitude toward the father (Loewen, 1988). But, as mentioned already in connection with the Wallerstein and Blakeslee (1989) study, this cannot be attributed to all fathers and is restricted to a minority. Kruk (1991) also examined the reasons why fathers disengage themselves from their children's lives following divorce and found that non-custodial fathers felt they had lost their child. These fathers thought that they were no longer involved in the everyday issues and problems that normally exist in an intact father–child relationship. Because of their feelings of being pushed out of family matters, these fathers responded with disengagement.

Both the courts and the mother and children normally assume that a father who loves his child will also visit him or her regularly. This assumption ignores exactly how difficult it is to maintain the sensitive, intricate father–child relationship once the family has been dissolved. The visitation relationship can be disturbed by the strong emotions which persist after a divorce. In addition, these fathers want to repress the painful feelings they associate with the failed marriage. Each visit can arouse anew feelings of pain, anger, shame, loss, worry, guilt and longing. In addition to this, visits inevitably are connected with goodbyes, and that can lead to depression and sadness in fathers who love their children. When fathers observe that their children are growing older, and that they see them only quite seldom, they sometimes develop guilt feelings about having left them. Moreover, the visits emphasize the discontinuity of the relationship. With each visit the father recognizes that he no longer belongs to the children's lives. Wallerstein and Blakeslee (1989) illustrated this typical situation with an example of such a father, Bob Catelano, who loved his children deeply and enjoyed being with them, but, for the reasons mentioned above, found it difficult to visit them. Bob could not bear this situation any longer. He solved the problem by only stopping by to see the children for a short time. He would drive up to the house and stay for only about ten minutes. This behavior affected his children's feelings quite negatively, and they rejected and ignored him.

The age of the children does not seem to play a consistent role in the nature and quality of father visitation. As their children grew older, some fathers reported that they saw them more often. Other fathers found that their teenage children had full schedules of their own and were not very enthusiastic about arranging a visit, so the frequency of meetings decreased.

The Disneyland daddy

Another commonly described pattern of the non-custodial father–child interaction is reflected in the "Disneyland daddy" syndrome. Here the visitation relationship becomes transformed into a kind of "visitation stress." The fathers go with their children to the zoo, to ball games, to video shops and other amusement centers instead of addressing the more complex task of dealing with the child more personally. Because of the limited amount of time fathers are allowed to spend with their children, they tend to plan each meeting in advance, and try their best to have fun when together with their children. However, children and fathers become exhausted by rushing from entertainment parks to restaurants to cinemas. The drain on individual energy levels and on the budget cannot be maintained for too long, which may explain why visits tend to become less frequent after the second year (Furstenberg, 1983). The tendency for a Disneyland daddy to give up is surely born out of the strain put on the personal energy levels and the increased expenditures; moreover, it signals the need for a "normal daddy." Since a father who practices this type of visitation routine is excluded from the everyday routine of the child and has very little to do with many of the parental responsibilities, he no longer has a good idea of what really interests the child or what the child is concerned about; for example, the next class test, the marks in mathematics, the conflicts with friends, the interest in sports matches. The father cannot fulfill specific needs, and addresses the interests of his child by offering a "Disneyland program."

Taken together, children of divorced families may experience two possible non-custodial paternal attitudes: that of fathers whose interest in the child decreases over time, or that of fathers who engage their children in mutually enjoyable activities for short periods of time. These two tendencies crystalize deep-rooted conceptions of fatherhood. On the one hand, fathers tend to be distant and less involved with their children. On the other hand, when together with their children, fathers are more engaged in joint activities but less involved in their everyday care (Abelin, 1975). These two prototypes of non-custodial fathering described above expose the child to different models of relationships: disengagement or inconsistent involvement. Both of these relationship types may bear strongly on the child's development, and may be connected with problems in adolescence, when separation becomes a major concern again.

PROBLEMS FOR ADOLESCENTS: THE OSCILLATION BETWEEN FEELINGS OF NEGLECT AND IDEALIZATION OF THE FATHER

From the viewpoint of the child, the visitation relationship is complicated as well. Children almost always want to be visited and eagerly wait for the arrival of the visiting parent. Many consider the visit to be the high point of the week or month and are afraid that the father may not appear at the agreed time. Some children only show their best side in order to ensure that the father really does come. They do not dare make other arrangements with their friends or pursue their hobbies lest the father be insulted or disappointed and thus cancel his visit.

According to Wallerstein and Blakeslee (1989), the frequency of a father's visits is less decisive than the kind of relationship the child enjoys with him, as well as the father's personality. To their surprise, these authors established that the feelings of loss that children experience have nothing to do with how often they are visited. Most adolescents visit their fathers regularly; however, many of them have the feeling of having lost them. In one interview a son explained: "I'm not welcome in his house. I don't feel comfortable there. I don't do anything except watch television while he talks with his friends" (Wallerstein and Blakeslee, 1989: 282).

A 14-year-old girl in our counseling program described when she arrived at her father's house for the weekend, her father told her that he had to leave because of an important commitment. Her father did not apologize for the change in his plans, and even asked his daughter to stay and babysit her two younger half-brothers until he and his wife returned.

It can be understood, then, that a distant non-custodial father is often perceived as "lost," as Drill (1986) has described, which may lead to a higher depressive effect in the child. Furthermore, whereas father-absent children tend to develop flexible images of adult men in their search for a father surrogate, children of distant non-custodial fathers tend to become less involved with other adult men, while hoping that their fathers become more involved. In some cases, adolescents may develop a very negative image of the unavailable father (Loeb, 1986) which may have detrimental effects on the adolescent (Spiegelman and Spiegelman, 1991). Children may also develop a "theory" that explains the father's distance. This is especially the case when the father lives in the near vicinity yet hardly ever visits. The child who feels unwanted comes to the conclusion that he/she does not deserve the father's love

(Neubauer, 1989). All in all, children may develop a negative perception of either themselves or their distant fathers.

In addition, misunderstandings may arise, for it is not uncommon that fathers and children have different views about the visitation relationship. Wallerstein and Blakeslee (1989) reported on many such misunderstandings. For example, it often happens that the father believes he has done his best, whereas the child thinks he or she is lacking something. The father thinks he has fulfilled his responsibilities, whereas the child feels pushed aside. The father thinks he has been loving, but the child feels rejected. The father claims to be neutral and sincere; the child thinks he is lying. The result of such misunderstandings is that most fathers in this study thought that they had fulfilled their obligations, and three out of four children had the impression that they did not mean very much to their fathers. They thought that their fathers were physically but not emotionally present. This shows that the needs and interests of children and fathers who no longer live together are hardly met. A further reason for the dissatisfaction of the children could be traced to the high expectations placed on the father. In the Catelano family mentioned above, Billy identified with his father. However, he felt unloved by his stepfather and was thus alienated in the new family situation. Although Billy knew his father's weaknesses all too well, he refused to give him up as a role model; he loved him and forgave him for everything. In contrast, Bob's failures as a father enraged the mother. She simply could not understand why Billy worshiped him. Billy desperately sought for all the things he had missed in his father over the years. In his view, his father was more friendly and gentle than his stepfather. Thus, because he felt that there was nobody to whom he could turn, Billy could not give up his hopes.

The claim that children idealize their absent fathers must certainly be stated more precisely. A child from a failed marriage may indeed know his or her "real" father, his good and bad sides, but as a rule the child does not form the same conclusions from such information as an objective observer would. Without recognizing the inherent contradiction, the child simultaneously has a list of rejections and failures *and* a positive image of a loving father in his or her head. In other cases, continuous longing for the idealized "absent" father may persist, to the point where the child or adolescent looks for any omen that indicates that the "good" father is coming back. The child fantasizes that if the father were present, he would fulfill his/her wishes and help in coping with day-to-day problems.

Similar dynamics can be found in the case of the "Disneyland daddy." Custodial mothers usually complain of the unfair competition they feel in comparing themselves to their ex-husbands. These mothers claim that they have to support, care for, guide and discipline their children on a daily basis. Just as occurs in intact families, conflicts with their children arise from time to time. In contrast, the non-custodial father is freed from dealing with the "dirty" daily problems, and in particular, is not expected to discipline his children. What these mothers mainly are afraid of is that the children will develop a negative perception of them and a positive one of the father. Indeed, although the father's encounters with the child are limited, the time he has available may be planned with generous surprises, fun and interesting activities, or simply may be more relaxing owing to the absence of the everyday problems mentioned above.

The idealization is not fixed to a certain age group and in many cases is reported to last for many years, sometimes never ceasing to exist. Billy's longing for his father – a problem which he considered to be the great tragedy of his life – did not wane over time. Billy knew that he could never live with his father, therefore he longed for the fantasy father that he never had but needed, and for the real father whom he missed, loved and felt sorry for. He yearned for his father despite being completely aware of the fact that his longing could never be satisfied. In the group investigated by Wallerstein and Blakeslee (1989), many 13- and 14-year-old girls especially longed for their fathers. As Kelly, one adolescent girl in this group, reported: "But now I would really like to be closer to him." Another girl in this study, who hardly knew her father, wrote the following letter to him after her thirteenth birthday: "Dear Papa, do you remember me? Here I am, your daughter." She was thrilled when he wrote back, but the exchange of correspondence died out soon thereafter. Another 13-year-old girl sent her father her diary entitled "The Bleeding Chronicles" because it disclosed all her heartaches, her anger and her sadness. She wanted to share her most secret feelings about herself and the world with her father, because, as she put it, "he'll understand me." The father had only seen his daughter during the school summer vacations. He was completely bewildered and hardly understood what this type of correspondence meant for his daughter as she entered puberty. He flipped through the emotional poems, the fragments of songs and the confessions without grasping the fact that she had paid him a great honor by confiding to him in this way. Nor did he recognize the cry for attention that was expressed through the act of sending him her diary.

Since boys and girls in puberty perceive a growing inner need for their fathers, they eagerly collect all the information they can obtain to construct an image that corresponds to this need. When the mother is very strict, then the "phantom father" becomes tolerant, a sympathetic knight who, if necessary, hurries to rescue the child. When the mother is curt and distant, the idealized father is then tender and attentive. In our own study comparing clinical and non-clinical adolescents stemming from divorced families, an idealized image of the father was found only in the clinical sample. As can be seen in Figure 6.1, the clinical sample had much higher scores in duties, shared roles, communication and emotional relationship with the father.

Although the construction of a fantasy father and the idealization of a father about whom one knows very little has also been observed in intact families (cf. Freud, [1905] 1952), these fantasies in adolescent children of divorced parents are particularly problematical since during this stage of development, adolescents are expected to become disengaged from parental images and to develop a mature and realistic perception of their parents (Steinberg and Silverberg, 1986). Separation and the differentiation between self and object can hardly be achieved under conditions where the images of the father are fragmentary or where the father is over-idealized and the fantasies about him do not correspond to reality. Once the perception of the

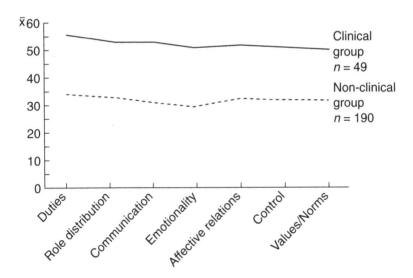

Figure 6.1 Perception of the father in clinical and non-clinical groups of adolescents stemming from divorced families

father becomes very negative, the image of the father might be "destroyed" (Winnicott, 1965) and the father becomes practically non-existent for the adolescent. Under such conditions some form of pseudo-autonomy is the most that can be expected to develop. When the adolescent or child is "bribed" by the weekend father, a seemingly positive relationship might be witnessed. But in this case, too, the process of optimal disengagement from the paternal image and a re-evaluation of the relationship can be hampered. The following case represents the possible scenarios described above.

The G. family sought help in family therapy a few months after the father had left home and moved in with his lover. The mother, aged 47, was a professional and highly regarded in her field. Mr and Mrs G. had one daughter and two sons. The daughter, Noga, was 19; the two boys, Leo and Simon, were 15 and 11. At the time, the father was not able to invite his children to his new residence so meetings were held on "neutral grounds." Noga tried to be minimally involved in the conflict between her parents. Though she resented her father's move, they met on a regular basis and discussed matters of mutual interest. Leo was very angry at his father. He even commented once that though he understood that his father "wanted to fuck," this was not a sufficient reason to break up a family with three children. Leo refused to see his father or speak to him on the phone. He invested all his energy in peergroup-related activities that resulted in misbehavior and loss of interest in his studies. Simon met his father often; they went to movies or out for pizzas, and it was clear that Simon looked forward to being with him. Simon was the least critical of his father, as if he was trying to maintain the relationship with him at any price.

The two boys' attitudes toward their father reflect the two possible tendencies of children's and adolescents' behavior with non-custodial fathers. After criticizing and condemning his father's behavior, Leo cut off any contact with him. He even refused to attend family therapy meetings, insisting that he did not want to hear about his father anymore. Simon was rather quiet during the family therapy sessions. To some extent, it even seemed that Simon felt that maintaining a good relationship with his father might convince him to return to the family. Only the oldest daughter was able to view the situation from a more mature perspective and thus deal with her father on more realistic terms.

The ability to develop a more balanced relationship with the non-custodial father is not only related to the maturity of the adolescent but is strongly influenced by the nature of the father–adolescent encounters. When non-custodial fathers are capable of bringing their children into their real lives, children will be able to perceive them more realistically. In one example, Rosenthal and Keshet (1980) described a shift from the former to the latter pattern:

> When John learned to expect Cynthia to amuse herself with whatever was available to her while he prepared dinner, he had learned to be with her instead of doing things with her. This is the second stage of single-parenting – when the father learns how to be with the child without the constant distraction, and perhaps emotional distancing, keeping busy or even bribing the child with objects and activities. Life becomes normalized and routines set in. Trips to the laundry or the bank are something to be done together. Such daily routines are opportunities for the child to participate in the realities of the father's life, and they shift the burden of activities from the child's interests – for example, what film the child might like to see – to the real survival needs of this family unit. Such a shift reasserts the proper balance of authority. It is the father who is in charge again, who defines the needs of the unit, and who responds to them. When a father is no longer indulgent out of insecurity, guilt or a lack of firm definition of parenting behavior, the child loses the inappropriate centrality in the relationship.
>
> (Rosenthal and Keshet, 1980: 93)

THE CUSTODIAL FATHER

Loewen (1988) has suggested that successful visitation relationships between father and child can develop once the visitation routine is integrated with the different roles these fathers have to fulfill in their lives. In such a case, the relationship with the child is reality-bound and will probably not fluctuate between extreme disengagement and closeness. It is especially important for adolescents to be able to develop a balanced relationship with their non-custodial father, and to be able to perceive the father as a separate "person" (Steinberg and Silverberg, 1986) and to shed childish perceptions and expectations of their father.

The metamorphosis of contemporary family structures has introduced an additional form of child custody – single custodial fathers (Hanson, 1988). Such fathers have physical (though not necessarily legal) custody of their children and thus carry the primary parental responsibility without a co-parent living at home. Demographics from the USA showed that in 1985 11 per cent of single-parent families were headed by fathers and the number increased by 27 per cent between

1970 and 1984 (US Bureau of the Census, 1985). In 1994, a study of the Federal Republic of Germany's Ministry for Family Affairs showed that 9 per cent of fathers in divorced families care for the child or adolescent. The rates are higher for adolescents (16 per cent) than for children (5 per cent). It is important to be aware that one-fifth of all children of divorced parents change their custodial parent at some point. Most shifts are to fathers, as a result of problems in the mother–child relationship, and take place when children become older or are adolescents (Furstenberg and Spanier, 1984).

In general, custodial fathers report better child behavior at home than do custodial mothers, and children of custodial fathers verbalize their appreciation of their fathers (Ambert, 1982). The higher level of single fathers' well-being can be attributed to their tendency to employ problem-focused coping strategies in comparison to custodial mothers who prefer emotion-focused coping behavior (Cohen, 1991). Some of the competent single fathers have been described as revealing a higher level of androgynous sex role perception (ibid.). However, it would be too simplified to assume that all single fathers turn into outstanding caregivers as portrayed by Dustin Hoffman in the film *Kramer vs. Kramer*. While some custodial fathers may perceive their children as the core of their lives, others may pursue their own lives regardless of the child's needs. One case that came to our attention involved a young lady who came to the clinic requesting therapeutic help for her youngest sister.

The mother of the family had died two years prior to the referral. Two older daughters were married, and the father lived at home with the youngest daughter, Minnie, who was 14 years old when her mother passed away. A few months after the mother's death, the father started to go out and socialize with other women. Slowly the responsibility for the household was transferred to Minnie. She was supposed to shop, clean and cook. The father became less and less interested in Minnie and in what it meant for her to be responsible for the household. The father started to come home late at night. It seemed to Minnie as if she was being granted full independence. Although Minnie's relationships with her sisters were good, she felt as if her father and the family had more or less deserted her. Minnie's interest in schoolwork and in her social life decreased; she looked depressed. Although father and daughter lived together, the emotional distance between them was great.

This situation is reminiscent of cases of the parentified child (Boszormenyi-Nagy, 1965). In other cases, the custodial father may develop a strong connection with his son or daughter. The adolescent may then fulfill certain of the father's needs and the father may seem very supportive of the adolescent. For example, he may help his son to make the transition to manhood, as Blos (1985) has described. On the other hand, the question remains as to whether the boundaries between father and son were somewhat blurred (Lidz, 1980).

The issue is more complicated when a custodial father lives with his daughter. Adolescence is the stage when the oedipal conflict must be resolved. Identification with the same-sex parent is an essential ingredient for gender differentiation and resolution of the oedipal conflict (A. Freud, 1958). If the father has remarried, additional conflicts may arise. In an intact family, the mother and father help their daughter to deal with her sexuality. Following a divorce, the adults in a newly formed family are not always adequately prepared for dealing with the sexual development of a growing girl. First of all, the stepmother has not known the daughter since birth. Second, from the daughter's viewpoint, the father's new partner introduces a new aspect in her relationship with the father. Therefore, increased sexual interest and sexual arousal can become potentially more important factors operating on the father–daughter relationship. These impulses are not necessarily realized actively, but they contribute to the tensions in the family, and under certain conditions can put a dangerous strain on the marital relationship. According to Wallerstein and Blakeslee (1989), such tensions leading to the breakup of a marriage were much more frequent than the incidence of practiced incest. It is more common that boys and girls grow up with a stepfather than a stepmother (see Chapter 7). This at least was the case for 55 out of 113 children in Wallerstein and Blakeslee's (1989) study, and the relationships of the male and female adolescents to their stepfathers were considerably more strained than in the few families where a stepmother lived with the family.

When a daughter lives alone with her father and her relationship with her mother is conflictual, some additional difficulties may emerge. The following case may illustrate this point.

Dennis, a divorced man in his late thirties, applied for treatment because of problems with his only daughter, Karen, aged 13, who lived with him. He complained that Karen seemed to be incapable of maintaining long-term relationships. Karen would become highly involved with friends, but the friendships consistently "evaporated." The father added that he was afraid that Karen would behave toward him in a similar fashion and might some day disappear from home. When Karen was 3 years old, her parents divorced and Karen lived thereafter with her mother. The father used to visit them three times a week. When Karen was 7 years old, her mother remarried and had two sons. Karen's relationship with her mother was very stormy and oscillated between love and hatred. The summer prior to the referral for treatment, Karen spent a few weeks with her father during the school summer vacation, as she had in the past. When the time came for her to return to her mother, she called to inform her that she had decided to stay and live with her father and had already registered at a different school close to the father's residence. When the mother heard this, she fainted and was hospitalized for three days. At first, the relationship between Karen and her father was easy and relaxed. Dennis prepared the meals for his daughter and she helped him clean the house. Karen also invested time in cultivating her social relationships and developed close friendships with girls in her school. She continued to visit her mother, but treated such visits as a duty she was obliged to carry out. This "honeymoon" ended after a few months, and then the father sought help.

In the sessions it became clear why the father was worried that his daughter might suddenly leave him one day. Their relationship oscillated between extreme closeness and extreme distance. Karen would go to a folk-dance club with her father where they danced as a couple. Karen complained that her father was too stiff while dancing and did not move his legs flexibly. When Dennis received phone calls from women, Karen would sit on his lap, listen to the conversation and suggest what her father should say. It also came out that Dennis often walked around the house dressed in his underwear. When Karen was younger and came to visit her father, they slept in the same bed. However, father and daughter often had disagreements. Dennis complained that his daughter stopped helping him around the house and acted as if she was living in a hotel with no obligation to contribute to the household chores. She even took her meals to her room and ate them there. Furthermore, Dennis complained that once he returned from work, Karen locked her room and did not allow him to enter. Karen complained that her father did not respect her privacy and would enter her room without knocking while she was dressing.

It was evident that father and daughter had to negotiate and balance the level of closeness between them. The father acted toward Karen in opposing fashions: he treated her like a lover yet also as a little girl. Karen perceived her father's behavior as containing sexual overtures and responded accordingly, yet she also wanted it to stop. Conceptually, the pattern of oscillating between closeness and distance was also evident in Karen's relationship with her mother.

However, closeness to the father also consists of sexual and oedipal components. The coherence between patterns of relationships has been described in the literature (Sroufe and Fleeson, 1986). It was interesting that at first Karen was more willing to discuss her relationship with her mother. After she and her mother were able to renegotiate their relationship so that the mother could accept Karen's new situation, Karen's relationship with her father also improved and became more balanced.

As this case shows, custodial fathers may become very involved in the lives of their children. Atkins (1989) argues that this trend may help fathers to stabilize their own lives, once they recognize that they have to care for their child. In cases of fathers and daughters, especially when the latter become adolescents, the father's tendency to become over-involved may interfere with an adolescent's striving for independence and consolidation of a differentiated and mature ego identity. Although this pattern may seem more relevant for custodial fathers, it is important to be aware of these dynamics in cases of non-custodial fathers as well.

An additional finding regarding single fathers should be addressed and incorporated in our discussion. More men than women were found to become involved in romantic relationships after separating or divorcing (Cohen, 1991). Romantic involvement with a new partner may leave the father with less energy for his children, and patterns of behavior associated with the absent/disengaged father may emerge from time to time. When children have reached adolescence and become more interested in sexual and romantic relationships, the encounter with their father as a lover may arouse the oedipal issues (A. Freud, 1958), though in this case the third angle in the triadic relationship is a strange woman. As the cases presented above have suggested, the custodial or non-custodial father may become over-involved or disengaged and thus interfere with the adolescent's own interests in extra-family relationships. The single father's ability to maintain both hierarchy and closeness enables the adolescent to pursue his/her own interests.

Taken together with what has been discussed in the other chapters so far, we have to stress that father absence is a relative construct, both in intact and non-intact families. Some fathers are very present, even if they are no longer married to the children's mother. Other fathers, from intact families, may spend so little time with their children that they seem to them like strangers. Non-custodial fathers basically show two different types of reactions, which parallel the overall trend of fathers' activity and relationships with children: too much closeness, i.e. over-involvement, or too much distance, i.e. neglect. Similar patterns of father–adolescent relationships can be found in the rare cases of custodial fathers. Some may lead their own lives regardless of the child's needs, leaving a great numbers of family duties to nannies, while others place their children in the center of their lives.

7   Adolescents and their stepfathers

When a step-parent – who is frequently a stepfather – joins a family there are many new changes and dilemmas which each family member faces. Given that the parent–child relationship precedes the new relationship between husband and wife, the new family situation may potentiate already existing conflicts related to the emotional demands involved with "sharing" an adult or child.

Clinicians and researchers report that adolescents have a particularly difficult time in new stepfamilies (Visher and Visher, 1979; Peterson and Zill, 1986), especially concerning matters of discipline (Lutz, 1983), and/or when there is differential treatment of stepchildren within the household (Ihinger-Tallman, 1987; Pasley, 1987). The practical difficulties and emotional strain involved when children have parents in two different households may become more salient for the adolescent. It is not uncommon that adolescents move back and forth between two households. In this regard it may not be surprising that adolescents tend to leave their stepfamilies to live on their own at an earlier age than they do in biological families (White and Booth, 1985).

In this chapter, we review research findings on the relationships adolescents have with their stepfathers. We begin by describing different types of stepfamilies, including stepfather families, and follow with a discussion of the typical problems occurring in stepfamilies, in particular in those with a stepfather. Finally, the association between the developmental tasks of the adolescent and the life cycle of his or her stepfather is analyzed. We discuss the question of whether the adolescent may profit from stepfamilies.

TYPES OF STEPFAMILIES

Of course, there are many different types of stepfamilies. Some are formed following the death of a spouse; others are created after a divorce. Some stepfamilies may have few or no children residing in the household. In some stepfamilies, only one spouse has children; in others, both have children, and all live together under one roof. These different patterns produce different dynamic configurations. We will deal in the following with three different types of stepfamilies.

Stepfather families

Stepfather families are those in which the man is the step-parent. This is the most frequent type of stepfamily. Research findings indicate that this type tends to have less stress than the other types of stepfamilies (Visher and Visher, 1979; Crosbie-Burnett, 1985). Male children and adolescents in particular respond favorably to having a stepfather join the household (Santrock *et al.*, 1982) and many develop satisfying relationships with their stepfathers (Bohannan and Yahraes, 1979). How can we explain the positive effect of stepfathers on male children? After divorce, fathers usually move out and the contact with the male person with whom they identify most strongly becomes limited. After a remarriage, children as a rule live with a stepfather, so boys regain an important male figure. Maintaining contact with their biological fathers tends to enhance the ability of boys to form good relationships with their stepfathers. From the latter's perspective, having no children of his own increases his ability to bond with his stepchildren (Furstenberg and Spanier, 1984).

Stepmother families

Stepmother families are those in which the woman is the step-parent. These families exhibit much more tension than stepfather families (White and Booth, 1985; Hetherington, 1987). Not only do step-mothers report high stress levels, but the children also experience greater stress when they are living with their father and stepmother than when they are living with their mother and stepfather (Jacobson, 1987). Compared to stepfather families, the positive identification with the same-sex parent could not be found in stepmother families. Strained relations between a child's mother and stepmother may contribute to the difficulties occurring in stepmother families.

Complex stepfamilies

Complex stepfamilies are families in which both adults have children from a previous marriage. The greatest difficulties reported by complex stepfamilies concern the children. In fact, although several investigations have demonstrated that the presence of stepchildren increases the chances that a remarriage will end in a divorce (e.g. Becker *et al.*, 1977), this is even more likely to occur in complex stepfamilies (White and Booth, 1985).

In any kind of stepfamily, each individual is confronted with many new tasks. Not only must the stepfamily as a whole achieve a new identity, but each family member must cope with loss and change, as well as with conflicts related to the distribution of power, issues of loyalty, defining and respecting personal and physical boundaries and maintaining the balance between closeness and distance. In the following, we shall focus on discussing these issues as they pertain to the adolescent in stepfather families.

QUALITY OF RELATIONSHIPS BETWEEN STEPFATHERS AND ADOLESCENTS

Change and loss

The characteristic feelings of teenagers in stepfamilies can be characterized best by statements made by an adolescent talking to stepfamily peers:

> When I am with my mother, I cry because I miss my father. Then I go to my father's house and I cry because I miss my mother. You just have to go with the pain. Don't fight it. Just accept it, so you don't miss out on seeing both of your parents.
>
> (Visher and Visher, 1988: 91)

A stepfamily is formed because there has been a divorce or death of a parent. In the case of divorce, adolescents lose everyday contact with a parent – usually their biological father – and wonder whether they will continue to see that parent. They may feel that their biological father is being replaced by a stepfather. Adolescents may act out their feelings rather than verbalize them. In addition, they may construct a fantasy father who is never cross, always giving, and a paragon of virtue. The remaining parent (usually the mother) or the step-parent (usually a stepfather) can never compete with this idealized image. The fantasy that the biological parents will get together again is created by a large percentage of children and adolescents, and is one that often persists following a remarriage. Even though this fantasy may remain dormant, adolescents nevertheless experience a loss since they interpret a remarriage as reducing the likelihood that their divorced biological parents will get together again.

In the newly formed stepfamily household, there are numerous changes that take place, many of which represent loss for the adolescent. One marked change involves the adolescent's ordinal position in the family. The addition of new family members which alters previous family living arrangements is quite sudden. The household composition of stepfamilies, especially in complex stepfamilies, may change every day of the week, so that the child's position changes from day to day. Adolescents may feel displaced by a new step-parent and by step-siblings, so strong feelings of alienation may result.

Sharing space is another issue related to change and loss. Stepfathers as well as adolescents are faced with sharing living space at home with individuals who may be virtual strangers. For adolescents, a common situation is the necessity of sharing a bedroom with a step-sibling. Unfortunately, the adults are not always sensitive to the tension that can be created when adolescents are asked to share a room with other siblings, especially if they hardly know them.

Papernow (1980) has found that one characteristic of a smoothly functioning stepfamily is that such changes are perceived as normal. Members of stepfamilies must learn to experience a sense of family stability, despite continual shifting in the household composition. The feeling of stability also applies to the relationship the children have with the biological parent not living in the household. Lutz (1983) found that teenagers in stepfamilies perceived not being allowed to visit their biological father as one of the three top stressors in their lives. Thus, continuity in relationships is very important to them. Hearing their parents talking negatively about each other or hearing the mother and stepfather argue were the other leading stressors reported. Such stress might be related to a fear of additional loss.

Closeness and distance

In stepfamilies, the new challenge of getting on with one another under one roof, which includes not only sharing the parent, but also sharing family rooms and facilities, can instantly create much tension between stepfamily members. Such tension is often increased by attempts to contrive a closeness between family members that has not developed naturally. Adults in stepfamilies are sometimes upset by the lack of strong emotional ties between step-parents and stepchildren. Visher and Visher (1988) reported that adolescents may not share this concern; in fact, they may feel quite happy with their stepfathers although they do not show much affection or engage in joint activities. Visher and Visher reported the case of Steven, 18 years old, who lived with his mother and stepfather. Although Steven did not converse much with his stepfather, he continued to care a great deal for him, and considered him a role model. Steven's mother and stepfather, however, thought that he should show more interest in communicating with his stepfather or spending time with him. The authors comment that step-parents are often too hasty in trying to forge close relationships with their stepchildren, without allowing time for familiarity and trust to be established gradually. Adolescents often feel uncomfortable about becoming close to a step-parent. If a child already has an emotionally close relationship with his or her biological parent, he or she may feel guilty about creating an even closer relationship with a step-parent. As Thies has noted, such guilt may arise since "children are reared to love and trust only their natural parents" (Thies, 1977: 59). Although Steven described his relationship with his stepfather as being excellent, he also indicated his closeness to his father: "My dad is irresponsible and sort of a flake, but I love him. I am not sure why. I guess it's because he's my dad" (Visher and Visher, 1988: 227). As in all families, over the years the nature of contact between the adults and children changes, both qualitatively and quantitatively. While preschool children may easily accept the emotional warmth provided by a stepfather, adolescents may require much more time to feel comfortable with closeness. Teenagers may even be living on their own before they relate warmly to step-parents.

Loyalty conflicts in the adolescent

Before, during and after divorce, adolescents may find themselves caught in the middle between threatened and hostile biological parents. Parents are frequently unaware of the ways in which they involve their children in their own conflicts. Compared to younger children, however, adolescents are more able to remove themselves from a central position, leaving their parents to deal with their problems with each other. Nevertheless, after a divorce, virtually all adolescents experience loyalty conflicts, the severity of which may depend on the post-divorce relationship between the two parents. After a remarriage, the adolescent feels very little loyalty to the stepfamily group, and there is usually an exacerbation of problems related to loyalty as a step-parent enters the family system. Conflicts between parent and same-sex step-parent are also frequent. According to Isaacs (1982), this is one of the situations causing overt discord in stepfamilies. In this situation, the adolescent is caught in the crossfire between the step-parent and the parent of the same sex. Even when animosity between the two adults is at a minimum, adolescents can suffer from guilt because they fear that liking their new step-parent means being disloyal to their own parent. In this context, Mead (1970: 29) commented: "Each American child learns early in childhood that his whole security depends on that single set of parents." The message that adolescents need to hear is that it is acceptable to love more than two parents. Fathers are still expected to be more peripherally involved than mothers in raising the children, managing and running the household and assuming responsibility for the emotional climate. It is logical then that children might feel the pulls of allegiance to their mothers and stepmothers to be more intense than to their fathers and stepfathers.

Custody and visitation

Following a divorce settlement, legal custody of the children and visitation arrangements are set down. After a remarriage, however, it may become difficult to maintain such arrangements, and any previous flexibility in parent–child contact may suddenly be compromised. Adolescents who are cut off from a parent report feeling stressed (Lutz, 1983). In addition, they show a poorer overall adjustment and have greater difficulty in forming relationships with their step-parents. In particular, these effects have been documented by research on stepfather families (Furstenberg and Nord, 1985). Clinical observations have shown that many adolescents cut off from a parent build idealized images of that parent and that they often have no opportunity to confirm the reality of their fantasies. This finding was discussed in Chapter 6, where we presented data describing the situation of father idealization seen in clinical and non-clinical adolescents stemming from divorced families. We should emphasize, however, that a collapse of a parent–child relationship may occur despite the fact that the parent does care for the child. On the contrary, the parent may care a great deal but be unable to cope with the pain of separation. The case of Bob Catelano, presented in Chapter 6, illustrates this mechanism.

Joint custody is one possible arrangement that encourages continued contact with both parents following divorce and remarriage. This arrangement has been shown to support the father's involvement in parenting his children (Bowman and Ahrons, 1985). However, although adolescents in stepfamilies may desire to have contact with both parents, they are often uncomfortable with joint custody arrangements (Crosbie-Burnett, 1985). It may be that teenagers in both single-parent and step-parent households reach a point in their development where they are beginning to distance themselves from the family and become more inclined to interact with their peers. In this case, teenagers may prefer to reside in the parent household that is located in the vicinity of their friends. Adolescents may also be wrestling with questions of identity and thus often choose to live on a regular basis with the parent of the same gender. Such changes frequently take place even without a legal change of custody, and are often beneficial, particularly for boys (Giles-Sims, 1984). Similar changes for girls can be more problematic (Ihinger-Tallman, 1987).

In summary, the issue of beneficial custody arrangements following remarriage needs clarification. Much of the research on custody issues has made no distinction between single-parent households and stepfamily households following divorce. However, there are structural and emotional differences between these two types of households and it may be that the most beneficial custody arrangements in single-parent households are different from the most beneficial arrangements after a remarriage.

When sole custody is awarded to the mother or father, there may be different effects on the adolescent which are related to gender. When sole custody is awarded to the father, girls are likely to perceive this arrangement as a severe rejection by the mother. For boys in the same situation, it can make logical sense to them that they live with their same-sex parent. However, additional research is required to uphold these impressions.

Permeable household boundaries

To adolescents, the issue of household boundaries is especially important. Because of the need to move between households, Messinger *et al.* (1978) consider that stepfamily households need to have "permeable boundaries" to allow the adolescents the freedom to go back and forth easily and gain from the diversity of experiences offered by the different households. On the other hand, each household needs to feel that there are clear psychological and physical boundaries defining it. Often, adolescents would like their biological parents to maintain frequent contact, celebrate holidays together and feel free to enter the living space of the other parent. In most households, however, if the former spouse feels free to enter the house when not specifically invited, the other adults in the household might feel that their household boundaries have been trespassed. Thus, each household must define and respect the boundaries of the other. On the other hand, each household must be prepared to experiment with introducing changes in such boundaries to meet the needs of the children as they develop and adjust to the new stepfamily system. Fesler (1985) illustrates a case of an adolescent girl who wrote to stepfamily adults about her experiences and suggestions:

> I am 12 years old and I live in a stepfamily. My mother got divorced from my father when I was 2 years old. Now I live in two houses. I change to a different house every week. I have been doing that for two years now. It works very well for me. The one thing that's nice is that both of my parents live in the same town. That way I can go to the same school and also have the same friends. It was my idea to go to each house every week. At first, my parents disagreed about this. They tried it. After a while they liked doing it that way. I like it very much also.
>
> (Fesler, 1985: 6)

Another issue concerning the boundary problem is the control in the household. Commonly, there is less control in stepfamilies than in nuclear families, because of the presence of more, and different, people. To complicate matters, step-parents in the USA and in Europe often have little or no legal relationship to their stepchildren. This may make the step-parent's role in the newly formed "stepfamily" ambiguous.

Boundaries within stepfamily households can also be ambiguous. For one thing, the absolute number of individuals residing in the household may fluctuate, often dramatically. For example, one day two individuals may live in the household, the next day there may be ten. During the school year the children are present; during holidays these children may not be living in the house, but two others have taken their place. This dramatic change in the size of the household may mean that stepfamily members feel deprived of enough time, space and/or privacy. This is especially true for adolescents living in stepfamilies, because they need their own room and an atmosphere of privacy. Visher and Visher (1988) reported on a 14-year-old girl, Jessica, who had been an only child until she was 11 and then suddenly, after the remarriage, had to share a room with a stepsister. As for the rest of the house, she found someone in every room, including the bathroom. She kept wondering what was wrong with her because all this activity did not seem to bother anyone else. One solution to this problem would have been to make arrangements for each girl to have some private time in the shared bedroom.

Power issues

Aponte (1976) suggested that the distribution of family power is manifested in "the relative influence of each family member on the outcome of an activity" (Aponte, 1976: 14). Most studies on family power have examined the balance of power between couples in nuclear families. Recently, attention has been directed at examining the types of power structures exhibited in stepfamilies (Visher and Visher, 1979; Crosbie-Burnett, 1984; Furstenburg and Spanier, 1984). In stepfamilies, there are many factors to be taken into consideration, such as the number of children each partner has or custody and visitation agreements. Other factors which influence the nature and distribution of power in family relationships include age, sex, educational background, financial assets and previously existing alliances within the household. More power is associated with having custody of the children, being older, being male, being better educated, having a higher income, providing more financial support for the stepchildren and children and having interpersonal alliances (Crosbie-Burnett *et al.*, 1986). While the relationship between spouses in a remarriage has been found to be more egalitarian than in first marriages (Giles-Sims, 1987), other factors can create significant imbalances in stepfamilies. When the children have parents living in two different households there may be marked differences in power structures. There seems to be a prevailing hierarchy of power: the residential parent possesses the most power, followed by the spouse of the residential parent, the non-residential parent and the spouse of the non-residential parent.

Stepfathers, for example, have considerably less authority over their stepchildren than do the children's parents. In some stepfamilies, this inequality can exist without causing difficulties, for example, in stepfamilies formed when teenagers are in the process of leaving the household. Hetherington (1987) showed that stepfathers were less authoritative and much more disengaged than fathers in non-divorced families. Many fathers tended to minimize the amount of time, effort, and interference with their own needs and their marital relationships that childrearing demands. To some extent, stepfathers were like polite strangers. A frequently heard complaint was "I married her, not her children." When confronting problem behavior on the part of stepchildren, stepfathers tended to comment "That's the mother's problem, not mine." A sequence analysis of observed family interaction in Hetherington's study indicated that the pattern of "mother command/child non-comply/father intervene" was less frequent in remarried families than in non-divorced families. Also, the stepchildren rarely consider the step-parent to have the authority to enforce rules or carry out disciplinary measures. This is especially true for stepfathers. In fact, in the specific area of discipline, empirical and clinical evidence clearly shows that stepfathers who attempt to take on a disciplinary role too quickly impede rather than enhance stepfamily integration (Stern, 1978; Brown, 1986). Moreover, Fine *et al.* (1993) showed that the more stepfathers engage in control and supervision activities, the poorer becomes the quality of the relationship between children and their biological mothers. Hetherington *et al.* (1982) described stepfathers who tended to remain disengaged for about two years after remarriage, but got into angry and prolonged interchanges, especially with stepdaughters, on issues of parental authority and respect for the mother. Mills (1984) points out that stepfathers should be flexible about their roles.

For the adolescent, there may be sudden changes in their authority in the new stepfamily. For example, when adolescents have been given too much responsibility during the single-parent household phase, they may be quite surprised, even angry and resentful, when their parents remarry and their position in the power hierarchy is suddenly altered. Adolescents thus need to find new areas of responsibility and control.

In nuclear families, adolescents often find ways to play one parent off against the other, when the parents are not getting on well together. With their biological parents in two different households, adolescents in stepfamilies may gain an inordinate amount of power by playing one household off against the other. They move more freely between the households and they can use this position against their biological parents or biological parents and step-parents. This power struggle between households can be very dramatic. A pediatric allergist, in reflecting on his case load, realized that 90 per cent of his emergency night-time calls were for children and adolescents who were in a single-parent household or a stepfamily (Visher and Visher, 1988). In most instances he detected underlying hostility between the two households. He observed that as the children changed households, medications or the instructions for their administration were forgotten, or the other household had not been informed of current allergic difficulties. Even in this way, one household was in control and putting the other at a disadvantage.

ADOLESCENTS' DEVELOPMENTAL TASKS AND INTEGRATION IN NEW STEPFAMILIES

Does the stepfamily affect adolescent development?

Teenagers do not usually welcome the birth of a stepfamily. Usually they have lived in the nuclear family for some time and their ideals of family are more fixed than they are for younger children. Older adolescents have reached a stage in their individual development in which they are trying to understand who they are and are striving for independence (see Chapter 3). They are moving away from the family unit in the direction of peers and close friends and starting to form romantic relationships. This gradual developmental progression may become disrupted by parental death or divorce. In the subsequent period of living in a single-parent household, the children may assume the role of parental companion or spouse surrogate. Upon a parent's remarriage, the adolescent is often quite suddenly assigned the task of helping to establish the new family unit. All these events may occur while they are working on their own developmental tasks of individuation from the family. It is no wonder that one 16-year-old lamented, "Two parents are too many – who wants any more?" (Visher and Visher, 1988: 156). Frequently, in their search for a new identity, teenagers in stepfamilies elect to live with the biological parent who first moved out of the household, usually the father. This wish may cause conflict as the residential adults attempt to consolidate their stepfamily unit. In the early years of a new stepfamily's existence, the new step-parent may be inclined to interpret the teenager's increased interest in his or her friends as an expression of rejection of the new step-parent. As a result, the new couple often tries to force the adolescent into participating in family activities. This may result in even more tension and friction between the adolescent and other family members. Bray (1987) reported that demands for greater adolescent participation in the new family were associated with higher rates of behavior problems among stepchildren. However, this scenario mostly reflected families in the early stages of remarriage. New fathers were then perceived as intruders or competitors for the mother's affection. In the long run, stepfathers became a source of support and a model with which to identify for their adolescent stepsons (Hetherington *et al.*, 1989). In line with the contentions presented in Chapter 4, one of the father's functions for the adolescent son is to resolve the ambivalent relationship with the mother. The introduction into the family of a mature male who is not too close to the adolescent and is involved with the mother may facilitate these developmental tasks. The scenario for the adolescent stepdaughter is different. Adolescent stepdaughters exhibited more problems even at later stages of the remarriage. Hetherington suggested that for daughters independence is achieved within the relationship with the mother (see Chapter 5), and the introduction of the new stepfather threatened this delicate balance. Stepdaughters tended to be more sulky, resistant, ignoring and critical toward their remarried mothers and stepfathers.

Some adolescents do not continue living under these conditions. As noted above, adolescents in stepfamilies are more likely to move out of the common family household and into a place of their own at an earlier age than teenagers in nuclear families (White and Booth, 1985). Hetherington and Clingempeel (1992), for example, found that about one-third of adolescent children who are confronting their parents' marital transitions tend to disengage from the family. This is sometimes a response to exclusion by the adults who are attempting to protect their own relationship from unresolved and severe conflicts between themselves and the adolescents. When an adolescent's attempts to gain autonomy and independence are constantly thwarted by a parent and step-parent who are in the "nesting stage" and thus eager to create a new family unit, more conflicts may arise and persist. Again, moving out may also seem to be the most convenient solution to dealing with this conflict. Nevertheless, although an adolescent may gain independence by moving out, he or she may be burdened with the increased responsibilities of living alone, and may feel disconnected from the family (see Grotevant and Cooper, 1986).

Life cycle discrepancies

In Chapter 3, we discussed the relationship between the developmental tasks of the adolescent and his or her father's life cycle. In biological families, these cycles are usually congruent. In stepfamilies, they often are not. In biological families, there is an ordinary progression of events marked by marriage, the honeymoon period, birth and development of children, career advancement, gradual departure of children from home, and dealing with deaths of parents and grandparents. In stepfamilies, the new couple may have come together at very different individual stages in their lives. There is no marital stage without children, since children are there from the beginning, often moving toward independence and individuation rather than wanting family closeness. Sager *et al.* (1983) consider such developmental discrepancies as often being incompatible. Similarly,

McGoldrick and Carter (1980) consider a wide discrepancy in life cycle stages as a predictor of remarriage difficulties. Such discrepancies may cause much confusion in several major areas of family life. Visher and Visher (1988) found that stepfamily members frequently need help in recognizing that their sense of confusion may be related to the life cycle differences that have produced competing and incompatible needs. In stepfamilies in which only one of the adults has a child, the discrepancies in the couple's expectancies can vary considerably. Although it is more common that childless stepmothers want to have a child, the wish to experience biological parenthood is by no means restricted to women. Childless stepfathers frequently want to have children with their spouse.

Sexual attraction in stepfamilies

The common discrepancies in developmental tasks and life cycles seen in stepfamilies also involve the issue of sexual attraction. Sexuality is a prominent ingredient in stepfamilies, especially when the newly married couple is living through the "honeymoon period" in the presence of the children. There also may be step-siblings of different sexes who are dealing with the sexual issues of puberty and adolescence.

By far the most serious problem of sexual attraction in stepfamilies concerns crimes of sexual abuse of children and adolescents (see also Chapter 11). Present figures indicate that young girls below the age of 14 have a 10 per cent greater probability of being molested by a residential stepfather than by a biological father while living in a nuclear family (Russell, 1984). Unfortunately, accusations of child abuse are often made by worried ex-spouses and angry stepchildren to express their bitterness over their unwanted situations. Visher and Visher (1988) described the case of one stepfamily in which the teenage daughter reported her stepfather's intimate approaches long after they had ceased, around the time when she noticed that her mother and stepfather were beginning to share a warm and loving relationship. The girl perceived this as a loss of closeness with her mother and she used the most powerful weapon she could think of in her attempt to return the household to its former homeostasis.

Since stepfathers and stepchildren do not have years of common family life behind them, the novelty of their relationships may enhance sexual arousal. Furthermore, the new stepfather is likely to have a sexually charged aura for the child, since he was brought in as the mother's sexual object. Although we must recognize the increased potential for sexual abuse in stepfamilies, we have to be aware of the "normal" attraction between stepfathers and stepchildren, especially when they approach adolescence. This conscious or unconscious sexual attraction may be repressed or covered up with a disguise of hostile behavior. Visher and Visher (1988) described several cases in which adolescents exhibited angry and sarcastic behavior toward their stepfathers in order to mask or control sexual attraction. Sexual attraction may also exist between step-siblings, especially when they reach adolescent age. The sudden confrontation of young people and adults of the opposite sex seen in the stepfamily, especially when the individuals have not lived together for long, immediately brings sexual questions and interests into consciousness. To adolescents who are dealing with their emerging sexuality, these issues are particularly important. It is therefore necessary that parents introduce household rules that help reduce open displays of sexuality or intimate behaviors, such as undressing in the presence of others or not respecting others' privacy when using bathroom facilities. Visher and Visher (1988) reported a case of the provocative behavior of a 17-year-old adolescent coming downstairs dressed only in a pair of pants. He was advised by his stepfather to go back and get dressed properly before he came downstairs to meet the family. In another stepfamily, when the husband's 21-year-old son and his wife's 18-year-old daughter became intimately involved, the young man was asked to move into an apartment of his own. The relationship between the two young people continued, but without the acute discomfort previously experienced by the others in the stepfamily household.

Do adolescents profit from stepfamilies?

Step-parents have very negative images. The stereotype of the evil stepmother portrayed in fairy tales such as *Cinderella, Snow White* and *Hansel and Gretel* persists in our culture, and similar stereotypes can be found to exist in other ethnic lore. The negative image of stepfathers has also been described in several fairytales. Although research efforts have generally emphasized the problematic aspects of stepfamilies, positive results of such family constellations have also been documented. Among the older studies, Duberman (1975) found that 64 per cent of stepfamilies rated themselves as having excellent relationships; only 18 per cent reported that they were experiencing poor relationships. Burchinal (1964) studied 1,500 US high school students and found no evidence that divorce or remarriage had any significant, long-term detrimental effects. More recent studies have reported similar findings.

For example, Santrock *et al.* (1982) found that there were few differences in social behavior between stepchildren and children in nuclear or single-parent households. Direct observations in a controlled experimental situation revealed that the social development of boys in stepfamilies was more competent and mature, although girls tended to be more anxious. Bohannan and Yahraes (1979) reported the results of a survey conducted in San Diego, California. They found that stepchildren considered themselves as being just as happy, successful and accomplished as children in nuclear or single-parent households. The experience of living in stepfamilies has been found to ameliorate many of the negative effects of divorce for adolescents (Peterson and Zill, 1986). Crohn *et al.* (1982) have also discussed the positive aspects of remarriage. A successful remarriage may be beneficial for both adults and children. The love relationship established between parent and new spouse is often strengthened by maturity, life experience and stability in identity, and benefits from the process of regaining independence and freedom of decision-making. Adolescents may observe the remarried parent in a stable and loving marital relationship, and refer to this model in creating their own future emotional relationships. They may receive affection and support from a new step-parent, and feel more secure through being part of a new, complete family unit. Upon remarriage, new lifestyles, opinions, feelings and interests introduced by the integration of a new family member may enhance family life, and may enrich existing relationships or help to establish new ones. An adolescent may learn to appreciate and respect differences in people and ways of living. If an only child, he or she may benefit by learning to co-operate and get on with other children.

Hetherington and Clingempeel's (1992) longitudinal studies can explain the reason for the possible benefits for adolescents of remarriage. After working to establish a relationship with the stepchild and supporting the mother in her parenting, stepfathers could allow themselves to become authoritative parents. When adolescents experienced awareness, warmth, involvement, concern, and monitoring of their activities with their stepfathers, they showed increased competence and lower levels of behavior problems. When stepfathers were capable of assuming, over time, a positive role of parenting, adolescent children may benefit from the authoritative fatherhood (Steinberg *et al.*, 1991).

To summarize,

normative changes and stress encountered by children as they enter adolescence may be exacerbated by their marital transitions. As the early adolescent child's demands for autonomy increase, parents become increasingly disengaged, less controlling, and emotionally involved, and spend less time with the child. Moreover, heightened conflict often tends to accompany this early surge of independence on the part of the child. For remarried and divorced mothers, this pattern of disengagement from their children may be accelerated and accompanied by more pronounced conflict and negative affect, and autonomy may occur earlier in children who go through their parents' divorce and spend time in a one-parent household. The introduction of a stepfather may further complicate problems in the development of autonomy or lead to a precipitous or inappropriate disengagement from the family.

(Hetherington and Clingempeel, 1992: 204)

However, stepfathers are not only a source of risk, they may also become a source of strength. When stepfathers move too quickly into a relationship with the adolescent child, become either too close and affectionate, or a strict disciplinarian, the chances for conflicts are high. When stepfathers introduce themselves gradually, and are capable of balancing closeness and individuality (as elaborated in Chapter 2), combined with some measure of supervision, they can become a source of strength – at least for their adolescent stepsons.

The problem of comparing stepfamilies with idealized nuclear families

Given that 30 per cent of all marriages today involve the remarriage of at least one of the adults (Glick and Lin, 1986), it seems reasonable to reconsider the traditional understanding of the family life cycle. As Goldner (1982) once stated, "The first marriage is no longer the happy ending to childhood." It seems that the concept of marriage has to be adapted to include divorce, cohabitation and remarriage as parts of the whole cycle of coupling. At the present time, the nuclear family is no longer meeting the needs of a great proportion of families. There are a number of possible explanations for this phenomenon. For example, although increased life expectancies have introduced the potential for couples being married longer, there is also more opportunity for partners to change and drift away from one another. The women's movement has altered women's expectations of marriage. Religious values appear to have less influence in questions of marriage. More individuals today are less concerned about economic survival than about the qualities of their lives.

There is a tendency to evaluate stepfamilies by normative impressions that apply to biological families rather than using suitable norms that apply to stepfamilies. Nuclear or biological families are idealized, and other types of family models, including stepfamilies, are considered to be inferior, or are viewed with skepticism or disapproval (Ganong and Coleman, 1984). This inaccurate, often damaging prejudice about stepfamilies needs to be carefully re-evaluated. The general characteristics of stepfamilies diverge from those of a biological family. For example, they have a complex structure. There are many possible inter-family relationships, each of which can cause problems, particularly at the beginning, because there may be connections to other households. Age and gender of children, as well as the type of stepfamily (stepmother or stepfather family, complex stepfamily structure), can affect the process and duration of integration. Satisfactory family integration generally takes some time; the minimum seems to be about two years (Stern, 1978). Very often, relationships are severed. In a sample of divorced couples, 75 per cent of the children had no further contact with their fathers (Furstenberg and Nord, 1985).

As discussed above, there may be many conflicts of loyalty. The stepfamily will always have strongly fixed sub-systems, to which members remain loyal. Also, the roles in the stepfamily are often ambiguous, in particular for the step-parent. A positive aspect of this ambiguity is that it provides freedom of choice, and there are a variety of possible roles that step-parents may assume in their new family situation. Nevertheless, Bernard (1956) has said that parenting in a stepfamily is one of the most difficult of all human assignments. Recent studies continue to support this statement (Furstenberg, 1987). While it is not an easy task for stepmothers or stepfathers, there is strong evidence that stepmothers have considerably greater difficulties than stepfathers in assuming their new role in the stepfamily (Nadler, 1976; Adams, 1982). This may be rooted in expectations that women are primarily responsible for the ambience of the home and the care of the children, including stepchildren. In fact, many women still derive much of their self-esteem from their role as parents, and should stepmothers be unable to succeed in their role as "second mother," they may be disappointed, frustrated or angry. This in turn may affect the entire family climate adversely. As discussed above, the finding that there is less tension between a child's father and stepfather may also influence the acceptance of the stepfather. In this regard, it is interesting to note that although boys exhibit more problems than girls following divorce, girls have greater difficulties than boys following a remarriage (Wallerstein and Kelly, 1980). In particular, stepmothers and stepdaughters appear to have the most difficulties in establishing a good relationship (Ferri, 1984).

8 Adolescents' chronic illness and father–adolescent relationships

In this chapter, we will try to analyze the father's role in the process of autonomy development, in particular with attention to the way the father may help the adolescent, despite his or her severe illness, to gain autonomy and establish independence. This role may vary depending on the severity and duration of the adolescent's illness. When the adolescent's illness can be self-managed and does not restrict his or her life too much, the role of the father clearly will be different from when the illness is life-threatening, the adolescent needs constant supervision while being treated for extensive periods, or when the prognosis is uncertain. What is more, family structure and family climate may change according to the characteristics or type of the illness involved. Thus, fathers of adolescents with chronic illness face situations that demand continuous change and flexibility. Before addressing the special topic of the father's role in the development of adolescent autonomy despite chronic illness, we will deal with the impact of chronic illness on the adolescents and then focus on the distinctive roles of fathers with chronically ill children and adolescents.

DOES CHRONIC ILLNESS INTERFERE WITH DEVELOPMENTAL PROGRESSION IN ADOLESCENCE?

In the spontaneous statements of adolescents, the issues "health and illness" do not arise as problem areas, perhaps because adolescents are very preoccupied with their physical development and feel healthy. At the same time, it should not be forgotten that currently at least 10 per cent of all families all over Europe are caring for chronically ill adolescents (Eiser, 1990). Although chronic illness is relatively rare, its existence in adolescents may have considerable consequences for autonomy development. A 14-year-old adolescent will clearly be affected in quite different ways by the onset of a chronic illness than a young adult who has already solved most of the developmental tasks that an adolescent is confronted with.

In fact, empirical studies have shown that the mastery of relevant developmental issues is impeded or delayed by illness. For example, Hauser *et al.* (1983) found specific arrests in ego-development among diabetic adolescents. Other authors have focused on friendships, heterosexual relationships and/or the establishment of an occupational identity. A frequent finding has been that since medical treatment frequently interferes with school and leisure activities, sick adolescents are more socially isolated (Weitzman, 1984; Grey *et al.* 1980), have fewer friendships and start dating later than healthy ones (Sinnema, 1986). Future plans become unpredictable, and thus career plans are reported less frequently by ill adolescents, compared to healthy ones (Becker, 1979). It is also striking that twice as many ill adolescents never take part in joint family activities – 32 per cent compared to 12 per cent of healthy adolescents (see Orr *et al.*, 1984) – and that ill adolescents are less likely to obtain a driving licence – 65 per cent compared to 88 per cent in healthy young people (ibid.). Finally, role expectations and role assignment tend to shift within the family and the normal process of separation from parents becomes very difficult (Hauser, 1991). Such findings uniformly point to the strong impact of chronic illness on autonomy and separation/individuation. We may thus conclude that while attaining individual autonomy in the family is a general developmental task in adolescence, it may be delayed or disturbed by the onset of a chronic illness. In some cases the onset of a chronic illness also leads to developmental progression. However, only a few studies have documented this phenomenon empirically and, in addition, have usually examined progression in relation to aspects of premature cognitive development.

How can this strong yet negative impact of chronic illness be explained? According to the focal theory of Coleman (1978), adolescents tackle and solve relevant developmental tasks continuously. With each new stage during adolescence, certain developmental tasks come into focus and are dealt with while others may make fewer demands on the adolescent. This "stretching" out of tasks enables the adolescent to keep the stress level low and to solve one issue after the other. The onset of a chronic illness, however, represents a major stressor, thus increasing the strains already inherent in this developmental phase. Coping with the chronic illness may thus become a major concern and be put ahead of other relevant developmental tasks (see Seiffge-Krenke, 1994). In addition, family conditions may lead to a situation where the adolescent is reintegrated into the family as the "ill child" for a long period. This situation, coupled with a general restructuring in the family and stronger control and monitoring of the adolescent by the family, may exacerbate the problems introduced by the illness. Thus, from the viewpoint of the young adult nothing seems possible without some trouble, and he or she cannot approach mastering the relevant developmental tasks as they would if they were not ill.

DISTINCTIVE ROLES OF FATHERS WITH CHRONICALLY ILL CHILDREN AND ADOLESCENTS

If one reviews the existing literature on chronically ill children or adolescents and their parents (for a summary, see Seiffge-Krenke and Brath, 1990) then it becomes evident that adolescents are typically included as a sub-group of a larger population of individuals of a broad age span. Of the 249 studies we analyzed, only 30 per cent restricted their samples to adolescents, aged from 12 to 25 years. The typical procedure has been to select mixed groups from a large age span without further differentiating within the years of adolescence. Another striking characteristic of these studies is that analyses of how the family deals with the onset of a chronic illness have focused almost exclusively on mothers' reactions to the illness. Similarly, it is mostly the mother's perspective that has been investigated in studies on the course of the illness or on dealing with death and dying. It seems as if the chronically ill child or adolescent is perceived as someone whose needs for caring, help and assistance can only be provided by or fulfilled best by the mother. Thus, we find hardly any studies which deal with the father's contribution toward the process of autonomy development in the ill child or adolescent. In contrast, numerous studies have dealt with the worries and problems of mothers who must care for a child or adolescent with chronic illness – which reflects a tendency to focus on regression (in the afflicted child) and caring (by his/her mother). The few studies which address the father's perspective, however, have indeed revealed that the roles of fathers and mothers in the illness process are clearly different. The problems in sharing information and feelings about the illness may vary because mothers and fathers are likely to encounter different experiences in the course of an illness. Mothers are more likely to assume the major responsibility for an ill child's physical care, and the intensive nursing involved often intensifies the bond between the mother and the child or adolescent (Cook, 1984). Fathers, in contrast, are expected to be supportive yet must control their emotions; furthermore, they must continue to carry out their duties as breadwinners (Gyolay, 1978). Moreover, fathers and mothers experience different demands on their time as they and the family attempt to deal with the illness. Owing to their different roles, mothers typically report family conflicts and, more specifically, conflicts between the sick child and other children (Cain *et al.*, 1964). Fathers experience more conflict between the requirements of their jobs and their wishes to spend more time with their ill child or adolescent (Schiff, 1972). Other studies have reported that the differences in mothers' and fathers' roles are even more pronounced. In many cases men withdraw from their families (Binger *et al.*, 1969) or are even excluded from family interaction (Schiefelbein, 1979).

It is interesting to note that a similar distinction between mother and father roles with ill children has also been seen in parents of developmentally delayed children. Goldberg *et al.* (1986) showed that fathers were less involved than mothers in caring for a developmentally delayed child. Fathers' lower involvement paralleled their lower level of self-reported symptoms, and fewer feelings of distress. Fathers had higher self-esteem, which was also reflected in feelings that they had more control of their lives. Mothers were, in general, more involved, more distressed, and reported having less control of their lives. Goldberg *et al.* suggested that the distinction between the roles of fathers and mothers of children with health problems "simply reflects the traditional role divisions in the family" (ibid.: 616).

These differences in perceived roles are especially prominent in the behavior patterns and feelings of parents of terminally ill children. A study conducted by Cook (1984) provides many illustrative examples. She interviewed the parents of 240 children who were being treated for cancer or blood disorders. At the beginning Cook expected that both parents would commonly experience a series of problems during the child's fatal illness. However, interviews revealed that owing to their different involvement with the child's illness and with other family members, fathers and mothers experienced quite different problems.

Mothers were primarily involved in managing the care of the chronically ill child as well as in co-ordinating the family's activities to meet the demands of caring for that child. They felt obliged to prevent others from learning upsetting information, and were concerned about helping the child to overcome feelings of depression or fear and maintain his or her morale. They complained of the intense emotional strain caused by the child's illness. Marital problems were often reported as well. For example, some mothers reported that their husbands felt neglected – even to the point of being envious of the attention their wives directed toward the ill child – or that their husbands seemed to be emotionally estranged from them.

Fathers continued to fulfill their responsibilities as economic providers and were involved in co-ordinating and maintaining extra-familial contacts such as with institutions, insurance companies or hospital bursars. Owing to this splitting of responsibilities, the fathers tended to be excluded from the family's everyday realm and they either withdrew from the mothers' over-involvement with the child or were more or less forced out by the mother or other family members. The consequences of this situation appeared to be more problematical for the fathers than the mothers. More specifically, fathers disclosed problems that could be characterized according to the following four main areas of concern: conflicts between job responsibilities and family obligations; being excluded from the family; the mother's over-involvement with the ill child; and finally, the desire to be with the wife and child. Many fathers described the child's illness as a time when they were faced with two competing sets of obligations: those relating to their job and those connected with their home and family. Especially when the child was in hospital, fathers felt the burden of assuming additional tasks which their wives had previously performed, such as childcare, cooking, chauffeuring and housekeeping. Taking on these new, additional tasks often disrupted the fathers' normal job routine and made them feel that they were being pulled in many different directions at the same time.

Another problem described more often by fathers than by mothers was the feeling of being excluded from participating in the active care of the sick child, or of being unable to provide any support in this matter. Since mothers usually accompanied their children to the hospital and were thus in a better position to speak to the hospital personnel, fathers were seldom involved in decision-making discussions relating to the child's illness. Sometimes the hospital even precluded the father's involvement. Many fathers felt that the attending physicians and nurses did not demonstrate as much concern toward them or were not as helpful as they were to the mothers and children. As one man put it: "as the father I was sort of a forgotten entity" (Cook, 1984: 83). In other situations the wife or other family members excluded the father. One father described the situation in this way: "I felt shut out. I felt that my wife became closer to her family and farther from me.... I felt like a fifth wheel or something" (ibid.: 83).

A further problem reported solely by the fathers, which is strongly related to the preceding one, was the reluctance of the mother to leave the hospital or home for any reason. Mothers usually felt that their place was with their children in hospital or at home, should it be possible to continue treatment there. The fathers frequently perceived their wives' commitment to the child or adolescent as being over-involved. Accordingly, they felt that their wives ignored them and other family members. This may have caused marital conflict.

A final problem mentioned primarily by the fathers was the conflict between their strong desire to be with their sick children and their wives, and their inability to be. One man said: "I would have liked to be with my daughter every minute. This was constantly on my mind" (Cook, 1984: 84). It might appear that the desire to be with the wife and child was related to conflicts between the responsibilities of work and family as described above. However, the context of that problem focused on the father's role "overload" and his inability to meet others' expectations. In contrast, the problem at hand involves the conflict between a strong desire to be with a sick child and the feeling that the responsibility to provide for the family is more important.

Although Cook's impressive study was conducted on a very special sample of terminally ill children, we can nevertheless draw important conclusions from the findings. These findings parallel those from other studies showing that the new demands involved in dealing with a sick child can result in changes of family roles and responsibilities. Both parents had to redefine their roles. In particular, fathers learned new roles; they found themselves more involved in caring for the remaining children at home and managing household matters. The observations and descriptions of the father's role obtained through Cook's research reveal the picture of a "pushed out" father, or at least a quite distanced one. Because of role splitting, the responsibility of fulfilling the child's primary needs is solely reserved for the mother. The father is occupied with other tasks necessary to ensure that family life continues to function, yet he is kept away from the afflicted child. In some cases the allocation of roles between mothers and fathers was rigid enough to lead to an active expulsion of the father from the family arena. However, as Cook's (1984) results show, this does not tell the whole story. Fathers regretted not being involved, and even if they continued to be the breadwinners, their thoughts and emotions remained directed toward the sick child. Considering the economic hardship which chronic illness sometimes places upon families, this special function as a breadwinner may become critically important. Thus, the father's conflict between being compelled to go to work and provide an income for the family and yet wanting to stay with his child is augmented.

In Chapter 3 we commented on the functions of the father in separating "one body for two." This function appears to gain increased significance in a situation where the wife is intensely involved in caring for a child with chronic illness whereas the husband is more concerned about his wife. In this regard, it is interesting to note that a frequent complaint among the fathers in Cook's study concerned their spouse's over-involvement with the sick child. Men also thought that their wives' over-involvement was damaging their physical and emotional well-being. Accordingly, some fathers tried to alleviate the close fusion between the ill child/adolescent and the mother, for instance by encouraging their wives to spend less time at the hospital.

A recent case at our out-patient clinic illustrates this issue. The father was very critical of his wife's behavior toward their 20-year-old chronically dysfunctioning son. The father wanted the son to resume some degree of independence. Such attempts were undermined by the mother, who continued to treat her son as a totally helpless person. The father even arrived at a stage where he insisted that either he or his son must leave the house.

ILL ADOLESCENTS AND THEIR FATHERS

The ability of parents to balance care and encourage autonomy becomes even more important in the case of ill adolescents. Generally speaking, any elevated level of closeness to an adult in a developmental phase in which autonomy from parents is a central developmental issue may well cause additional problems. It is therefore not surprising to find that ill adolescents dependent on the assistance of others over longer periods of time are often resentful and show highly aggressive behavior toward the caring adult, usually the mother (Lepontois, 1975). It is known from studies on adolescents with less serious diseases that even in periods of relatively good health they are excessively mothered (Ritchie, 1981). Furthermore, it is very difficult for the parents to ignore the illness or handicap of their children – even for just a short time – and to allow the adolescent to develop individuality in at least a few areas (Minde, 1978). Supportive and sustaining as the family network may be to the sick adolescents, their parents' – especially their mothers' – unlimited care and concern may nevertheless become enormous problems for them. As outlined above, separation and autonomous development are thereby retarded, postponed, or even obviated altogether. Over-protection is the most common manner by which the central developmental task of achieving autonomy is interfered with. We are thus not surprised to find that studies investigating families coping with illness show that the coping strategies which contribute most to successful adolescent adjustment include normalization (maximal integration of the chronically ill adolescent into society) and the establishment of a wider social support system through which the burden of the illness can be shared effectively (Holladay, 1984; Shulman, 1990). It is interesting to note that in most of these families, over-protectiveness actually decreases during the course of an illness whereas in less well-adapted families, dependence and parental control tend to increase. We may thus conclude that during the course of an illness, a shift from an over-involved relationship to a more separated and individuated one is most appropriate. While the close relationship with the mother may serve to reduce the emotional strain caused by the onset of the illness, the father's role in helping the adolescent in his or her search for autonomy, despite the illness, may be very important, perhaps even more so as the illness continues. The ability to balance closeness and individuation was also indicated as an important predictor for the well-being of families with a developmentally delayed child (Trute and Hauch, 1988). In those families, parents showed the ability to discuss and debate alternative and different choices in family activities while maintaining a high commitment to their marriage.

Unfortunately, only a few studies deal with the specific roles and functions of fathers of chronically ill adolescents or how fathers contribute toward adolescents' progress and adaptation in the illness process and to developmental progression overall. Individuation in the illness context has only been addressed very recently in the research by Hauser and his co-workers (Allen *et al.*, 1994) on diabetic adolescents. A general finding was that ego development in diabetic adolescents was at a lower level than in the control group of non-diabetic adolescents. This contrast was especially marked for the diabetic males, whose ego development was significantly lower than that of the females. Self-esteem was also more impaired in the diabetic adolescents who had a longer duration of the illness.

From 1991 to 1994, we conducted a longitudinal study on a sample of 109 families with chronically ill adolescents with a recent onset of diabetes and a sample of 108 families with healthy adolescents (Seiffge-Krenke *et al.*, 1996). Development in quite different areas (e.g. school, work, friendship, romantic relationships, family, physical maturity and health) was analyzed in order to determine whether the recent onset of such a major stressor as illness hinders or delays adolescent development. The impact of diabetes was major and placed various demands on both the afflicted patient and his or her family. Not only were long-term issues such as anticipation of future health problems and longevity affected, but so also were daily concerns such as mealtime routines, daily body care, physical exercise and travelling alone. During childhood the task of administering insulin by injection was usually taken on by the mother or the father, but most adolescents learned to administer the injections themselves. Over 80 per cent of our chronically ill 12- to 16-year-old adolescents assumed the responsibility for self-injections and, in part, for watching their diet. In the management of diabetes, it was necessary to monitor the adolescents' metabolic control by examining urine or blood samples at least once a day. Parents could monitor the adolescent three times daily and make sure that he or she followed the restrictions about food intake, consumption of alcohol, etc.

Nevertheless, while adolescents may manage their diets, injections and urine and blood checks almost completely by themselves, it is obvious how much of the family routine may be restricted and influenced by the illness. When asked about everyday stressors and hassles, it was striking that parents reported higher levels of stress and strain and a greater number of stress-related symptoms than the adolescents themselves. The highest level of reported stress was found among the fathers of diabetic adolescents. This high level of stress-related symptoms in parents was not only related to a redistribution of family responsibilities and a reorganization of routine. The necessity of taking on new tasks and the uncertainty of the course of the illness represented an enormous strain for both parents. In our interviews conducted with parents and adolescents in the diabetic sample, a marked change in family roles and duties occurred shortly after the diagnosis. Mostly the mothers were attached more closely to the ill child, and the adolescents managed the medical regimen and diet together with the mother or under her close supervision. Fathers felt excluded from the family and reported their wives' over-involvement with the ill adolescents, and named many hassles and minor stressors. In comparison, mothers reported feeling emotionally over-taxed and depressed. Such findings parallel those found in parents of terminally ill children as reported by Cook (1984).

The diabetes management was, generally speaking, very good in our families. Over two-thirds of all afflicted adolescents belonged to the group with good or medium glycemic control, and only 11 per cent belonged to the group with brittle diabetes with unstable or poor glycemic control. An analysis of developmental progression revealed, however, that there was a delay in mastering several developmental tasks relevant for this age group such as establishing heterosexual relationships, gaining autonomy and creating close friendships with peers. While the ill adolescents showed age-appropriate development in relation to tasks such as developing an occupational identity, tasks which include processes of separation and individuation were impaired. Such tasks were less completely realized in ill adolescents than in healthy ones of the same age. In addition, sick adolescents did not strive for future realization of these tasks as strongly as their healthy peers did (Boeger and Seiffge-Krenke, 1994).

Our analysis of family climate measured by the Family Environment Scale (FES, see Moos and Moos, 1981) revealed that an achievement-oriented family climate was established in all families shortly after the diagnosis (Seiffge-Krenke *et al.*, 1996). Compared to families with healthy adolescents, the climate in families with diabetic adolescents was characterized by highly organized and structured activity, an emphasis on achievement-orientation and less autonomy for the adolescent. While such a family climate was apparently very appropriate for managing the illness, it could lead to a rigid family interaction detrimental to the development of other family members. This characterization of the family climate from the perspective of the adolescent corresponds quite well to the parents' evaluations. Figure 8.1 illustrates that adolescents and their fathers shared the same views and gave rather similar descriptions of the family climate.

It can be seen that in comparison to families with healthy adolescents the climate in families with a chronically ill adolescent undergoes marked changes. The family appears to take on a solid, if not rigid, structure and becomes highly organized. Family activities are planned and controlled and a strong achievement orientation dominates. Thus, our diabetic families correspond to the "achievement-oriented family type" (Billings and Moos, 1983). This type is consistently found in families of adolescents with good as well as with poor metabolic control. The only difference between the two groups can be found in a better quality of interpersonal relationships in families with a diabetic with good glycemic control.

It is reasonable to suggest that the structured family climate is tailored to address the needs of the sick child or adolescent appropriately. The way these families function, though different from families with healthy adolescents, may just seem "different" and not "deviant" (Kazak *et al.*, 1988). However, as French (1977) has proposed, the adherence to strict routines in cases of prolonged stress may lead to structural changes in the family. Changes that start as

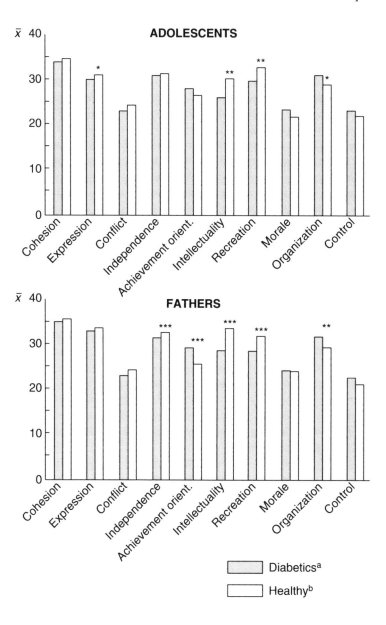

Figure 8.1 Family climate as perceived by ill and healthy adolescents, mean age 13.9 years, and their fathers
Note: [a] = 109; [b] = 108; * = f<0.05; ** = f<0.01; *** = f<0.001

organized and integrated responses by the family to address efficiently the specific needs of the ill child may end up as routines. Lewis (1986) has claimed that even the structure of well-functioning families may tend toward increasing rigidity.

However, difficulties are not restricted to the family. The relationships of the diabetic adolescents with their friends also point to a developmental delay. While in our two groups the number of friends was comparable, an analysis of friendship level and friendship characteristics in the diabetic group revealed that their relations were typically lacking in intimacy and closeness. In this regard it should be mentioned that the social network of ill adolescents as compared to the healthy group was large and intact. Parental divorce in the ill group was less frequent than in the healthy group. Thus, although the objective characteristics of the diabetic's family structure and network of friends were positive in themselves (e.g. as revealed by low divorce rates in diabetic families and the existence of a large circle of friends and acquaintances), the incidence of unusually high achievement-orientation and reduced emotional expression in the family as well as low levels of intimacy with friends suggest that the quality of the relationships in these networks appeared to be somewhat deficient. On the basis of the results from annual investigations in our longitudinal study from 1991 to 1994, the family climate was not perceived by fathers and adolescents to have undergone major changes. The achievement-oriented family climate in families with a chronically ill adolescent was consistently described by fathers and adolescents in all four investigations. It was not influenced by variables such as age or gender, duration of illness or medical adaptation of the adolescent (good or bad glycemic control).

In summary, we found that with the onset of a major long-term illness, a restructuring in family climate with a clear emphasis on achievement and organization occurs as a typical consequence. This more structure-oriented climate in the family was uniformly perceived by ill adolescents and their parents. In the light of these findings, the question arose as to whether such a family restructuring also involved an increased participation on the part of the fathers. As mentioned above, the general finding has been that most fathers of chronically ill children felt excluded from the family. With this in mind, we would like to examine in the following section the characteristics of paternal involvement in families with adolescent diabetics.

DIFFICULTIES IN GETTING THE FATHER INVOLVED

In most of the cases we observed, the fathers of diabetics, besides complaining a lot about the burden of the illness, were much more distanced than in normal families. More specifically, the feelings of stress and strain due to the illness of their child did not lead to an increased involvement of fathers in settling family matters, assisting in the illness management or nurturing a relationship with the afflicted child. It seemed as if they were "frozen in inactivity." This passivity is also described in Stuart Hauser's work on how families cope with diabetes in adolescence (see Hauser *et al.*, 1988). In our study, an analysis of family communication patterns according to the Family Interaction Task (FIT) as developed by Grotevant and Cooper (1985) revealed this phenomenon quite vividly. In the FIT, families were requested to sit together and solve a given task. For instance, they had to plan several weeks of holidays together for which they could spend as much money as they liked. In trying to solve this problem, fathers were very passive and uninterested, compared to the mothers, and hardly contributed to the discussions. The following protocol of such a discussion illustrates the distant and inactive position of a father of a chronically ill boy and the numerous attempts of his son to get him involved:

CHRISTIAN   Well, then, let's go to the USA this time. What about San Diego? Oh, wait, that's California. Yeah, hey, we'll go to San Diego. What do you think, Dad?

MOTHER   It would be better if we went on a winter holiday.

CHRISTIAN   No, no, San Diego, that's cool!

MOTHER   A week of winter sports, everyone together...

CHRISTIAN   Okay, but also a week in San Diego.

MOTHER   No!

CHRISTIAN   Come on, we have enough money; let's go to San Diego with Benny. Yeah, then after that we can go do some winter sports!

MOTHER   No! We'll go to a nice hotel in the mountains where we can go skiing.

CHRISTIAN   But we can still do that anyway!

MOTHER   No! I don't want to go to San Diego!

CHRISTIAN   Why don't you say something, Dad? You're the one who is going to pay for it all!

FATHER   I can't really say anything!

CHRISTIAN   Why not?

FATHER   What should I plan, when this is all just nothing?

CHRISTIAN   Man, you really have no fantasy at all; you're so uncreative! I think we should go to San Diego, for a week...

MOTHER   No, we'll go skiing for a week and then in summer we'll go to Majorca for two weeks.

CHRISTIAN   San Diego!

MOTHER   Just laze about in the sun and lie on the beach.

CHRISTIAN   No, no, San Diego, San Diego! I think San Diego is pretty cool. Come on, think about it, we could spend all the money that we have.

MOTHER   No!

CHRISTIAN   Of course! I say that we should go to California, to San Diego. But I think that a polar expedition also wouldn't be so bad. Yeah, or something a bit unusual, like to, um, what's that place called...

MOTHER   Now I think you're really beginning to have some wild ideas.

CHRISTIAN   Somehow, like in a tropical rain forest, somewhere, something like that would really be pretty amusing! So...

MOTHER   I don't find it funny at all. I think we should do it like we've always done it: go for a week of winter sports. Now, during the Easter break.

CHRISTIAN   No!

MOTHER   A nice week of ski school...

CHRISTIAN   Does my fat sister have to come again, too? No, I'm not going to do it; I just don't feel like it. But maybe snowboard skiing, yeah, that would be O.K. But I'm not really sure. San Diego is pretty cool and unusual. I don't really know. Say something, Dad!

FATHER   I really can't say much. I can only say something about how our last vacations were.

MOTHER   Yes.

CHRISTIAN   The last time Lisa went with us.

FATHER   I already went on holiday with Mom – you weren't even with us!

MOTHER   Yes, we could go without you.

FATHER   All the holidays were nice.

CHRISTIAN   OK. We've decided that this year we'll take a winter vacation. We'll have a nice time. I'll be on the snowboard slopes; my father and my mother will dreamily jump around on their skis.... We hope you have a nice day [laughs] and say goodbye for now, okay?

The difficulty of getting the father involved is also obvious when one looks at the small group of ill adolescents in our sample who were raised by their fathers alone ($n = 5$). Single fathers who raise their diabetic children demonstrate extremely compliant behavior. While they encourage their sons or daughters to express their wishes and interests and respond to their comments by confirming or accepting them, they seldom make suggestions themselves and put their own interests in the background. This type of interactional behavior can be illustrated quite clearly in the following stretch of a conversation between a 15-year-old daughter, a diabetic, and her father. Again we refer to the protocols from the FIT:

FATHER   So then, you want a week with Nadine [a friend]?

DAUGHTER   At least!

FATHER   Or maybe two? Or all three?

DAUGHTER   Yes, maybe!

FATHER   With Nadine alone or with her parents, too?

DAUGHTER   Yes, with her parents!

FATHER   Oh, hm, and what about me? Do I have to be there? Should I be there? Could I be there? Would you like me to be with you or not? Hm?

DAUGHTER   Yes, but you don't have to!

FATHER   But, I should go with you, shouldn't I? Would it bother you if I went on vacation somewhere else, or, for example, if I drove to the Eifel area?

DAUGHTER   Oh, God!

FATHER   I only meant it as an example!

DAUGHTER   [as if bored] If it makes you happy.

FATHER   I'm only asking whether you would like me to be around when we spend our vacation together.

This tendency to be very accommodating to the needs and interests of the adolescent while at the same time hardly articulating their own interests is also evident among single mothers of adolescent diabetics. Compared to the fathers, however, this imbalance is not as striking.

WHEN THE FATHER IS TOO INVOLVED

It is difficult to explain why most of the fathers of chronically ill adolescents in our study were so uninvolved. It may be that the strict division of roles between husband and wife and the latter's over-involvement with the child left little opportunity for them to introduce or follow up on their own initiatives for involvement. It is also striking that while on the one hand they were relatively uninvolved, on the other hand they experienced considerable stress. This could be an indication that even less involved fathers are quite troubled about their child's illness or concerned about what consequences the illness might introduce for the child's future. Perhaps it is more difficult for fathers to express their feelings openly and/or to react appropriately in order to solve illness-related problems. In this regard it is quite possible that culture-specific conditions which discourage German fathers from openly displaying their emotions kept them from expressing feelings of sadness, fear and depression. It was indeed noteworthy that all of the foreign (non-German) fathers of adolescents in our sample were able to speak relatively openly about how concerned they were about the idea that their child would probably never marry and have children. This was especially the case among the fathers of Mediterranean descent (e.g. Italian, Spanish), who lamented the "defective bodies" of their children and openly indicated their sadness about the loss of a healthy body.

Whereas in most families with chronically ill adolescents the distant and inactive position of the father was predominant, there were a few cases in which the father was unusually intensely involved. These examples, however, have a clearly incestuous character, as the following case vignette reveals.

The interviewer was received by the patient's mother, who was dressed all in black and had a glassy expression on her face. The suspicion that something was wrong with her was confirmed later when the interviewer was informed that the mother had epilepsy. The 13-year-old daughter, who had been suffering from diabetes for six months, was rather pale and thin, yet precocious. She obviously felt flattered by the visit. The interview was interrupted several times by the mother. For example, she claimed that she had to place some orders by telephone, and later, she placed some cake right in front of her daughter but remarked that the cake was only for the interviewer, not for her. The patient herself reported that her relationship with her father was better than with her mother. This closeness of the father–daughter relationship was confirmed when the daughter's demeanour clearly brightened when her father entered. In contrast, her interactions with her mother appeared very strained.

In family conversation, the father clearly dominated. The mother seemed weak and inferior. She made some very differentiated and sensitive comments about the daughter's illness but her contributions were often drawn out, and she was frequently interrupted by her husband and daughter. She said that she often felt absolutely at the mercy of her daughter's aggressiveness. The father reported that his wife suffered from epilepsy and was often forgetful so that he preferred to take care of errands and other things himself. The mother protested, saying that she did get things done. The father confirmed that his daughter turned to him with all her problems and not to his wife. He was very proud of his daughter and her independence. In this context he mentioned that his daughter was very interested in sex and sexuality – she talked about such topics constantly. She even showed visitors condoms. This comment prompted the mother to mention that since the onset of the illness, her daughter had been sleeping with her husband in the double bed while she herself slept in her daughter's bedroom.

The importance of sexuality in this family, at least on a verbal level, was quite conspicuous, as was the open provocation of the mother by the father and the daughter. The interviewer had the impression that the daughter's relationship with her father (whom she very much idealized) had already reached a preincestuous level, and that she was in full command of both her parents in a very self-confident way, as if she were the "queen of the family." Obviously, the onset of the illness had occurred at a time when the relationship between father and daughter had already developed a strongly incestuous character, whereby the mother was consequently excluded. The recent onset of the illness was used to legitimize the close physical contact between father and daughter. It was regarded as problematical that the father undoubtedly accepted his daughter's offers and did not regard the exclusion of his wife as a problem.

This case is an example of the "darker side" of the way a father's involvement with his child may develop. Indeed, the daughter's behavior was neurotic, but since neither the patient nor the parents regarded such behavior as inadequate or unusual, the development of pathological elements in the family was left unbridled. More specifically, not only did the father try to justify his sleeping habits as a way of supervising his daughter, but the mother was excluded from the father–daughter unit. In a way, father and daughter exploited the daughter's illness and the mother's dysfunctioning as means to fulfill their own needs.

One year later, when we interviewed the family again, this incestuous relationship had become even more obvious. When the female interviewer tried to enter the house, she got the impression that she, like the mother, was like a third object disturbing the father–daughter relationship. When the father and daughter were physically close together, they reacted very aggressively toward the interviewer and, at the end of the interview, literally threw her out. The interviewer had to find her way in total darkness through the garden to reach her car parked in the street.

In some cases fathers may oscillate between the two opposing tendencies of sometimes being too close and at other times too distant, as the following case shows.

Simon, aged 17, was a twelfth-grade pupil who suffered from muscular dystrophy. His medical condition was discovered when he was 4 years old. Simon attended regular schools, was regarded as a brilliant student, and was well accepted by other students. At this stage of his sickness, Simon was very dependent on the help of his parents in day-to-day functioning. He needed help in rising from a seated position. His father had to drive him to school and help him to get out of the car. The bathroom door could not be locked in case he fell. As a result of this condition, the father was very involved in Simon's life. He stayed at home and would not let Simon be on his own. He screened phone calls and monitored the visits of friends. When Simon received correspondence from a friend who had moved to a different town, the father opened the letters, though Simon did not need this help. On the other hand, there were occasions and circumstances when the father showed lack of interest. For example, the mother often took Simon for different treatments, which required them to stay away from home. The father did not contact or visit his wife and son for long periods. Simon also wished to establish some distance from his parents and asked them to be less intrusive. However, he was afraid to address his father's behavior openly, for fear that the father would punish him by forgetting to take him to a place he had to attend. Simon, therefore, was subject to his father's extreme tendencies of either being over-involved or uninterested.

DOES THE ILLNESS REINFORCE EXISTING PATTERNS IN THE FATHER–ADOLESCENT RELATIONSHIP?

To comment on the cases presented so far, we would like to emphasize that having an overly distant and passive father or one who cultivates an incestuous-like intimacy as illustrated above, clearly has negative consequences for the adolescent. In the first example presented above, the 15-year-old male was, despite several attempts, unable to involve his father in the decision-making process, and in the end agreed to his mother's suggestions for vacation plans, although he really was not enthusiastic about them. Not only was the mother very much involved in the discussion, but she knew what she wanted and was successful in asserting herself. The son made many attempts to suggest going somewhere different for a change, somewhere more interesting; however, his suggestions appeared to conflict with the family routine. The son probably expected some assistance from his father, but was unsuccessful in rallying his support. The father remained disengaged and passive. This example might be regarded as a prototype of the interaction that exists in families with ill adolescents.

The second case illustrated the situation of a father and daughter having different ideas, for example, about how to spend their holidays. The father was uncertain about whether he and his daughter should travel together. While he showed interest in the needs and wishes of his daughter, albeit in a distanced manner, he let himself be excluded. His daughter got her way completely without showing any consideration for her father.

It is our impression that the onset of illness strengthens some existing patterns in the father–adolescent relationship. For example, if the father has been distant, he may become even more so. Similarly, if the father has been involved, he may become even more involved, as can be seen in the last case, where a quasi-incestuous relationship between father and daughter had been established and the mother was "pushed out." It is quite obvious that a reinforcement of negative patterns already existing in the relationship imposes negative consequences for the afflicted child's further development. Such a relationship lacks flexibility for an autonomous and more mature development and fixates the adolescent in an overly childish or adult-like position. Both pathways are powerful ones and may lead to enormous gratifications for the child, which are difficult to give up.

An issue which has only been touched on briefly so far concerns the question of whether it is more difficult for fathers or mothers to deal with bodily distortion, disruption of normal physical functions and loss of physical strength in the sick adolescent. One of the most important aspects of adolescence, the process of separating and becoming independent, becomes more complicated and more demanding for physically handicapped adolescents insofar as, owing to their illness, they remain like children in a state of dependence. This means that in a way, they cannot separate themselves from their parents and learn to live independently. While this more child-like behavior can probably be tolerated more readily by mothers, fathers, who are supposed to emphasize separation, may be more burdened or irritated by caring for a life-long child. As already mentioned, in our longitudinal study we observed that fathers from countries such as Italy, Turkey and Spain expressed irritation and even narcissistic injury concerning the body distortion much more vividly than the sons or daughters themselves. For example, one father, an Italian, was nearly in tears when he spoke with the interviewer about the illness of his son, emphasizing that this was his only son, who, with such a damaged body, would probably never have children.

Pursuing our line of thought that the illness may reinforce certain aspects of the father–adolescent relationship, our last example may illustrate the value of an intact body for the father. In Chapter 3, we outlined the fact that historically, a child's body belonged to the father and that the line of inheritance was bound to the child's physical health and bodily integrity. It is thus understandable that even today, a child, especially a boy, whose body is diseased can represent a narcissistic injury for the father. Although this is probably the case for many fathers, only those of southern European descent were able to acknowledge openly this kind of inner reaction.

Finally, we wish to comment on similarities in patterns of parenting under elevated stress. It seems as if the stricter role division between fathers and mothers and a more ambivalent paternal style is characteristic for families experiencing a divorce or caring for a chronically ill adolescent. Until now we have been primarily concerned with the distancing process of the father in intact families. Yet, in the light of the ongoing shift of family structure and the significant role that parents play in Insulin Dependent Diabetes Management (IDDM) treatment and management, it seems important to examine the link between family structure and adolescent adaptation to illness. The case presented on page 139 concerns single fathers who raised a diabetic adolescent – a rare pattern indeed. It is of course more frequently the case that single mothers have to cope with the chronic illness of their children. Because there is considerable evidence that boys are more vulnerable than girls to the deleterious effects of "father absence" (see Chapter 6), we might ask if the effects of the absence of the father in families with a chronically ill male adolescent potentiate the negative effects of chronic illness. Some studies found no differences in metabolic control or social competence between chronically ill adolescents from fatherless families and those from intact families. Although the sample size was rather low and the range of variables restricted, the result was unexpected. The authors suggested that the fatherless adolescents adapted to the difficulties associated with single-parent households by assuming greater respon- sibilities for their own health care. This interpretation is consistent with findings that the loss of a father may promote the development of adult-like behavior in adolescents (see Chapter 6). It was also striking that in families without fathers, mother–daughter support was higher than mother–son support, a result that also parallels findings on divorced families. Because of these differences in maternal support, we may consider father-absent adolescents with diabetes as an at-risk population. This is possibly more true for boys, but may also apply to girls since the mother–daughter relationship may be too close to enable autonomous development.

9 Fathers and adolescent psychopathology

In the preceding chapters, we examined the role of fathers in normative development, and, more specifically, the distinctive role of fathers in relation to adolescents' penchant for autonomy. We then turned to fatherhood under stressful conditions, like a divorce, a step-parent family or in a family caring for a chronically physically ill adolescent. In this chapter we want to examine the relationship between an adolescent's health and his/her relationship with the father with respect to psychopathology. Interestingly, in adolescent psychopathology the relationships with significant others are either too close or too distant. In this chapter, the contribution of fathers to adolescent psychopathology is examined, focusing on the dysfunction of fathers in supporting the adolescent in his or her separation/individuation process.

FATHERS AS FORGOTTEN CONTRIBUTORS TO CHILD AND ADOLESCENT PSYCHOPATHOLOGY

As long ago as 1975, Lamb argued that there was an urgent need to pay more attention to the role of fathers in the socialization of children. A more integrated view, examining the role of the father in the normative and pathological development of his offspring, was not developed until 1990. According to Phares (1992), the failure to include fathers in studies of child and adolescent development may be the result of several factors. There may be difficulties in recruiting fathers, not only in general, but also owing to the high incidence of divorce and resulting distance of the father from the family. Moreover, the relative contribution the father makes to child and adolescent development has been neither fully nor universally appreciated. Although the father's role in normative developmental processes such as attachment and social development has been examined in most of the studies presented in Chapters 1 and 2, his influence on the development of children showing patterns of deviant or dysfunctional behavior was not fully discussed. This may be due to the general tendency to blame mothers when their children show signs of maladjustment (Caplan, 1989).

This standpoint has a close connection to the myth of maternal instinct (Badinter, 1993) and the idea of an exclusive bonding of the child to its mother (Winnicott, 1965). Concepts such as primary motherliness (ibid.) as well as the idea of a symbiosis between mother and child (Mahler, 1979) are similar in that they both propose an ideal unity that cannot or should not be destroyed. Not only do such concepts legitimize the exclusion of the father but they also have the consequence that the mother is blamed solely for the unsuccessful development of the infant. This tendency to place sole blame on mothers for the maladjustment of their offspring was evident decades ago, yet has persisted and been incorporated into modern concepts such as that of the "schizophrenic mother" (Watzlawick *et al.*, 1974). In theories of the pathological effects of certain types of family systems (e.g. the psychosomatic family, see Minuchin, 1974; or the diabetic family, see Minuchin *et al.*, 1978) the emphasis placed on the influence of the mother is also unusually marked. One characteristic among these theories is that a weak, distant or absent father is not able to correct the influence of a dominant, aggressive and unempathetic mother.

Caplan and Hall-McCorquodale (1985) found in their review of publications over three different years that more than 70 different kinds of child psychopathology were attributed to maternal influence, while none was attributed to fathers. Mothers were mentioned at a rate of 5 to 1 compared with fathers in studies on child and adolescent psychopathology. More importantly, in these studies mothers were never described in solely positive terms. In contrast, among the rare instances where fathers were mentioned, their influence on children was judged only in positive terms.

This points to the distinctive perception of fathers as the parent correcting negative mother–child relationships. We must point out, however, that the empirical base for conclusions is rather limited owing to the lack of studies which have investigated both mothers' and fathers' influence on child psychopathology. A basic tendency to seek the roots of child psychopathology within the mother–child relationship may explain only a part of this deficit. Structural variations in families with disturbed children and adolescents have to be taken into account, too. Children and adolescents referred for treatment predominantly have a disrupted family background. They have grown up within single-parent families, their parents are divorced and/or they live in foster homes. Consequently, the father is usually absent or missing. Frequently the mother is the only family member available with whom the researchers may be in contact. It can thus be expected that the mother's influence on the psychopathology of the children is often over-estimated, whereas an inquiry into the father's function and the meaning of this "missing father" for the development of disturbances is hardly pursued. Accordingly, two different, possibly mutually potentiating influences are characteristic in familes with disturbed children and adolescents: a mother who is dominant, powerful and partly disturbed herself, and a missing father. The question whether the presence of a father would have enabled a correcting experience and provided the child or adolescent with an alternative model must therefore remain open. In the following section we will first concentrate on the possibly damaging effects of fathers in general before dealing with more specific pathologies and disturbed father–adolescent relationships.

DO FATHERS CONTRIBUTE TO ADOLESCENT PSYCHOPATHOLOGY?

In a recent contribution, Phares and Compas (1992) addressed the question of whether fathers contribute to adolescent psychopathology, and more specifically, if the paternal effects are limited to certain types of problems in children and adolescents. In addition, the mechanisms that are responsible for paternal effects were examined. In order to pursue these questions, the authors reviewed and analyzed the results from empirical studies published from 1984 to 1991 involving parents and their pre-adolescent or adolescent sons and daughters exhibiting psychopathology. In their analysis of more than 577 articles, they in fact determined that fathers continue to be rather under-represented in the literature of psychopathology. Over 48 per cent of the studies involved only mothers, 26 per cent involved both fathers and mothers analyzed separately, 25 per cent included both fathers and mothers who were not analyzed separately or referred to as "parents" and only 1 per cent involved fathers only. The differences in numbers (48 per cent of the studies included only mothers, 1 per cent of the studies included only fathers) are striking and illustrate that the general approach has not changed since earlier reviews by Lamb (1975) or Caplan and Hall-McCorquodale (1985). As a group, fathers continue to be excluded in the literature. Phares and Compas (1992) selected those studies for review which could be classified according to one of the following sample types:

1 clinically referred children and adolescents and the characteristics of their fathers;
2 clinically referred fathers and the characteristics of their children;
3 non-referred children and adolescents and fathers.

In the following, we will deal only with those studies including adolescents and their fathers.

Clinically referred adolescents and their fathers

It has to be emphasized that "fathers of diagnosed offspring" is a broad category. Fathers may have children of different ages, different gender and/or with different types of disorders. The fathers of clinically referred children were investigated in studies dealing with certain types of child psychopathology, most commonly, attention deficit, hyperactivity and behavioral disorders. Fathers of clinically referred adolescents, however, were investigated in studies analyzing quite different types of disorders such as delinquency, substance abuse, depression, suicidal behavior, schizophrenia and eating disorders. Since we can assume a continuity from childhood to adolescence in only some of such disorders, for the most part the studies on adolescents deal with illnesses or disorders that have been diagnosed for the first time during this developmental period. Moreover, while research has tended to concentrate on specific illnesses and disorders with varying degrees of interest, this trend is not related to the prevalence rates of these disorders. Very few studies have investigated the relationship between adolescent alcohol and substance abuse and paternal characteristics, and the findings have been quite equivocal.

Many more studies, however, deal with paternal factors associated with adolescent delinquency, including lack of paternal supervision and discipline, inconsistent communication patterns, high amounts of paternal defensive communication, high levels of paternal deviance, aggressiveness and conflict as well as high levels of alcohol abuse, of which the latter was found to be more prevalent among fathers of delinquents. Also, high rates of paternal child abuse have been reported in several studies. The majority of research on juvenile delinquency is concerned with samples of male delinquents. As an exception, Henggeler *et al.* (1987) compared fathers of female and male delinquents and found that fathers of female delinquents were significantly more neurotic than fathers of male delinquents and also had more conflicts with their spouses.

Concerning depression, the vast majority of studies have analyzed the role of mothers in adolescent depression. In general, it has been demonstrated that mothers of depressed adolescents have high rates of depression themselves, while there was no difference in rates of depression in fathers. More studies can be found which relate paternal psychological symptoms to anxiety, but not to depression of their offspring. As a rule, fathers are less likely than mothers to have a history of depression, but they are more likely than mothers to have a history of substance abuse and antisocial pathology in the samples of depressed children and adolescents (see, for example, Mitchell *et al.*, 1989). Thus, overall there does not appear to be a strong link between paternal factors and depression in adolescence.

In the few studies analyzing fathers and suicidal behavior in adolescence, however, fathers of adolescents who attempted suicide were significantly more depressed than fathers of non-attemptors. But in general, fathers of suicidal adolescents did not appear different from fathers of non-suicidal adolescents, and the impact of mothers in suicidal behavior in all studies analyzed by Phares and Compas (1992) was much greater. Similarly, there has been a long history of focusing on mother–child interaction in explaining the etiology of schizophrenic disorders. Only very recently has harsh paternal discipline been found to be associated with the incidence of adolescent schizophrenia and paternal hostility to be associated with re-admittance of adolescents to psychiatric in-patient units (Angermeyer, 1982).

In contrast, numerous studies have investigated interactions in families of anorexic, bulimic and non-referred adolescents (see, for example, Garfinkel *et al.*, 1983; Humphrey, 1989). Very frequently, differences between anorexic adolescents and normal controls in the perception of parent–child relationships have been found. For example, Humphrey (1986) has found that bulimics and anorexics perceive their parents to be less affirming, understanding, nurturing and comforting than non-clinical adolescents. More specifically, bulimic adolescents perceive greater deficits in parental nurturance than the anorexic and non-clinical adolescents do. In a follow-up study, Humphrey (1989) found that the interaction of both fathers and mothers with their anorexic daughters was rather contradictory in nature. Although the parents showed signs of nurturance and affection, they neglected their daughters' needs. Both fathers and mothers of bulimics were hostile toward their daughters and tried to control them. Taken together, these studies suggest that the investigation of paternal relationships may be helpful in distinguishing between sub-types of eating disorders. Furthermore, while such studies have revealed no difference between fathers and mothers in their respective involvement in the etiology of eating disorders in adolescents, there does appear to be a difference between the parents of adolescents with eating disorders and weight control problems and the parents of adolescents showing normal eating and weight patterns.

Taken together, we may suggest that the characteristics of fathers are more consistently related to adolescent externalizing behavior than to internalizing behavior. Also, as a rule, the nature of the father's pathological interaction does not seem to differ significantly from that of the mother. At this point, we should emphasize that the empirical basis for these suggestions is rather limited. More representative research involving both fathers and mothers might reveal those patterns of family dynamics in which both father and mother interact negatively with the adolescent and potentiate their destructive influence. It is also likely that more representative research involving fathers would reveal the distinctive manner in which fathers contribute to the psychopathology of their adolescent offspring. At a later point in this chapter we would like to elaborate on the father's involvement in the fostering of some special types of adolescent pathology, for example, adolescent delinquency, or the inability to separate one's self from parents and create one's own identity.

Clinically referred fathers and their offspring

According to Phares and Compas (1992), another type of research methodology has involved studies of children and adolescents whose fathers have been referred for clinical treatment or have received a psychiatric diagnosis. Fathers with a variety of diagnoses (antisocial personality, criminality, depression, alcohol and substance abuse, schizophrenia) as well as fathers who physically and sexually abuse their offspring have been analyzed and the behavioral and psychological adjustment of their offspring have been determined. As a general result, adolescents from clinically referred fathers have been found consistently to be at risk for a variety of emotional and behavioral difficulties. In this regard, the effects of alcoholic and depressed fathers were most severe. It should be mentioned, however, that in the samples of depressed fathers, the incidence of depression among mothers was typically high as well. The majority of these studies failed to find any differences in the offspring's risk for maladjustment as a function of which parent is identified as depressed (see, for example, Billings and Moos, 1983; Orvaschel *et al.*, 1988).

Research on fathers who physically and sexually abuse their children and adolescents is quite extensive and will be dealt with more specifically in Chapter 10. Here it is only necessary to mention the general finding stemming from those studies comparing paternal and non-paternal abusers. Victims who have been sexually abused by their fathers suffer greater psychological trauma than those abused by other adults or family members. As an example, children abused by their fathers were significantly more likely to be diagnosed with a psychiatric disorder (45 per cent) than children who had been abused by another relative (26 per cent) (see Sirles *et al.*, 1989). Taken together, these studies suggest that consequences for the child or adolescent resulting from paternal abuse are more severe than from being victimized by other individuals. Apparently, the important role of the mother who consciously or unconsciously tolerates the abuse has not been investigated. Thus, we would suggest that because of the mother's implicit consent she may not perform any compensatory function or help to ease the effects of abuse.

Although the possible effects of maternal illness on children and adolescents have been studied frequently, hardly any studies have focused on physical illness of the father and the consequences for their offspring (see Chapter 8). In contrast to findings from studies on families with severely psychologically disturbed fathers, we do not know what changes occur in the family when fathers are "absent" owing to severe chronic physical illness. In summary, results from studies investigating clinically referred adolescents and their fathers as well as results from studies including clinically referred fathers and their offspring converge in that the level of maladjustment is similar in adolescents regardless of the father or the mother having been diagnosed or referred for treatment. This underlines the idea of basic similarities in parental behavior, but may be due also to the restricted samples and type of research questions pursued. Also, several very important topics such as the consequences for adolescent development resulting from physical illness of the father have hardly been investigated.

Psychopathology of non-referred adolescents and adolescent relationships with fathers

In recent years, the investigation of adolescent symptomatology in normative samples has contributed to our knowledge of disturbed and healthy development. Also, a relationship between adolescent and paternal symptoms can be observed in normative samples. The last studies to be dealt with here therefore involve the samples of non-referred fathers and their offspring. As shown in the review by Phares and Compas (1992), the majority of these studies are correlational, examining the degree of association between an index of psychological symptoms in the father and a comparable measure in the child. Most of the studies revealed an association between, for example, delinquent behavior or aggressive behavior of the father and aggressive delinquency in male and female adolescents (Neapolitan, 1981). In addition, adolescents who drank more heavily had fathers who were also rated as heavy drinkers. Furthermore, fathers' personalities and child-rearing practices were directly related to their sons' marijuana use. A similar pattern was found in the analysis of father–daughter relationships (Brook *et al.*, 1983; 1986). Moreover, in non-referred samples, there is relatively strong support for a connection between depressive mood in fathers and the incidence of depression in their adolescent daughters (Forehand and Smith, 1986).

Several studies have demonstrated the negative effects of paternal stress on adolescent development. Since the early studies of Elder (Elder *et al.*, 1985), it has been shown that female adolescent behavior is strongly and adversely influenced by the father's feelings of rejection connected with unemployment. Also, Cohen *et al.* (1987) and Holahan and Moos (1987) have reported some evidence that fathers' stress and adolescent maladjustment are correlated cross-sectionally. This points to the fact that the effects of stressful events on fathers should be studied more thoroughly.

If we summarize the results, it is evident that the father's behavior, personality characteristics and psychopathology are significant sources of risk for adolescent psychopathology. Even in non-referred samples, the evidence for the contribution of factors such as paternal stress or paternal unemployment is quite clear. As expected, a positive relationship between paternal effects and externalizing behaviors in adolescence has been found. In addition, adolescents of referred or diagnosed fathers – regardless of the type of problem identified in the father – have been found to function far more poorly than those in control groups. However, the mechanisms of these effects have not been clearly identified. The lack of data on the mechanisms underlying paternal effects is perhaps not surprising in light of the relative paucity of studies on fathers and adolescent maladjustment. Nevertheless, the studies provide a clear, affirmative answer to the question of whether fathers contribute to the incidence of psychopathology in their offspring. Apparently, the effects do not differ greatly from those caused by maternal factors, although a clear relationship between paternal factors and externalizing behavior in adolescence is evident. Variables that may moderate paternal effects have hardly been investigated. For example, the gender of the offspring may be of greater consequence for some types of problems than for others.

We have tried to show that fathers continue to be dramatically under-represented compared to mothers in research on developmental psychopathology. It is our thesis that this is related to the traditional idea that mothers are solely responsible for children's positive as well as negative development and, what is more, to the structural variations found in most "families" with disturbed offspring. While a summary of results from the studies reviewed by Phares and Compas (1992) has established the importance of the father's contribution to adolescent maladjustment in general, future research should enable more specific predictions of when and to what extent fathers are involved in the development and maintenance of psychological disorders in their offspring.

MECHANISMS OF FATHER IMPACT

The results of empirical studies summarized above have indicated that the effects of fathers on offspring psychopathology are non-specific. This seems to reflect the trend suggesting the overall similar socialization techniques by mothers and fathers (Lytton and Romney, 1991). Meta-analysis of parents' socialization techniques showed only one difference, i.e. mothers and fathers differ in their relations with boys and girls (Siegal, 1987). In general, mothers treated their sons and daughters in a similar manner. Fathers, on the other hand, interacted differently with children of different gender. Fathers were observed to be more involved with their sons in physical and active play and to treat their daughter more gently. Fathers tended to use more discipline techniques involving rejection (Siegelman, 1965) or even firm control (Siegal, 1987). As Siegal has suggested, fathers employ socialization techniques that emphasize gender-related characteristics and behavior. In Chapters 4 and 5 we discussed the different attitudes fathers exhibit toward their sons and daughters. Thus it can be understood that paternal differential attitudes may play a certain role in the consolidation of sexual identity of their sons and daughters. The reported unspecificity of the effect of fathers on psychopathology of adolescents might simply be a consequence of the fact that research carried out on fathers as a whole has been rather limited and selective.

Moreover, the approach taken in investigating fathers is limited as well: their activities and relationships have typically been measured according to the same dimensions applied to mothers. The tendency to evaluate fathers by dimensions that apply to mothers is inappropriate. It is important that the distinctive characteristics of fathers be acknowledged and that fathers are evaluated according to their own norms. Our suggestion is that a further discussion of the differential nature of father–son and father–daughter interaction in cases of adolescent pathology could highlight the mechanisms of fathers' impact on the development or intensification of offspring psychopathology.

The identification process: a dangerous pathway

The study of Brook *et al.* (1986) points to differences in processes related to the psychopathology of sons and daughters. In an earlier study (Brook *et al.*, 1984) these authors had shown that the sons' identification with paternal traits did indeed have an impact on the sons' own traits. More specifically, sons who identified with fathers exhibiting positive traits were more likely to possess these traits themselves. Similarly, sons who identified with fathers exhibiting negative traits were more likely to possess negative traits as well. Comparable results point to the significance of identification as a moderating variable in cases of drug abuse by father and son. While identification processes between father and son are in line with psychoanalytical and psychological theories, these same mechanisms could not be expected to apply to the relationships between adolescent daughters and fathers. In their follow-up study, Brook *et al.* (1986) analyzed father–daughter identification and its impact on daughters' personalities and drug abuse. As expected, correlations between the adolescent girls and fathers according to the identification index were rather low; similarities between father and daughter could only be found in traits which could be considered as more female. For example, similarities between fathers and sons were high for depressive mood, femininity and responsibility, while similarities between fathers and daughters were low for traits like anxiety, obsessiveness and rebelliousness. Thus, a daughter's identification with her father was not directly associated with her own personality traits, as was found for sons' identification with the father. However, when identification with the father was indeed evident, then its influence was significant, i.e. females who strongly identified with their fathers exhibited the same positive or negative traits. These results indicate a basic similarity in processes concerning identification, yet this process is much more relevant for boys than for girls. More specifically, girls identify with a father who possesses highly feminine traits.

However, when the mother is a disturbed and denigrated figure, the father's role and personality is crucial for daughters. Balsam (1989) presented several cases in which girls' mothers were emotionally disturbed for a long period and the fathers were thus very involved and played a more vital role in the lives of their daughters.

Balsam presented case studies of five bright young women between the ages of 18 and 20 years, all college undergraduates and outstanding in their academic achievement. All of them had fathers who were high-achieving professionals; all of their mothers were housewives suffering from long-term psychiatric illnesses. The fathers had not been directly involved in childcare during their daughters' early childhood. All the patients reported memories of being angry that their fathers had failed to protect them from upsetting interactions with their mothers at home. It was only in high school that these fathers became directly involved. The major complaints of these young women were that they had such a hard time with their mothers and did not want to turn out like them. In addition, they felt that there was something wrong with their relationships with men. These young women were obsessed with food and fatness, had been episodically bulimic or had other eating disorders. Growing up and becoming sexual women were particularly difficult for them in light of the disturbing influences of a distorted model of femininity, namely their unconsciously denigrated mothers.

The fathers, excellent models in dealing with the outside world, were greatly admired by all the women, who were highly talented, educated and achievement-oriented. While growing up, the patients spent a great deal of time with their fathers pursuing athletic activities, discussing their school papers, going to the cinema and theatre and joining their fathers in managing the household, cooking and organizing family life. Often they assisted in the process of the mother's rehospitalization. From these examples the intensity of relationship to the father is apparent. It can also be seen that most of the adolescent girls' activities involved the father while the mother was ignored. Yet, when a father is so emotionally involved with his daughter in her adolescent years, not only may he unconsciously become the admired adult male in her life, but in her fantasies he may be her "true husband." Sexual fantasies may be aroused and become difficult to deal with. Accordingly, in these cases the father not only became a part of the daughter's ego ideal, but the girl's sexual fantasies were also directed solely toward him. Concerning sexual development, it was apparent that masturbation was taken up very late as was the transition to non-virginity. None of Balsam's patients had had intercourse before finishing college. Their main problem with intercourse was related to a fantasy of being out of control in their female bodies. Their fantasies about intercourse were aggressive and in them, the women often assumed "male" roles. None of these patients was an overt lesbian in her choice of sexual partners and all had enjoyed positive experiences with men. This feeling was the main one expressed during therapy.

In recognizing the positive effects of the father in compensating for the disturbing influences of the mother, a main focus of the treatment was on making amends with the image of the mother and on creating more distance from the idealized, possessive and omnipotent father. One outstanding feature of all these patients was an irrepressible vitality. Greenacre (1966: 198) spoke of the "vigor and power" acquired through the participation with the father. The young women were actively engaged in solving their problems and willingly came for treatment. And, as already mentioned, they were all, like their fathers, highly energetic and achieving. But their fears of passivity were associated with their fantasies of the basic ingredients of womanhood. Perhaps because of their reduced contact with a nurturing mother, these young women were especially hungry for whatever stability the stronger, healthier father provided. It is also possible that the father unconsciously compensated for an earlier deficit in the girls described by Herzog (1982a) as "father hunger."

These case studies illustrate a facet of identification with the father which may occur should the mother not be fully available: namely, the development of a very active, problem-solving personality at the cost of denying femininity and passivity. Other case examples from our own practice have shown that when the mother is inaccessible owing to her own problems, the identification with the father can proceed so far that the daughter assumes the perverted perspective of her father, as in the case of Sophie.

This 25-year-old female patient came for psychoanalytic treatment because she suffered from sexual problems. The patient reported that her family had been preoccupied with the parents' divorce for over 10 years. As a teenager she had felt torn between her seductive yet unreliable father and her aggressive mother. The discord and the fighting began in her early adolescence and reached a climax when the patient was 15. At that time, both parents had other lovers. The father had a girlfriend from the patient's own class at school; the mother saw an older man. It is striking that neither parent chose a sexual partner of the same age and that they involved their daughter in their conflicts.

The patient described her mother's behavior in quite a peculiar manner – as if she saw her mother through the eyes of her perverted father. As an example, on one occasion she recounted the following: "When I was 14, my mother, wearing garters and high heels, secretly left the house to go down the garden path and get in her old lover's car. This was a secret between me and her." Somewhat later she spoke about her mother's suicide attempt which took place in the kitchen, again without any sign of emotional involvement and as if through the eyes of a perverted man. There is little evidence of any fear or terror that might have been present in the 15-year-old: "When I came into the kitchen, I saw my mother lying on the sofa with her arms and limbs all twisted, dressed in a black bra and panties. One strap had slipped down and her breast was partly revealed."

The identification with the seductive yet perverse father (he collected and read child pornography and had affairs with young girls) is evident in the transference to the therapist (I. S.-K.). The patient often dreamed about her, and in her dreams the female therapist appeared dressed like a man; once she approached her at a party and then suddenly "pulled down her pants," which frightened the patient very much. She also fantasized that the therapist, like her father, was interested in lingerie and had a particular penchant for black lingerie. The identification with her father during adolescence might certainly have been a "life preserver," since her deeply depressed, sadistic and aggressive mother provided her with little support.

Similar to Balsam's patients described above, this patient demonstrated difficulties in starting and maintaining relationships with men. She had problems in relinquishing control, taking on a passive role or "letting herself be stimulated by a man." It was always important for her to "keep her head up" during coitus, i.e. not to lose control. Like the patients described by Balsam, she developed rather masculine sexual behavior, marked by a strong aversion to desires of passive submission.

The child's identification with the father can be an urgent need; on the other hand, it may be a dangerous pathway especially in respect to the identity formation and separation of daughters. Identification with the father may lead to the denial of female aspects of identity. Moreover, the over-involvement with male aspects may result in a distorted, even perverse, view of relationships, as was the case in our last example.

The father's inability to dissolve the symbiosis between mother and child

While identification with the father may have a stronger negative impact on daughters, the father's inability to undo the mother–child symbiosis is more detrimental for sons. Through the idea of an exclusive bonding of the child to the mother as well as the idea of a mother's natural predisposition to nurture her child, not only is the exclusion of the father legitimized but the symbiosis between mother and child is supported as well. The small girl's repeated physical contact with her mother's body is advantageous in respect of the attainment of female identity. For the development of a masculine identity, however, the absence of close physical contact with the father is very problematical. Badinter (1993) has even maintained that the lack of physical closeness and warmth with the father in the first five years of life of the male child might be more critical than those effects introduced by the absence of the father at a later age.

In addition, Badinter reports that in France, a working father spends six minutes a day being involved with the actual care of his children. Other studies in the USA confirm that fathers spend four times less time with their children than mothers do (cf. also Chapters 1 and 2). If this finding is compared with the data derived from divorced-parent families (cf. Chapter 6), then the situation is even more unfavorable. The effects on the adolescent of losing the father owing to a dissolved marriage are such that while dramatic consequences for identity and autonomy can be empirically demonstrated for boys, such marked changes are not evident in girls. Boys living with their mothers after a divorce may have serious difficulties in school, may demonstrate antisocial behavior and/or become socially isolated, and may have identity problems as well. Although as a rule divorce takes place in the first four to seven years of a child's life, the effects have been shown to be long lasting – until adolescent years (Hetherington, 1979). The effects are quite similar to those following the loss of a father, due, among other reasons, to the father's death. Depression, suicidal tendencies, psychosomatic disorders and psychotic developments have been observed in adolescents who lost their father or grew up without one. Of course, in attempting to consolidate these findings, one must proceed with caution since the loss of a father usually introduces even more stressors (i.e. poverty, conflict in the remaining family, depression or other psychological disturbances in the mother) so that one is actually dealing with the effects of a very complex deficit.

As a result of their physical absence, these fathers cannot hinder a bonding of the adolescent with the mother that may possibly become too strong, nor can they provide a correcting new experience. Quite frequently one finds in clinical case studies of patients without fathers that they look for a "father replacement" who can provide these functions. But as we have seen, even in families with both parents, the father may be "there" but not necessarily present. Above all, sons complain about the emotional unavailability of the father. Osherson (1993) has reported that men complain that they do not know anything about their fathers, and their need to be recognized by and receive approval from their fathers is met with a wall of silence. Badinter (1993) has related this emotional non-availability in fathers to the initiatives of the men's movement. Participants of this movement meet together in order to share their experiences about their miserable relationships with their fathers. These men, for the most part settled 40-year-olds, try to articulate their "mutual longing for the father" (Badinter, 1993: 182). If this need to understand their relationships with their fathers and to achieve an independent masculinity has become so pressing for some "established" adult men, one can easily imagine the significance the emotional (and physical) absence of the father has for an adolescent whose identity is in flux and who is seeking a male role model.

In the case of the father's physical absence, or as a result of his emotional non-availability, the mother takes on an inappropriately powerful role as the sole person of reference available. Badinter described this "omnipotence of the mother" coupled with an absent father quite impressively:

> The longer the symbiosis exists, the more intimate and pleasurable the relationship between mother and son is, the more likely the chance is that the son will become effeminate. This effect will persist if the son's father does not dissolve this bonding both qualitatively and quantitatively.
>
> (Badinter, 1993: 66)

The physical closeness with an ominpotent woman is not unproblematical. Since the fathers are not around, "the sons are smothered by the protective love of their mothers" (Dubbert, 1979: 23). However, if the mother is a disturbed figure, the father is extremely necessary to dissolve a dangerous symbiosis, as in the case with the "schizophrenic mother" or the cases presented in this chapter.

Generally speaking, the results of a strong maternal influence in early childhood can be observed in many historical examples. Boys were often dressed like girls by their mothers until they were 6 years old and their hair was allowed to grow long and curly (cf. Badinter,

1993). In adolescence, when a boy would like to identify with his father in relation to competence, autonomy and self-sufficiency, the physically absent or emotionally non-available father leaves a large gap. It is thus more difficult for the adolescent to develop a distinctive male identity which is clearly differentiated from his mother. The results we have reported in Chapter 7 on stepfathers underline this mechanism. Although male adolescents are experiencing loyalty conflicts toward their biological father, the presence of a stepfather as a male role model is beneficial and helpful in gaining autonomy. An even darker side of the father–adolescent relationship, and in particular the father–son relationship, can be seen in the case of paternal hostility and ambivalence. Chapter 10 deals with this issue in more detail, focusing on delinquency in particular. Paternal hostility and violence is also the topic of Chapter 11, where we deal with a very negative and detrimental father–daughter relationship: child abuse.

THE ABSENT FATHER: A CAUSE OF PSYCHOPATHOLOGY?

Not all adolescents who grow up without a father necessarily have problems; neither is there any guarantee that the development of those who live with their fathers in the same household will proceed normally. Up to now, we have endeavored to elucidate those processes and mechanisms by which fathers can influence adolescent psychopathology, and thereby have encountered the different pathways for sons and daughters, as, for example, the importance of gender-specific father–child interaction. For daughters, identification with the father as a powerful and attractive figure has positive as well as negative consequences. We found that pathology develops when, owing to the presence of a weak and disturbed mother, the daughter over-identifies with the father and thus is unable to develop a feminine identity. Abusive relationships are a further pattern of negative interaction between fathers and daughters that may have longstanding and destructive effects on a daughter's development and will be further elaborated in Chapter 11. As regards sons, the inability of the father to break up the pathological symbiosis between mother and child has a strong impact on the son's well-being. The consequences of having a weak or absent father will be described in Chapter 10 and are more detrimental for sons than for daughters. The great importance of the fathers in cases of delinquents differs from that of fathers of neurotics.

It is our impression that the absent father or the emotionally unavailable father is clinically of great importance for both sons and daughters. Whereas in Chapters 1 and 2 we discussed the positive aspects of a distant father, i.e. that he can provide room for autonomy and serve as a model for separation, in this chapter we are dealing with the negative side, with a father who is too distant, i.e. physically or emotionally not present. We have tried to show that the impact is greater on sons than on daughters because a distinctive identity including a differentiation from the mother cannot be developed. Also, a parental model for separation while remaining connected is not present. For daughters, the problematical pathways can be identified in an overly close relationship with the father which restricts their development of a female identity and over-emphasizes independence. For sons, the missing father is an important, although not necessarily an openly discussed, issue in the psychotherapy of males.

As Gunsberg (1989) has shown, fathers are not discussed very much in the treatment of men. When a man comes for therapy, there is often little, if any, mention of the father. Sometimes the therapist has to introduce the father's presence, even in the face of strong opposition from the patient. Also, only negative aspects of the father may be mentioned and the therapist may have to elicit mention of positive character traits and achievements of the father and encourage the patient to recall positive experiences in order to relax the fixedness of denigrated images of paternal figures. However, issues of aggression in father–son relationships are mentioned comparatively frequently. Many patients claim that as children they were abandoned by their fathers – either psychologically or as a result of divorce – and that fathers also tended to place their children in dangerous situations, which might have been experienced negatively, as, for example, a castration threat. To a certain extent, boys and even adult sons need to be able to display aggression toward their fathers. But it is apparent that a warm, loving and constructive relationship, i.e. the early model for the pre-oedipal father–son attachment, is hardly mentioned in therapy. Relying on the information from case studies poses the risk that the image of the father will be distorted owing to current disturbances in an individual. For example, depressive patients typically describe their father as harsh and cool, delinquent patients portray him as aggressive, demoralized and weak. Here one must be reminded that such descriptions, as well as being the portrayal of the father in therapy, are in fact "constructions" (see Freud, [1937] 1952). However, these constructions represent a psychological reality for the patients, and this is what matters.

The question of whether the absent father is a cause for psychopathology has also been investigated in empirical research. Steinberg (1987b) has investigated the biological intactness hypothesis and came to the conclusion that there is only marginal support for the idea that youngsters living with both natural parents will develop less symptomatology. In an earlier study, Dornbusch *et al.* (1985) found that boys living in stepfamilies had rates of deviance comparable to their peers living in single-parent households and girls living in stepfamilies had rates of deviance lower than girls in single-parent homes, but higher than girls living in mother-only families or girls living with both natural parents. Apparently, according to the Dornbusch study, an additional adult at home makes little difference in terms of adolescent deviance if that additional adult is a stepfather. Indeed, the findings reported by Dornbusch *et al.* suggest that it is the biological intactness of the adolescent's household – *which* adults, rather than the number of adults present – that attenuates rates of deviance. Steinberg (1987b) took up this biological intactness hypothesis and the additional adult hypothesis and investigated both hypotheses on a sample of 865 adolescents in grades 5, 6, 8 and 9. In particular, he investigated adolescents from intact families, living with both their natural parents, adolescents from divorced families and adolescents from stepfamilies. First, the study demonstrates the lower incidence of deviant behavior among adolescents living in biologically intact homes. This finding is paralleled by their lower level of susceptibility to pressure from their friends to engage in antisocial behavior. Second, the findings offer little support for the notion that adolescent misbehavior may be deterred by the presence of an additional adult in the home and indicate, instead, that the deterrent effect of an additional biological parent is likely to be stronger than the deterrent effect of a step-parent. The study also supports the view that youngsters living in stepfamilies are as much at risk of involvement in deviant behavior as their peers living in single-parent households. He discusses his results in light of the "additional adult" hypothesis. In view of the fact that the presence of an additional adult is hypothesized to lead to greater control of adolescents' behavior, and, presumably, less deviance, one would surmise that youngsters from stepfamilies would exhibit rates of deviance lower than youngsters living in single-parent households and comparable to youngsters living with both natural parents. But although an additional adult was present in the adolescent stepfamily, this was not enough to prevent antisocial behavior.

ADOLESCENTS AND THEIR FATHERS AS PART OF A PATHOLOGICAL FAMILY SYSTEM

In the following we would like to consider adolescent relationships with fathers from the perspective of the systems approach in family therapy. In this connection a point which has already been suggested should become clearer, namely, that often it is not a pathological father per se that impedes the developmental progression of his children but rather, a pathological system. This approach takes into account that the relationship of a father to his offspring only becomes understandable in light of the relationship to his spouse.

The suggested pathways between father characteristics, adolescent personality variables and possible psychopathology pointed mainly to situations where the adolescent is close to the father, greatly identifies with him and is highly involved with him in a positive or negative manner. A systems approach can further highlight under what circumstances such phenomena will take place. Family systems consist of the parental sub-system and the child sub-system (Minuchin, 1974). Parents have the authority and resources in the family, and children naturally turn to them in time of need. When the mother does not function, they may turn to the father. This situation was evident in the case studies presented by Balsam (1989) discussed above, in which the mothers did not function and the only functioning adult figure left in the family system was the father.

Systems approaches elaborate further on the meaning of psychopathology in the family and the dynamics that are related to the emergence of psychopathological behavior in one of the family members. According to Bowen (1976), a basic premise in the functioning family is the ability to balance the relationships between members. Family members are supposed to balance relatedness and differentiation among themselves. In such families there is enough personal space for each individual within a close and supporting environment. When spouses are not differentiated, they may establish various patterns of behavior that are basically aimed at keeping both partners close together. One pattern described by Bowen (1976) is the "undifferentiated ego mass," i.e. a situation lacking room for individuality within the family system. Another possible pattern is when one partner assumes an independent role at the expense of keeping the other dependent. Bowen describes several cases of successful husbands with dependent and housebound wives. While a man seems to function in an adaptive manner, it is necessary that his spouse always be available and contribute to his superior functioning.

There are other cases when partners are unable to establish a stable pattern in their relationship and tend to oscillate between being very close and loving, and being apart and fighting. A symptom is then understood to reflect a maladaptive relational pattern between spouses or family members.

As we have attempted to outline in this book, issues of closeness and separateness are also the central dilemmas of adolescence (see Shulman and Klein, 1982). As discussed in the previous chapters, adolescents are supposed to separate themselves from their families and to consolidate their individuality. Adolescents revealing a variety of symptoms have been found to belong to family systems that did not successfully balance between being close and being separate (see Minuchin, 1974). Either an enmeshed or a disengaged pattern of relatedness could be revealed in these families. A symptom in an individual thus can be understood as a message reflecting a deviant pattern of relationships in the family and as an effort to effect change. Adolescents may display certain maladaptive behaviors that can be understood as a message to the family. Furthermore, in line with the objective of our discussion, there are cases when an adolescent may act in a certain way while trying to support his father's demands on the family – at the expense of his own autonomy. The following two examples present cases of adolescent psychopathology where the adolescent actually acted "in the service" of the father in order to change the family dynamics and, more specifically, the mother's behavior.

Mrs K. turned to the clinic following a referral of her son Gad, aged 15, by the school counselor. Gad was skipping classes and was involved in "petty criminal behavior." He and some of his classmates joined up together to "collect" car emblems, or they went to the kiosk next to school, started fights and stole soft drinks. A family session was set up. The family consisted of the father aged 39, a bus driver, the mother, aged 38 and recently employed in a managerial position in a hotel, and two younger children, a boy aged 12 and a girl aged 7. Gad was a handsome boy, athletic and talkative. At the first family meeting he dismissed the counselor's complaints and regarded them as an exaggeration. His father agreed with him. He added that on his bus routes he passed close by the school from time to time and all that he could see was a bunch of boys, including his son, making some noise but nothing else. The father added that he always had the feeling that this female counselor did not understand what it means to be an adolescent boy. It became quite apparent at the first meeting that we were facing a disagreement between father and mother regarding their expectations for their son and their conception of male adolescence. A deeper probe into the family history revealed that the mother had tended to be the housewife and the father the breadwinner. About a year prior to Gad's referral, the mother decided that the children were old enough for her to look for a job and pursue her interests. She took a short course related to hotel work and started to work as a receptionist in a hotel. After a short time the management was impressed with her competence and she was offered a higher position. This position required longer hours and she asked for her husband's and Gad's help in taking care of the youngest child. They were supposed to pick her up at school from time to time and prepare her lunch. At this point the problems in the family began. The father argued that though he worked in shifts he did not intend to become the housewife. Gad and the other brother were then supposed to help with their younger sister.

Further sessions revealed that the family dynamics became even more interesting. It turned out that Gad missed school days because he went windsurfing instead. He planned on becoming a champion and decided to practice as much as possible. More interesting was the fact that his father was his coach. It looked as if the two men had set up a conspiracy against the mother. The father even added that just because he was 39 there was no reason why he should not be able to enjoy the beach any more. He worked in shifts; he had free mornings from time to time and, according to him, it certainly did not harm anyone when a man went to the beach. And as for his young daughter, he claimed that nothing would happen if she learned to heat up her own meal once in a while.

The family dynamics here appeared quite obvious. The couple was in the midst of a conflict over their roles as spouses and as parents. The mother insisted on change and expected a new division of home-related responsibilities. The father was unwilling to accept the change. It seemed to us that Gad's unconscious intention was actually to bring the family for treatment, and thus his symptoms represented a message to the family. It is important to realize that Gad acted in the service of his father. He practically sided with his father and spent long hours with him on the beach. Through his problems at school and his unwillingness to help care for his younger sister in the afternoons, he tried to bring about the reinstatement of the former division of responsibilities in the family. Thus, as the school counselor had suggested, Gad undoubtedly was revealing some maladaptive behavior. However, this maladjustment was family-related (Sroufe and Rutter, 1984) and mainly served his father's needs. Father and son had created a sub-system and behaved like adolescents who attended to their own needs without caring about their family responsibilities.

The case of Ronen, aged 13, shows even more clearly to what extent an adolescent would go to act in the service of his father. Ronen was the youngest in the family of three boys. The father, aged 46, was a bus driver and the mother, aged 44, worked in the computer department of a bank. The father was of Middle Eastern origin and the mother's family was of European origin. When the children were young, the mother was not employed, and managed the household. This arrangement fitted the father's expectations that a woman should take care of her husband and her children. When Ronen turned 9, the mother decided to look for a job and to pursue her interests. She ended up working in a bank, and arranged to work in shifts so that the family routine would be minimally disrupted. The mother's job was a continuous source of disagreement between husband and wife; however, it appeared that this did not much affect the children's functioning for a certain period of time. As Ronen grew older, he started to assume some of the household responsibilities. He knew how to clean and cook and was even able to bake cakes at the age of 12. It seemed that Ronen was parentified (see Boszormenyi-Nagy, 1965) in the service of his mother.

Half a year prior to Ronen's referral to the clinic, he began to have social problems at school. Ronen, who was known to be a co-operative and sociable boy, turned into a bully. His school achievement deteriorated dramatically. A major change also occurred at home. Ronen started to fight with his older brother and to break things. The father tried unsuccessfully to stop the fights between his sons. One day he said he felt as if he did not have a say at home any more. His wife did whatever she wished, and his sons did not respect him either. He left the house. Ronen took the initiative to bring his father back home. First, he told his mother to quit her job. She refused. When she went out to start the car, Ronen threw himself upon it. She did not stop the car, but drove slowly away and Ronen fell off. Ronen then called his father and asked him to return. The father told Ronen that he would return on the condition that family members would allow him to be the "boss." No major change occurred after this ordeal. On the contrary, Ronen continually tried to stop his mother from going to work. She would sneak out and lock the door behind her without leaving a key for Ronen. The only access she left for him was an open window and since the family lived on the sixth floor, her message to him was quite clear.

As the case shows, and as became evident later during family sessions, Ronen was engulfed in the struggle between his parents. The family structure led Ronen to the position of a parentified child, where he tried to restore the status quo by fulfilling many of the mother's roles and thus appeasing his father. But this was not a solution that could last for too long and Ronen's functioning at home and at school deteriorated. However, Ronen's wish to appease and help his father was evident even in his clearly maladaptive behavior. He was torn between the needs of his parents, but no space and time were left for his own development.

The two cases suggest how adolescent males, in the service of their fathers' needs within the family system, can act in a maladaptive manner. However, serving the father's needs is not limited to males and can be found also among girls. Apparently, this is frequently the case in incest, which is dealt with in Chapter 11. But also in less destructive families, a comparable pattern can be found. Even the classical case of Dora can be reinterpreted from a systems perspective as Dora acting in the service of her father. Freud told Dora: "So you are ready to give Mr K. what his wife withholds from him." And when she married Mr K., her father could resume a formal relationship with his lover (Decker, 1991).

The problem behavior presented in the aforementioned cases can be seen both as a message and as an attempt to serve the father in the family system, and is different from common conceptions of adolescent psychopathology. In the first part of this chapter we referred to adolescent psychopathology in "DSM-III" terms, be it behavioral disorders, externalizing symptoms or anorexia nervosa. Drawing on the literature from social psychology and sociology, problem behavior or deviance can be defined as rule-breaking that occurs when a person fails to conform to applicable and normative expectations of the group. The problem behavior may thus represent a lack of will or motivation to conform to the expectations of the family or the group. The popular perception is that a healthy adolescent should appear to have some minor forms of problem behavior. A common description is of an adolescent with a labile mood oscillating between being depressed and "down" one day and elated and "high" the next. Adolescents are also expected to have conflicts with family, teachers and friends and to be explosive from time to time. The assumption behind this perception is that adolescents have to cope with a variety of physical and social changes, to attain independence from the family, and to form a mature identity. For these reasons it seems justified to expect adolescents to experience more emotional crises and to exhibit more problem behavior in comparison to other stages in life. Freudian theory also describes adolescence as the stage of "storm and stress" because of the elevated level of pressure put on the young individual to act like an adult.

It might be helpful to differentiate between "destructive" and "constructive" deviance in adolescence. There are cases when adolescents' unconventional behavior is actually aimed at emphasizing their own individuality. What might be perceived as simple rebelliousness is often, in fact, directed by internal values and preferences, and the real roots of the unconventional behavior lie in the search for an individual outlet. Combining this suggestion with the family system approach might then suggest that adolescents may, in certain family structures, employ rebellious behavior in order to be able to achieve some independence. The only outlet left for expressing individuality is to revolt against the father's control. The revolt is aimed not only at achieving independence but also is meant to serve as a message to the father that he should loosen his grip on the family.

In summary, it can be suggested that in some cases adolescent psychopathology is functional in that it might serve as a message to the family. We have presented cases where the message is in the service of the father's needs or expectations within the family system. In other cases adolescent behavior can be a message to the father that he should change his attitude toward family members in general, and the adolescent in particular. But all the presented case studies illustrate impressively how the autonomous development of the adolescent is hindered when he or she feels compelled to act in the father's interest. Thus, the father's main function of helping the adolescent to gain individuation and separation is inexorably negated.

10 Father–adolescent relationships and aggression

Another dark side of the relationship between father and adolescent, in particular as seen in the father–son relationship, is manifested in cases of paternal hostility and ambivalence. As Esman (1985) has outlined, we have a tendency to idealize female mothering behavior and to attribute cruelty and violence more to the male. Hostile, authoritative and castrating attitudes of fathers toward their sons have been reported only anecdotally so far. In mythology and religion, there are many references to fathers who are absent, aggressive, emotionless, resentful, or willingly turn their sons over to the clutches of the mother. For example, Cronos devoured his son, Laius commanded that his son Oedipus be put to death, and Abraham was prepared to sacrifice his son Isaac. Arlow (1951) has outlined the ambivalent role of the father in initiation rituals and infanticide. He also points out that aggressiveness is often mutual. This may take on extreme forms, for example, as manifested in the Laius complex. Here the father has a strong interest in killing or destroying his son, and likewise the son, eager to assume his father's position, has similar intentions.

It is paradoxical and perhaps indicative of cultural ambivalence regarding male aggression that some of the same qualities that are valued in males, such as boldness, may also encourage them to challenge authority figures, engage in socially deviant activities or have trouble with the law in general. What is more, society is ambivalent in its tolerance of male aggression exhibited within the family realm. In recent years, research efforts in various disciplines have been directed toward understanding aggression. Developmental psychologists are, for example, concerned with determining the factors involved in the etiology of aggressive behaviors in the developing child. In this chapter, we focus our discussion on the mechanisms underlying the propagation of aggressive behavior from generation to generation. In particular, we examine how aggression between the child's parents or between father and child may be associated with aggressive behavior in the child, and how children are affected by exposure to aggressive or violent behaviors depicted in televised media. Finally, we examine the influence of paternal hostility, aggression and violence on the development of socially deviant behaviors such as delinquency.

AGGRESSIVE BEHAVIOR: ANIMAL MODELS

There have been many attempts to understand and explain the nature of human aggression. In psychology, aggressive behavior is believed to be induced by frustration and concomitant stress. Learning theorists such as Bandura (1971) consider aggressive behavior to be learned, i.e. acquired and maintained through modeling and reinforcement contingencies. A great body of literature refers to findings drawn from animal models of behavior. For instance, influenced by their observations of animal behaviors, Freud ([1930] 1958) and Lorenz (1966) considered aggressive behavior to be related to central drives within the organism. They hypothesized that innate aggressive drives are controlled by neural and hormonal mechanisms and are expressed as aggressive behavior. Over the years, research on animal behavior in ethology, sociobiology and psychology has generally emphasized the importance of interactions between sensory stimuli and the intertwining activities of nervous and endocrine systems, the development of which is regulated by the genotype. Such interactions represent the physiological mechanisms underlying the elicitation and expression of diverse behavior patterns, including aggressive behavior. It should be emphasized that an understanding of the interactions and links between genotype, neurophysiology, ecology and behavior is still in its infancy; there is also much controversy still surrounding the extent to which explanations of human behaviors may be drawn from findings obtained from animal models. Nevertheless, there are many findings which may assist researchers in understanding and explaining human aggressive behavior. For one thing, the research on aggression based on animal models has shown that there is a considerable diversity in the kinds of aggressive behaviors shown, and there is also intraspecific variation in such behaviors.

Aggression is defined by Moyer (1968: 426) as "behavior which leads to or appears to an observer to lead to the damage or destruction of a goal." He further divides animal aggressive behavior into several classes, including territorial, maternal and instrumental aggression. Classical examples of territorial aggression include the behavior of the stickleback fish (Tinbergen and Van Iersel, 1947). Territorial aggression in males is generally directly or indirectly concerned with access to females, and is often closely linked to other courting and reproductive behaviors. In many species, the display of territorial aggression behavior is strongly linked to environmental parameters such as season of the year or temperature, which in turn regulate hormonal activity priming such behaviors. Maternal aggression is primarily related to the protection and defense of offspring, such as is seen in attack behaviors of female grizzly bears or wolves when their young are threatened by an intruder. Instrumental aggression is aggressive behavior which is shaped and developed by conditioning or reinforcement.

In summary, the nature of aggression in animals is complex. Human aggressive behavior is, of course, no less complex. It is indisputably diverse in its expression, and subject to being inhibited, promoted or at least shaped by cultural and learning factors. For example, in contrast to animals, the expression of aggressive behavior in humans may also be more contingent on the extent to which it is a response to stress, i.e. aggressive behavior in humans may have a stress-reducing or coping function. It is not the aim here to elaborate further on the argument concerning the problem of generalizing from animals to humans. Nevertheless, further discussions on human aggression will certainly continue to draw on findings derived from animal models, and may indeed have relevance for explaining many aspects of human aggression behavior.

THE VIOLENT AND AGGRESSIVE FATHER

Family violence is now recognized as a major social problem in the United States. Incidence rates of couples experiencing interspousal aggression at some point during the course of their marriage may be as high as 60 per cent (O'Leary *et al.*, 1985). Although the prevalence of child abuse has been clearly documented for some 20 years, family violence, especially paternal violence, has only recently become a matter of national and international concern. Violence increasingly affects all of us. According to a report by Langan and Innes (1985), 3 per cent of Americans, the equivalent of approximately 6 million people, are victims of violent crime every year. In most cases, the offenders are male. Of the total instances of violent crime, domestic violence is considered to be the most common. Brutal interspousal violence is a chronic feature of almost 13 per cent of all marriages in the United States (Straus, 1979). At least 1,200 children died in 1986 as a result of abuse and neglect (Widom, 1989). According to Straus *et al.* (1980), between 1.4 and 2.3 million American children have been assaulted by a parent at some time during their childhood. Several findings indicate that interspousal aggression is strongly associated with parental aggression. Hartstone and Hansen (1984) found that 23 per cent of the fathers of violent youths had battered their wives. Jouriles *et al.* (1987) analyzed the association between interspousal aggression and parent–child aggression on a sample of children who were referred for treatment to the Victims Information Bureau in New York. The type of aggression most frequently witnessed by children was the father pushing, grabbing or shoving the mother. Ninety-one per cent of the mothers indicated that their children had been a victim of paternal aggression in the past 12 months. Similarly, the mothers reported that the father had pushed, grabbed or shoved the child. The authors found a correlation of $r = 0.56$ between interspousal aggression and parent–child aggression.

DOES VIOLENCE BEGET VIOLENCE?

One of the most widespread claims in literature is that violent behavior is self-generating, i.e. individuals abused as children become child-abusers, or victims of violence become violent offenders. The theory that people who tend to behave more violently than the norm do so because their parents physically mistreated them is certainly compelling. The literature based on clinical experiences with adolescent aggression is rife with such concepts as "identification with the aggressor," "violence begets violence" and "the cycle of violence." There is, however, little evidence to support the theory of intergenerational transmission of violence. Widom (1989) has based her evaluation of the "violence-breeds-violence-hypothesis" on findings obtained in empirical studies from various disciplines, e.g. psychology, sociology, criminology, psychiatry, social work and nursing. According to Widom, much of the research conducted on this topic can be criticized on methodological grounds. Above all, many research studies employed methods of data collection that made the scientific validity of the results questionable. For example, many researchers relied on parental reports rather than on direct observations of behaviors. The accuracy of information provided in such verbal reports was thus not verifiable. Retrospective accounts of abuse or neglect may be distorted, especially if individuals are asked to recall events after a period of years. In the context of new circumstances and their present situations people may perceive and describe these events differently, or ascribe a different level of significance to them. Another methodological weakness commonly seen in studies on this hypothesis involves the use of inferior sampling techniques: often, opportune or convenient samples were studied, or data were obtained from physicians' patient records, anecdotal clinical accounts or individual case studies.

Another methodological weakness concerns the difficulties in isolating paternal aggression from its context. Paternal aggression may belong to a complex of problems affecting the family. Other factors, such as poverty, unemployment, parental alcoholism, drug problems or otherwise inadequate social and family functioning, are often associated with one another. Thus, the incidence of parental child abuse may also be a function of being poor or unemployed. In order to clarify this issue, control groups matched for socio-economic and other relevant variables are necessary.

In any case, more recent, well-controlled studies have identified physical abuse as a risk factor for later aggressive behavior. For example, Truscott (1992) examined the influence of experiencing violence in the family of origin on the expression of violent behavior in adolescent males, and attempted to assess the importance of psychological mechanisms in influencing this transmission. He analyzed male US high school students (grades 10 and 11). Subjects were defined as being violent if they reported having threatened someone with a knife or gun at least once in the past year, or if they had punched, kicked, bitten, beaten up or used an object to strike someone three times or more in the past year. Subjects were defined as having witnessed parental violence if they had observed their parents punch, kick, bite or hit someone with an object or beat up or threaten someone with a knife or gun at least once in the past year. Subjects were defined as having experienced parental violence if they reported that their mother or father had punched, kicked or beaten them up, or if their parents had threatened them with a knife or gun once or more in the past year. According to the results, 47 per cent had been the victims of violence themselves, 56 per cent had witnessed parental violence and 53 per cent had experienced parental violence. In order to test the hypothesis that a higher level of adolescent violence is associated with a higher level of witnessed and experienced parental violence, adolescent physical violence scores were entered as a dependent variable in a multiple regression analysis with parental physical violence and verbal aggression experienced and witnessed scores as independent variables after adjustment for age. The appearance of violent behavior in this sample of adolescent males was found to be explained by being physically abused by the father ($R^2 = 0.21$) and verbally abused by the father ($R^2 = 0.20$). In contrast, such adolescent aggression behavior was not explained by having witnessed paternal violence directed at another person. Also, no association was found to exist between adolescent violent behavior and having witnessed maternal violent behavior directed at another person or having experienced maternal verbal aggression or physical violence. Thus, such findings provide partial support for the hypothesis that violence is passed on intergenerationally from parents to their adolescent offspring, with paternal aggressive behavior being more strongly related to this transmission than is maternal aggression.

Several studies conducted in the 1980s contributed to explaining the relationship between paternal aggression and a father's own history of being abused as a child. Straus *et al.* (1980) interviewed a representative sample of 1,146 American couples who had children between the ages of 6 and 17 living at home. One child in each family was randomly selected as the referent child. The rate of abuse and violence by fathers who grew up in the most violent homes (16 per cent) was about twice the rate of those who grew up in non-violent homes. Using a different design involving a sample of 529 households (composed of 291 families characterized by child abuse, 89 by child neglect and the remainder having children served by various community programs), Herrenkohl *et al.* (1983) compared parents' descriptions of their being disciplined as a child with the disciplinary practices applied with their own children. An important feature of this research design was the inclusion of three control variables (social desirability, number of children and income level of parents). The authors found that 56 per cent of those parents who abused their own children reported having one or more abusive caretakers as a child. On the other hand, 44 per cent of those who reported being abused as a child did not abuse their children. The findings show some support for the hypothesis that exposure to aggressive discipline as a child increases the risk that a parent will employ severe discipline techniques with their own children. In addition, the authors suggest that other past and current life stress factors or a lack of support from family members appear to augment aggressive parental behavior.

In summary, the findings reported thus far seem to suggest that there is a relationship between interspousal aggression and parent–child aggression. There also appears to be an association between paternal aggression and adolescent violence. However, the assumption that adolescent aggression is a result of a direct transmission of violent behavior from parent to child, as the "violence begets violence" hypothesis suggests, remains unsubstantiated. We still do not know why the majority of abused children do not appear to become violent themselves. Indeed, there are certainly several other factors which account for adolescent violence and problem behaviors. Further research on this topic is thus necessary in order to understand the causal mechanisms and supporting factors involved in the expression, acquisition and shaping of such behaviors.

RELATIONSHIPS BETWEEN ADOLESCENT DELINQUENCY, PATERNAL AGGRESSION AND ABUSE

The association between paternal violence and violence in offspring becomes more obvious if we consider special populations of adolescents. Most studies conducted on this topic have used samples of delinquent adolescents that were divided into more specialized groups, i.e. abused and non-abused juvenile delinquents. In most of these studies, the authors examined the extent to which adolescents in the different sub-groups had experienced or witnessed child abuse and engaged in violent behavior. Many studies have provided evidence to support the hypothesis that adolescent violent behavior is a function of having experienced or witnessed child abuse. Widom (1989) reviewed the findings of such studies and determined that boys exhibiting violent behaviors were more likely to have experienced abuse or witnessed extreme physical abuse than non-violent boys. The correlation between the degree of adolescent violent behavior and ever having been abused was $r = 0.37$. Geller and Ford-Somma (1984) have published one of the most detailed and statistically sophisticated analyses of the relationship between special forms of violent behavior and a history of abuse. In their study, 224 incarcerated juvenile offenders (182 boys, 42 girls) completed self-report questionnaires and were interviewed about their experiences with violence. Two-thirds of the offenders reported having been whipped with a belt or an electrical extension cord at least five times and 32 per cent reported being beaten up at least five times. One-fifth had been threatened with a knife or a gun; 12 per cent had been assaulted with a knife or gun. The beatings were so severe that 33 per cent of these children were seriously bruised, 29 per cent bled and 8 per cent required hospital care. These juvenile offenders had not only been the victims of violence, but had also committed violent acts: 22 per cent had punched their fathers, 5 per cent had attacked their fathers with a knife or a gun, nearly 12 per cent reported having struck a sibling with a stick or other hard object and 9 per cent had injured a sibling severely enough to cause bleeding. Very few of the offenders reported that they had directed violence at their mothers.

In an impressive retrospective study, Wick (1981) examined 50 randomly selected case files from a total of 3,027 cases of troubled adolescents. Wick established that 29 per cent of the adolescents' cases were related to aggression, abuse or neglect. Mouzakitis (1981) investigated a group of 60 females convicted of delinquency and residing in a rehabilitation penitentiary for girls in Arkansas. Two-thirds of the girls, aged between 12 and 17 years, were white, one-third were black. Eighty-six per cent reported that they had received physical punishment by the use of hands, objects or belts. As a result of this punishment, 51 per cent of the girls recalled being bruised, 38 per cent had bled and 25 per cent were scarred. The majority of these girls reported that they had received such punishment before they were 10 years old, whereas only 3 per cent suffered such punishment after the age of 14. Given that most of these girls were punished at such a young age, it does not seem likely that the parents delivered this punishment in response to a child's running away or delinquent behavior. Kratcoski (1982) surveyed case files of delinquent male adolescents in four institutions for serious offenders in Ohio. Here, child abuse was carefully defined as a "non-accidental physical injury inflicted on a child by a parent or other caretaker deliberately or in anger" (Kratcoski, 1982: 436). Of the 863 cases in the population, 26 per cent had experienced physical abuse in some form. According to Kratcoski, most of the physical abuse took the form of severe beatings with fists or with objects such as belts, whips or paddles. A few cases involved sexual abuse, and there were also cases involving other forms of severe abuse such as stabbing or burning.

IMPACT OF OBSERVING OR WITNESSING VIOLENCE

Much has been written about the context of violence in our culture (cf. McCall and Shields, 1986) and the importance of physical force and violence in our society. A number of writers have argued that societal approval of such behaviors sanctions and reinforces the use of violence. There is also evidence of a high degree of acceptance of interpersonal violence in our society. Thus, given a cultural context in which violence is often tolerated, learning to become violent through "normal" childrearing experiences might not be too difficult or unusual (Goldstein, 1986). From a social learning perspective, the display of physical aggression between family members not only may encourage children to accept such aggression as being an appropriate mode of interaction with others in the family, but may provide a child with a potential model for the learning of aggressive behaviors (Feshbach, 1980). Children learn behavior at least in part by imitating someone else's behavior. Thus, children learn to be aggressive by observing aggression in their families and the surrounding society.

Up to this point, we have focused primarily on the direct effects of aggression, abuse or neglect on later behavior. Although early laboratory studies demonstrated that children and young adults imitate the behavior of aggressive models in experimental situations, these studies did not address the long-term consequences of such modeling (Bandura, 1973). Similarly, questions remained about whether the kinds of aggressive play observed in the laboratory situation may be related to violent behavior in the streets. In general, most studies which have been concerned with examining the impact of witnessing violence as a child on later behaviors belong to one of the following categories:

1 large-scale surveys that correlate self-reports of exposure to violence with adult approval of violence or interspousal violence;
2 studies of the children of battered women; and
3 studies on television violence and aggressive behavior.

One example of the first type of investigation is the US national survey conducted by Owens and Straus (1975). On the basis of information obtained from 1,176 interviews conducted with people 18 years of age and older, the investigators examined the relationship between certain aspects of early exposure to violence and approval of violence as an adult. The statistical correlation between exposure and adult approval was quite high ($r = 0.50$). Exposure to violence was found to be positively associated with approval of interpersonal violence as an adult, although at a lower level ($r = 0.30$). On the basis of these findings, Owens and Straus (1975: 193) concluded that "the amount of violence experienced in childhood by members of a society is one of the factors contributing to the development and maintenance of cultural norms supporting the use of violence in face to face situations."

The findings obtained from studies on children of battered women and violence also demonstrate the impact of a child's witnessing violence on his or her development. For example, Wolfe (1985) demonstrated that children of battered women displayed significantly more problem behaviors and had poorer social skills than children in a control comparison group. In their sample of 102 children coming from violent families, 34 per cent of the boys and 20 per cent of the girls could be shown to have clinically observable behavior problems.

Studies of television violence and aggressive behavior analyze the potential effects of television violence on attitudes and aggressive behavior of young children. The literature on this topic is abundant (for a review, see Freedman, 1984). A number of writers have questioned whether the findings on aggressive behavior measured in studies on television violence can be generalized beyond the laboratory to real-life behaviors of delinquency or criminality. Nevertheless, in their review of television violence and aggression, Friedrich-Cofer and Huston (1986) concluded that certain forms of aggression measured in studies of television violence are clearly related to the development of serious behavioral aggression. Viewing violence on television has been found to increase levels of aggression in the viewer; this effect is both short-term and long-term in nature. Exposure to television violence has also been found to result in emotional desensitization to the harmful consequences of violence, i.e. the viewer is less likely to respond to aggression exhibited by others. For example, children with a history of high levels of exposure to television violence have been found to show lower levels of emotional arousal in response to a moderately violent television program than children with a history of low level of exposure to television violence. Research on delinquent and violent offenders has shown that these individuals display similar characteristics, i.e. increased level of aggression after viewing television violence and an emotional insensitivity to violent behaviors (Wilson and Herrnstein, 1985).

THE ROLES OF MOTHERS AND FATHERS IN AFFECTING DELINQUENCY

The role of the parent–child relationship as the cause of delinquency has long been debated (see Farrington, 1995). Most studies have established that a close relationship between parent and child is strongly related to a low involvement in juvenile crime (as determined by self reports). However, almost all of these studies failed to differentiate between parental gender. Furthermore, most studies have used samples of male children. The study of Björkqvist and Österman (1992) showed that mothers and fathers affect sons and daughters differently. The Lisrel analysis of their data showed that mothers had a clearly stronger impact on sons, while fathers had a slightly stronger effect on daughters. Olweus (1980) found negativism on the mother's side to be a significant predictor of aggressiveness in adolescent boys, while no similar effect could be found on the father's side. In general, parental rejection is a predictor of adolescent aggressiveness. Olweus found mothers of aggressive boys to be permissive in regard to their sons' aggressive behavior. This can be explained by the social modeling hypothesis (Bandura, 1973), which suggested that if an aggressive model is rewarded for his or her behavior, then the observer is reinforced in adapting this particular behavior.

Indeed, the research findings concerning the role of parents in affecting delinquency in girls have been rather inconsistent. Some investigators have concluded that the role of parents is more decisive in causing delinquency in girls; others have found that the parental influence is more important in cultivating delinquent behavior in boys. Several studies found that family conflict has different effects on male and female delinquency. For example, Johnston (1987) examined the relative strength of parent–child attachments and their relationship to juvenile delinquent behavior across gender categories of both parents and children. More specifically, Johnston attempted to determine who is more delinquent (males or females), to whom young people are more attached (mother or father), and finally, which attachment is most relevant to delinquent behavior (the attachment to the mother or to the father). Johnston gathered his data from 734 high school students in Washington, DC: 41 per cent were white, 16 per cent Asian-Americans, and 33 per cent were black. First of all, he found that males in the sample were clearly more delinquent than females. Boys reported having engaged in an average number of 6.6 delinquent acts, girls reported an average of 2.7 acts. Sixty-five per cent of the males reported having committed at least one act in violation of the law, and 36 per cent reported having committed such acts more than three times. Concerning gender differences in attachment to mother and father, neither males nor females showed consistently higher levels of attachment to either parent. This lack of sex differences in the closeness to mother and father is important. It strongly suggests that these attachments cannot be used to explain the substantial gender differences in delinquent behavior. Thus, male adolescents are not more delinquent than girls because of weaker bonds to parents since their bonds are not weaker to either parent. In addition, the boys in this sample reported higher perceptions of parental supervision than girls did. This shows that boys do not break the law more often than girls because they feel less supervised by their parents. Since it might be possible that the pattern of parent–child ties differs in broken and intact homes, Johnston controlled for family structure in his study. Nevertheless, he did not find that divorce had greater negative effects on boys than on girls. More importantly, the splitting up of the family did not seem to make the child feel unloved by the father or create feelings of anger and rebellion toward him. In addition, fatherless adolescents did not seem to compensate by developing closer ties to mothers. Finally, Johnston looked for sex differences in the relevance of mother and father to delinquency. He found that father–child ties were consistently more predictive of delinquent behavior than mother–child ties.

In summary, the results of this study indicate that male adolescents report more delinquent behavior than females do, but that the differences cannot be explained by a presumed greater attachment to parents among females. Both males and females reported equally strong ties to their parents. However, moderate gender differences do emerge in the correlation between parent–child bonds and delinquency. The associations are consistently higher for males and the father's influence in causing delinquency appears to be somewhat greater than the mother's. Stern (1978) suggested that the father serves as the prime teaching and deterrent force in the family in his role as value transmitter and disciplinarian.

Studies on the sons of substance-abusing fathers highlight the role of fathers' aggression in sons' delinquency. In general, research has shown that children of substance-abusing fathers show more externalizing problems and are less able to concentrate while completing a task. Moss *et al.* (1995) interviewed substance-abusing fathers regarding their functioning and personality. Children's levels of aggressivity were also evaluated via a behavior checklist. Paternal personality characterized by aggression, stress reactivity and alienation were the most robust contributors to 10- to 12-year-olds' aggressive behavior. In a similar study, Ammerman *et al.* (1994) found that it was the negative affectivity of the substance-abusing fathers that predicted sons' externalizing symptoms. Tatar *et al.* (1993) showed that it was the inadequate paternal discipline practices of substance-abusing fathers that predicted the problem behavior of their sons. All in all we may then suggest that a combination of paternal aggression, inadequate discipline and negative attitude toward the child fosters aggressive and delinquent behavior.

MAPPING AGGRESSIVE BEHAVIOR OF FATHERS

Physical abuse and corporal punishment are generally believed to increase the likelihood of aggressiveness among adolescents, and many studies have provided evidence to support this view (Widom, 1989; Olweus, 1980). However, an explanation of the mechanisms underlying this relationship is lacking. Some investigators have attempted to understand this relationship in terms of the theory of social behavior modeling (Bandura, 1973). This theory maintains that if a model is rewarded for his or her behavior, then the observer is reinforced in adopting this particular pattern.

A study conducted on Finnish adolescents by Björkqvist and Österman (1992) represents one recent research effort oriented to this theory. These investigators were primarily interested in determining whether children acquire the same kinds of aggressive patterns as displayed by their parents. Their approach was based on analyzing the adolescents' perceptions of their parents' aggressive behavior as well as their own level of aggressiveness. A total of 85 girls and 89 boys (mean age = 13.6 years), divided into two groups according to the presence of hostile and non-hostile behaviors, were asked to "map" the aggressive behavior of their parents. They were asked, for example, what their fathers and mothers did when angry. Fathers of adolescents who belonged to the high hostility group scored significantly higher than fathers of the low hostility group on behaviors such as shouting, drinking alcohol, hitting, leaving the house, and sulking. Mothers of adolescents belonging to the high hostility group scored significantly higher than mothers from the low hostility group on three items, namely, shouting, breaking things, and leaving the house. The results of statistical tests of correlations between parents' and children's behavior when angry revealed that the adolescents adopted both aggressive strategies (such as shouting and hitting) and non-aggressive strategies such as constructive problem-solving (e.g. trying to resolve conflict by discussion), sulking or trying to hide anger. This finding thus lends support to the theory of social behavior modeling. The relative influence of the gender of the parent exhibiting aggressive behaviors on the acquisition of aggressive behavior in their children was also investigated. Interestingly, there were overall stronger correlations between mother–child behavior than between father–child behavior. More specifically, the analysis revealed that the behavior of fathers exerted a greater influence on their daughters' aggressiveness than the behavior of mothers (correlation of fathers' influence on aggressiveness in girls $r = 0.33$; mothers' influence on girls $r = 0.12$). In contrast, the behavior of mothers proved to be the sole important factor that predicted aggressiveness in their sons (correlations of mothers' influence on aggressiveness in boys $r = 0.62$, fathers' influence on aggressiveness in boys $r = -0.26$). Thus, these findings suggest that parental behavior is indeed an important determinant of adolescent aggressiveness. Yet, not only did fathers and mothers behave very differently, i.e. fathers hit and drank, mothers shouted, but the display of such behavior affected their sons and daughters differently.

These investigators were also interested in determining whether the display of aggressive behaviors in the adolescent was contingent on the emotional integrity of the parent–child relationship. Thus, the adolescents in this study were also asked to describe how they perceived their relationships with their parents. Adolescents belonging to high hostility groups perceived their relationship to both parents in significantly more negative terms than those belonging to the low hostility group. In particular, the relationship with the father was perceived to be especially negative. Furthermore, more girls than boys in the high hostility group considered their relationship with the father to be worse than with the mother. The most interesting result of this study was that in general, the emotional relationship to both parents seemed to be the strongest single predictor of children's aggressiveness, stronger than how the parents actually behaved when angry. In particular, to boys, the emotional relationship appeared to be more important than the actual behavior of the parents. The fact that the father's abuse of alcohol when angry turned out to be a predictor of aggressiveness in the girls cannot be interpreted in terms of the learning model, but rather in terms of producing a negative and frustrating home atmosphere. However, fathers may of course resort to more physical violence while intoxicated. From the point of view of identification, the opposite may perhaps have been expected. The authors suggest that sons of fathers who hit and/or abuse alcohol when they are angry may simply distance themselves from their fathers so much that they have problems identifying with them. In the long run, these sons may be less likely to adopt the aggressive behavior patterns exhibited by their fathers. Similar conclusions were reached by Olweus (1980), who investigated the relative effect of each parent on the display of aggressive behavior in their sons. To his surprise, he found that the behavior of the father had to be excluded from his model, since only the behavior of the mothers appeared to be an important predictor of aggressiveness in their sons. For example, he found that rejecting, cold, indifferent behavior of mothers toward their sons was a significant predictor of aggressiveness in adolescent boys, while no similar effect could be found on the father's side. Interestingly, it was also found that mothers of aggressive boys are permissive of their sons' aggressive behavior.

PATERNAL AGGRESSION PATTERNS, CONDUCT DISORDERS AND DELINQUENCY IN GIRLS

Research on aggressive behavior in children has almost exclusively focused on boys. This focus is possibly due to the findings of several early studies showing that males exhibit more verbal and physical aggression than do females. The assertion that males are more aggressive than females continues to be challenged, however, and recent research on gender differences in aggression suggests that females may engage in as much aggressive behavior (at least verbally) as males. What is more, the majority of research on juvenile delinquency has primarily involved boys. Only more recently have researchers begun to study female delinquency. In general, it appears that male and female delinquents are not as different as previously assumed. Nevertheless, some marked differences between male and female delinquent behavior have been documented.

The explanations for such differences appear to be related to several variables. For example, some researchers have noted a differential impact of family variables, such as broken homes, on male and female delinquents. For example, in their analysis of female juvenile delinquents and their family relationships, Henggeler *et al.* (1987) found that families of female delinquents were especially dysfunctional. Using a two by two (gender by delinquency status) design, 32 intact families were matched for demographic variables, and the male and female delinquents were matched for arrest data. Mothers, fathers and adolescents were asked to complete a self report personality inventory and were observed during family interaction tasks. Consistent with the literature, families of delinquents had low rates of facilitative information exchange. Delinquent adolescents were also more dominant toward their mothers than well-adjusted adolescents were. It was also observed that fathers of delinquents were more dominant toward their wives than fathers of the well-adjusted adolescents were. The mother–daughter dyad in delinquent families showed particularly high rates of conflicts, even higher rates than mother–son dyads in delinquent families. Fathers of delinquent adolescents were more dominant toward their wives than fathers of well-adjusted adolescents were and delinquent adolescents were also more dominant toward their mothers than well-adjusted adolescents.

In their study of two different populations of female adolescents incarcerated for delinquency, Lang *et al.* (1976) focused on the role of the father as perceived by female adolescent delinquents. Both groups reported a high degree of father absence or neglect, and perceived their fathers as being "cold, rejecting and uninvolved" (ibid.: 148). In her study on female delinquents, Duncan (1971) incorporated a non-delinquent control group, and found that parents of non-delinquents were clearly differentiated from the parents of delinquents with respect to several variables. In particular, non-delinquent adolescent females felt less rejected by their fathers than delinquents. Similarly, Kroupa (1988) compared the perception of parental acceptance and rejection among female delinquents and non-delinquents. Again, delinquent females felt much less accepted by their fathers than non-delinquent females; in contrast, acceptance by the mother was about the same in both groups. In addition, child avoidance of the father was much higher in delinquent families compared to non-delinquent families. Interestingly, although the girls in the delinquent group reported that their fathers rejected or neglected them, the fathers in this group were significantly more over-protective and over-indulgent than the fathers in the non-delinquent group. Overall, the findings on female delinquents are similar to those documented for male delinquents, i.e. male delinquents also tend to perceive their parents more negatively than non-delinquent males do. The results also suggest a greater ambivalence in the girls' perception of the mother–daughter relationship than in the father–daughter relationship. In addition, delinquent girls as a group clearly see their fathers more negatively (e.g. less accepting) than do non-delinquents. This suggested ambivalence in adolescent girls' perception of their mothers could account for the tendency reported in the literature that the father–daughter relationship is more significant than the mother–daughter relationship. The relative absence of positive father–daughter interactions and the relative presence of negative relations support previous findings which identified a "negative fathering" as being associated with female delinquency (Riege, 1972: 72).

Finally, we want to illustrate some aspects of father–adolescent aggressiveness in clinical material on delinquent adolescents.

Fathers of delinquent adolescents: some case illustrations

Christ (1978) has reported many examples of paternal aggression from his study on male adolescents in a juvenile prison. Fathers of male delinquent adolescents beat their wives, beat and humiliated their children and were obviously very disturbed, demoralized and weak. For the adolescents participating in therapy programs, dealing with the relationship to the father and with these negative experiences stood in the foreground.

The account provided in group sessions by a 17-year-old inmate, Werner, illustrates the kind of brutality that many of these young men witnessed or were subjected to. Werner recounted how he and his father went on a drinking binge at home while Werner was on home leave from prison. Around two o'clock in the morning, his father urged him to go out with him for another drink, since there was no alcohol left in the house. The boy's mother, most likely expecting something like this would happen, had put the house key under her pillow. His father had not dared to go and take it himself, so the boy poked around her pillows until he found it. When they returned home several hours later, his mother was waiting for them, furious. His father slugged her down right away, but then said meekly, "We were only out for a little fresh air."

In another session, Werner discussed his involvement in criminal activity. According to his account, his father had played a major role in encouraging or helping him to commit such acts. Indeed, his father had also been imprisoned for criminal behavior. His father did not want to work, and refused any job offered to him; he simply preferred to receive unemployment benefits. Werner spoke about the countless fights between his parents and of the situations in which his father had hit him. Martin, another inmate in the juvenile prison, described very similar experiences with his father. His father had stolen a car and ID in order to get married, and right after the ceremony, he visited his son in jail saying, "I would never be able to last here as long as you have. I would have either hung myself or escaped" (Christ, 1978: 192).

Throughout the various group therapy sessions, it became apparent that many of the youths maintained fantasies of paternal omnipotence. The influence of such fantasies on the behavior of the youths was encompassing, to the extent that father and son became partners in delinquent activity, united in a pseudo-grandiosity, in that they created their own set of rules independent of the existing law and order. Thus, the committing of delinquent acts by these young men could be understood partly as attempts to identify with the fantasy figure of the father instead of the malevolent, if not immoral, father. On the other hand, it was clear that the majority of father–son relationships were ambivalent in nature. Many fathers exploited their sons or openly rejected them. All too often the sons were forced to recognize that they could not depend on their fathers.

In one session, Burghard, another prison inmate, recounted the following incident, which best reflects the ambivalence in the father relationship. Once, while on a prison leave, he tried to get his father to accompany him to see a film. At the cinema, instead of treating his son to the show, his father bought only one ticket and a bottle of liquor for himself, went inside and left Burghard standing outside, irritated.

Another aspect relevant to the shaping of delinquent behavior in adolescents concerns the family structure in general. The psychological deficits that were established in adolescent delinquents, i.e. their inability to deal with tension and delays in fulfilling their needs, their defective superegos (see Eissler, 1966), can be explained by the lack of a father as a structure-building force in the family. The striking absence of mentions of mothers in the group therapy (only four times during the 52 group sessions) indicates that relationships with fathers were central for the structure and pathology of male adolescents. Nevertheless, it appeared that the mothers of these young men were powerful family figures, upon whom the father also depended. The experiences of separation from older sisters or brothers and from grandparents that had fulfilled compensatory functions also accentuated the feeling of being left all alone.

The group therapy setting that Christ (1978) created in the juvenile prison offered the boys the opportunity to experience other kinds of "male" behavior as exhibited by the therapist and thus, slowly, to correct the paternal experiences in the ego. The male therapist did not punish and was very permissive in dealing with the boys. According to Blos, this kind of interaction enabled "adaptive repair" (Blos, 1973: 244) to take place. The disappointing experiences, the authoritarian models, and especially, the strong ambivalence were not repeated in this new relationship. In assisting the adolescent to recognize the true nature of his relationship to his father and to achieve a corrected identification with him, the therapist ultimately enabled the boy to develop more independent and more mature behavior patterns. The boys increasingly learned to deal with conflicts verbally as well as to work out solutions within the group.

11 Incestuous relationships

"Incest" refers to a sexual relationship between family members. Two patterns of incest are widely known and discussed: father–daughter incest and mother–son incest. The mother–son pattern is found in many legends and stories (Roll and Abel, 1988), but in reality mother–son incest is quite rare. Father–daughter incest is more predominant in reality, and is an issue in domains of therapy and law. According to recent feminist writers this phenomenon reflects masculine tendencies to subordinate women, and may illuminate some aspects of father–daughter relationships (James and MacKinnon, 1990). This chapter focuses on father–daughter relationships in the discussion of incest, and only briefly addresses the less common father–son incest.

Freud's first assumption concerning the causes of neuroses pointed to an incestuous relationship between father and daughter. According to this seduction theory, true incest was the traumatic precursor leading to the development of a disorder in the daughter. Freud suggested that if an incestuous affair took place at an early stage and was repressed, later experiences associated with sexuality re-aroused incestuous feelings and led to the emergence of symptoms. The seduction theory was replaced in 1897 by the oedipal theory. This change was related to the death of Freud's father. In a letter to Fliess, Freud explained that if all neurotic cases were caused by perverted fathers involved in real incest, his own father would also have been accused. It was also difficult for Freud to accept that such a high number of fathers in Vienna were engaged in incest. Freud then transformed the real incest into a fantasized one, experienced through the subjective perception of the child, and to be considered as such.

Although the seduction theory was modified, it was never abandoned, as the sexual tension between parents and children – the oedipal conflict – continued to be a basic element in Freudian theory. In transforming the seduction theory, Freud re-emphasized the taboo of parent–child sexual relationships. It is interesting that psychology has not dealt widely with this issue until very recent years when sexual abuse of children became a major issue of concern for society. A computerized search of recent studies and articles under the heading "father–daughter relationships" revealed that almost half of the references are related in some way to an incestuous relationship. Incest is defined as an unconsented act of sexual interaction between family members. The prevalence of incest has been documented at between 1.3 per cent and 1.5 per cent of the population (Kinsey *et al.*, 1953; Finkelhor, 1979). Though this figure may seem low, it actually approximates the prevalence of schizophrenia (Finkelhor, 1979). Incest usually entails the exploitation of a relatively powerless person, almost always a child, by a trusted and more powerful family member (Gelinas, 1990). Female children constitute about 85–90 per cent of the incest victims, and male children approximately 10–15 per cent. It should be noted that even in cases of male victims, the offender is usually the father or another adult male living in the house, and not the mother as would be assumed. Therefore we may assume that incest can be understood as one of the pathological facets of father–child relationships.

HISTORICAL AND CULTURAL PERSPECTIVES OF INCEST

Bischof (1985) claims that an inspection of more than 1,000 cultures revealed that incest was found in only a few of them. Even among animals like the Canada goose that lead a monogamous life, incest is not to be found. The goslings remain with their parents for about three years. They then leave their "family of origin," do not mate with parents or siblings, but seek out geese from other families as mates (Aberle *et al.*, 1963). Bischof claims that the taboo of incest is a universal norm, and according to Lévi-Strauss (1970) it signifies the transcendence of mankind from nature to culture. Severe penalties exist across cultures for sexual relationships within the nuclear family. The only widely cited exception was the custom of brother–sister marriages in the royal families of ancient Egypt during the Pharaonic and Ptolemaic periods, and in the royal courts of pre-Columbian Peru and Hawaii.

Incest thus developed as a strictly forbidden encounter between parent and child. Even when presented in different cultures, the actors are unaware of their act. Oedipus did not know that he was marrying his mother. In the Bible, following the destruction of Sodom, Lot, his wife and two daughters escaped to the mountains. On their way, Lot's wife turned around, an act that was forbidden, and turned into a pillar of salt. Under this family condition of mother absence (or passivity), a father was left with two adult daughters in a remote cave. One night the older daughter gave her father wine to drink until he was inebriated. As the Bible relates, Lot was not aware of having intercourse with his daughters, subsequently producing Amon and Moab. Carrol (1984) describes a North American Indian myth in which a father has intercourse with his daughter only after he feigns death and appears as someone else. In his *Jokes* book, Freud presents a story of a father who leaves his adolescent daughter with a family friend while he goes for a long trip, charging the friend with protecting the daughter's virtue. Upon his return, the father discovers his daughter pregnant. When questioned, the friend admits that the girl slept with his son, but there was a screen between the two beds. The angry father retorts, "But he could have simply walked around the screen!" "Yes," mused the friend, "There is that. It could have happened like that." As Willbern (1989: 83) adds, "the incestuous displacements of this anecdote are obvious." Thus, when incest occurs it is depicted as enacted either unintentionally or by a substitute of the father.

In his comprehensive review on close relationships, Bischof (1985) describes only two circumstances where incest between father and daughter were allowed. Among the Thonga, a predominantly agricultural tribe in the south of Mozambique, once a year the males go out on a very long and dangerous hunting expedition. On the night before departure, it was customary for a father to have sexual intercourse with his daughter. Immediately afterwards he would leave with his sons for the hunt. The belief was that incest with the daughter turned the father into a killer, making him stronger and more capable of killing. A similar phenomenon is found among the Dierri in Australia, when on the night before an important battle, the father had sexual intercourse with his daughter, in order to become empowered for the fight. Bischof emphasizes that in these tribes a strong taboo against incest exists, and only under these special circumstances was it permitted.

FUNCTIONS OF THE INCEST TABOO

Meiselman (1978) summarized a few theories that explain the strict prohibition of incest relationships. Biological explanations claimed that inbreeding would lead to inferior populations. It has been shown that hybrids are superior to inbred individuals with regard to physical characteristics such as body size, fertility, longevity and resistance to disease. These differences have been demonstrated in a variety of species such as chickens, rats, mice and fruit flies. Freudian theory probably did not accept the biological explanation. A central foundation of Freudian theory emphasizes the existence of incestuous drives from the onset of life, exemplified by the oedipal complex. Malinowski (1927) presented a sociological theory: in his view, incest would violate age and generational boundaries within the nuclear family. In such a case, sexual attachment between partners, characterized by possessiveness and jealousy, could lead to disorganization of sentiments, violence, and ineffectual management of family transactions. According to White (1948), by marrying non-family members, humans were able to develop and extend larger networks of co-operation, making life more secure, increasing the movement of commodities and ideas and thus leading to cultural development.

Meiselman (1978) suggested that incestuous desires probably do exist among humans, and are repressed during development as suggested by Freudian theory. What does repression of incestuous desires contribute to individual development? When an infant is forced to give up his/her desire to become the spouse of the opposite-sex parent, identification with the same-sex parent develops, sex-role is consolidated and societal values are internalized. Parsons (1954) further suggested that erotic excitement and frustration is the "rope" by which the child is pulled up from a lower to a higher level in the "growing up" process. Chimpanzees, as well as other apes, promote growth in the younger generation by expelling them from the natal troop. Adolescent female chimpanzees tend to wander off and mate promiscuously with males from other troops (Goodall, 1984), a fact that can be understood both as a defense against incest and as a path toward growth.

Parker and Parker (1986) arrived at a similar conclusion after probing the antecedents of father–daughter sexual abuse. First they cite studies suggesting that a higher incidence of father–daughter incest is found among reconstituted families, namely by a stepfather or a mother's male companion. In their study, Parker and Parker found that when fathers or even stepfathers were with their daughters during the early socialization period, the risk of sexual abuse decreased. For example, almost 36 per cent of the abusers, but only 5.6 per cent of the non-abusers, were not living at home and could not have been involved in childcare and nurturing activities. At the other end of the continuum, only 5.4 per cent of the abusers and 37 per cent of the non-abusers were involved frequently in nurturing their child. Parker and Parker therefore suggest that "the essential explanatory variables [for a lower risk of father–daughter sexual abuse] appear to be sustained, prolonged, and perhaps early association [of father and daughter]" (Parker and Parker, 1986: 535). On the one hand it may appear that prolonged exposure to the daughter leads to lack of sexual interest in her, because a familiar object is less frequently chosen as a sexual partner. Yet this is combined with an evolutionary purpose. Taking care of the young increases the chances of survival and adaptation. Conceptually, we may then talk of two types of close relationships: one is erotic attraction and the other is bonding. The purpose of erotic attraction is not the development of the other. On the contrary, the development of one partner may lead to friction in the relationship. For instance, Bary and Ohlson (1985) have documented cases of sexually abusing fathers who reject their daughters once they reach adolescence. The other close relationship is bonding (Bowlby, 1969), whereby the young's needs are attended to and his/her impetus for development (and separation from the caregiving figure) is supported.

Paternal caregiving toward infants and young daughters also carries the message of "undoing of incestuous desires," an additional impetus for growth. The girl or boy is expected to look for a mate outside the nuclear and extended family. As we discussed in Chapter 2, separation from the family requires the attainment of various personal and interpersonal skills. If marrying within the family were permitted, individuals would have less need to develop these skills and would continue to rely on the parents. The following clinical case exemplifies this contention.

Keren, aged 18, was hospitalized following a psychotic breakdown. It was decided to apply family therapy and the whole family was summoned. Keren was the third daughter in a family of five children. At the first meeting it became clear that her older sister had also experienced a psychotic breakdown in the past. The younger brother, still in high school, was socially isolated and expressed ideas that sounded inappropriate. While exploring the family history it was revealed that the parents were first-cousins, a situation quite common among families of Middle Eastern origin. We do not want to raise the issue of possible inferiority of inbreeding since no genetic testing was done in this case. However, when the father was asked to recount how he and his wife got married, he replied: "What is the question, we are first cousins and we knew each other for all of our life. We decided to get married, so I moved to live in her house. We lived with my aunt/mother-in-law till after we had our fourth child. Then my aunt/mother-in-law stood up and told us that we are already grown-ups and it is time for us to have a house of our own." Thus, the custom of marrying within the family allowed the younger generation to stay close to the family and not undergo a separation process.

The taboo thus serves a developmental purpose. The dissolution of incestuous bonds is the impetus for growth and development of social contacts outside the family. This is particularly important during the formative years of adolescence, when the young girl (or boy) is expected to consolidate a sexual identity and start establishing relationships with the opposite gender. Support for this contention is found in a recent study by Sroufe *et al.* (1993). In this study, interactions between early adolescent boys and girls were observed during summer camp. Although at this age direct interactions between the genders are not common, members of the opposite gender are of interest during this period. Overall, two broad types of cross-gender interactions were detected and evaluated. The first type referred to "boundary maintenance behaviors," reflected in play-like encounters where interaction with the opposite gender was prescribed by rules that emphasized the distinction between the genders. The second type involved "boundary violation behaviors," reflected in intimate, too close interactions with the opposite gender, either while giving up one's sexual identity (for example, a girl socializing with boys and acting as a tomboy), or acting in an aggressive mode toward the opposite gender. The interesting finding was that developmentally appropriate or inappropriate behavior toward the opposite gender was related to family history. Adolescents who experienced or had experienced a seductive relationship with a parent where generational boundaries were dissolved, were found to be less skillful when interacting with the opposite gender. They were either not secure enough or too aggressive when approaching members of the opposite gender. It is thus reasonable to ask, under what circumstances do generational boundaries become violated and a parent adversely affects the child's development? What leads fathers to break this taboo and to engage in an incestuous relationship with their offspring? In the following section we will try to describe and define the incestuous "affair," the roles father and daughter play in the "affair," and to describe rationalizations given by abusing fathers in explaining their behavior.

THE INCEST "AFFAIR"

In most father–daughter incest cases, even in those where the daughter was thought to contribute by being seductive, the first actual move was made by the father. There are different ways in which an incestuous father approaches his daughter. Christiansen and Blake (1990) describe the grooming process in father–daughter incest. Fathers may start by building trust, which they do by spending time with their daughters and giving them presents. The daughters then get a sense of being favored, and step by step, efforts are made to cause them to accept later demands. When a sense of trust and closeness has been established, a stifling environment of secrecy is built by the father. Fathers often use persuasive and confusing rationalizations, for example, talking about the special relationships they have with their daughters, something that will not be understood by the mother or other family members. In the next step, the boundary between father and daughter which was previously blurred is also violated. Seemingly "innocent" behaviors such as entering the bathroom or watching the girl getting dressed develop into sustained closeness. Body touching and sexual behavior start to be commonplace. Sexual themes are then raised, and fathers use explicit sexual language in their discussions with their daughters. In this sexually laden atmosphere the father is ready to move to overt actions. As Christiansen and ·Blake describe, incestuous relationships between fathers and daughters follow a pattern similar to that seen in other heterosexual relations. It should be mentioned that there are cases where the sexual relationship begins abruptly, when the father induces the girl to co-operate. Arrangements must then be made in order to allow the "incest affair" to continue. A place and time must be designated, usually when the mother and siblings are not at home. Perpetrators use bribes and, more commonly, threats and punishment to perpetuate the incestuous relationship.

Although incest is abusive in nature, fathers tend to portray it as a sign of their close relationship with their daughters. The supposed "closeness" between father and daughter is reflected in rationalizations offered by fathers to explain their behavior. As Meiselman (1978) observed in earlier studies, fathers tend to describe their behavior as part of a father's *duty* to his daughter. Some fathers claimed that they felt they had to teach their daughters the facts of life. One said that his sex education program for his daughter would prevent her from becoming frigid like his wife. Another father claimed that his daughter was already promiscuous and explained that by having sex with him she would not have to seek it outside the family. Some of the men also emphasized the importance of family solidarity, and claimed that incest prevented them from being unfaithful to their partners by having an extra-familial affair. Of course there are cases when the father is psychopathic and has no guilt feelings. Thus, an analysis of the fathers' rationalizations suggests they were aware of their daughters' need to grow, and they "facilitated" growth in an absurd manner. In addition, for many of these men family cohesiveness was important and they related the affair with their daughter to their wish for family unity.

It is interesting that only in a minority of cases, approximately 20 per cent, did daughters overtly resist their fathers. In the majority of cases, daughters were either passive, or unsuccessfully attempted to avoid the sexual activity. For this reason some authors have raised the question of whether incest can occur because of the seductiveness of the daughter. However, as Meiselman (1978) indicated, there is no proof that daughters are interested in or enjoy the affairs. Our contention is that it is more probable that the girl is driven into circumstances that lead her to comply passively with her father's demands.

Originating from the definition of incest, physical abuse is only one aspect of the incestuous act. In incest the child is robbed of her rights to her body, stripped of power and thereby made a victim. She feels her trust in her father – who should be providing protection for her – has been betrayed, as he uses her to meet his own needs (Bierker, 1989). Therefore, as Furniss (1991) suggests, the child's passive compliance with the father's acts does not alleviate her experience of being abused. Once the child feels she is abused (regardless of the legal definition of incest, whether vaginal intercourse or various forms of sexual behavior), a variety of emotions may emerge. She may experience guilt, and she may be blamed, her implicit or explicit signals or calls for help rejected or denied (ibid.). Most of all, the child learns that she cannot rely on the parent as a source of support.

The lack of available parental support is even more crucial because the victim's mean age at onset of incest for girls living in intact families is 5.2 years, and the onset age for victims of stepfathers is 7.5 years (Faller, 1990). The incest affair may go on for some years. Changes were reported once the daughters reached adolescence. Negron (1988) described how fathers became more hesitant to continue the sexual relationship because of fears of pregnancy. Once the daughters get older they tend to end exploitation by leaving home, or by confiding in and obtaining help from others (Christiansen and Blake, 1990).

FAMILY PATTERNS ASSOCIATED WITH INCESTUOUS RELATIONSHIPS

Although the incestuous affair is hidden from other family members – from the mother in particular – in reality it takes place within the family scene and is not disconnected from the family milieu. McCarthy and Byrne (1988) suggest that incest reflects the confusion of the modern family, which is confined in itself, cut off from social enrichment and regulation, and sustained by the pursuit of proximity and meeting the emotional needs of its members. The inaccessibility of former role models and support leads families to oscillate between extremes of fusion and distance on the one hand, and between patterns of control and competition on the other. The incest affair is therefore an attempt to protect the family by establishing a coalition of what McCarthy and Byrne refer to as "mis-taken love." Analysis of family dynamics further reveals several family constellations that may lead to an incestuous affair between father and daughter.

One dynamic involves a constellation of a parentified daughter in an estranged marriage (Meiselman, 1978; Gelinas, 1990). In such a family pattern, the mother is unable to fulfill the emotional and daily needs of her husband and of the family. Step by step, responsibilities are transferred to a daughter, usually the eldest one. The daughter is thus parentified, assuming excessive household responsibilities such as cooking and looking after younger siblings. Family members learn that they have to turn to her when in need. Gradually, the daughter becomes the father's "buddy." She has dinner with him, listens to his stories, and they watch television together. The daughter is being set up as the alternative mother, as a source of emotional support for family members, and attains the position of female authority in the household. According to Gelinas (1990), under such circumstances, when the atmosphere between father and daughter becomes sexually loaded, the chances that the close father–daughter relationship will deteriorate into an incestuous affair are high. Physical contacts may turn sexual, culminating in a clearly incestuous affair. The daughter's development may then face an additional hurdle. Under such circumstances she may internalize her role of being responsible for others. Her identity may evolve as sensitive to others' needs to the exclusion of her own needs (Gilligan, 1982). According to Fullinwider-Bush and Jacobvitz (1993), such a girl may prematurely adopt an adult role without ever exploring personal alternatives. From the family's perspective the daughter serves the purpose of a mother, first by adopting her responsibilities, and second by reducing the father's sexual demands on his wife. For this reason the mother may be quite tolerant, and will not be active in terminating the incestuous affair. Paradoxically, Scott and Flowers (1988) found that recently molested adolescents who perceived that their mothers did not know of the incest demonstrated more pathology than adolescents who perceived that their mothers were aware. Research also supports these suggested family dynamics. Lavang (1988) presented families, with and without father–daughter incest, with family tasks. Recordings of family interactions revealed that incest families tended to communicate differently and to show less enjoyment and laughter. In addition a higher incidence of detachment between mother and daughter was found in the incest families.

In line with the constellation so far described, we can understand why the mother perceives the daughter as a rival, especially when the daughter becomes the father's favored child and partner. Although unconsciously the daughter may be acting in the service of her mother, on the surface the mother may be frightened by the emerging "affair." A different family pattern associated with incest is the constellation of a dominant mother and dependent father (Bierker, 1989). In this type of family the dominating, successful mother controls her passive husband and treats him like an incompetent child. She may repeatedly express her anger, saying that she is tired of attending to the needs of her additional child, and may withdraw emotionally and sexually as if to punish him. In his inability to assert himself and to feel "like a man," he may turn to his daughter to fulfill his needs. The following case exemplifies such a constellation.

Smadar was the second child in a family of five children. Her father died in a car accident when she was five years old. The mother, who lived in a small village, continued her late husband's activities. Two years after the death of her husband, she met a man four years younger than herself. At first the family continued to live in the village and two more children were born. The stepfather, who was a sensitive and artistic man, developed a good relationship with his wife's children, including Smadar. However, he felt that he could not fulfill his potential in the small village. For his sake, the family decided to leave Israel and moved to an English-speaking country where the stepfather started a business. He was unsuccessful, and the mother became the primary breadwinner. This was a difficult time for Smadar as well, involving a combination of pubertal development and adjustment to a new environment, resulting in low moods and absenteeism from school. The father, who also had considerable free time, stayed at home as well. In the house, he walked around wearing only his underwear, a practice also adopted by Smadar. The close relationship between Smadar and her stepfather turned into mutual consolation. Later it evolved into their sitting in bed dressed in their underwear. This mutual consolation almost progressed to what McCarthy and Byrne (1988) termed "mis-taken love," but the mother discovered them, and put an end to the practice. She decided to send Smadar to her grandmother; on the plane, Smadar experienced a psychotic breakdown.

Yet another dynamic involves a dominant and tyrannical husband and a very inadequate wife. In this case, incest involves a great deal of coercion and may be combined with physical violence against the victim, and against other family members. In this family pattern, the father has an exaggerated sense of entitlement (Gelinas, 1990). He may often use threats, intimidation and physical violence to pursue and fulfill his emotional needs. The basic attitude of such a father is that his wife and children are his possessions and therefore he has the right to dominate their personal lives. The father may experience particular control over the life of the incest victim, not allowing her to socialize or establish extra-family relationships. James and MacKinnon (1990) point to this type of scenario. According to these authors, writing from a feminist perspective, incest is a result of male tendencies to control their wives and children. James and MacKinnon suggest the development of the following interactional patterns which lead to father–daughter incest:

1 The father rules in an intimidating manner.
2 Afraid to disagree, the mother does not object to the father's behavior.
3 The father misperceives the mother's "agreement" as voluntary, as condoning his behavior.
4 The father continues to rule in an intimidating manner.

In his relation to the children

1 The father tends to control the children's behavior through verbal intimidation and threats of violence.
2 Afraid of the father, the children comply, but reject him, withdraw, and turn to their mother.
3 Feeling excluded and distrustful of the children's behavior, the father attempts to exert more control.

(James and MacKinnon, 1990: 85)

Because of his desire to control the household and especially to gain power over the female members, this pattern of intimidating behavior leads to sexual abuse of the daughter.

More complicated situations occur when the cause of incest is the father's own psychopathology, regardless of the family dynamics. For example, there are fathers who are diagnosed as "fixated paedophiles" (Groth, 1982) and their primary orientation is toward sexual interaction with children. In other cases, the father might be psychotic or a drug user and the daughter might be the available victim rather than an outlet for solving a family problem.

FATHER–SON INCEST

Father–son incest belongs to the category wherein the problem originates in the father. Meiselman (1978) describes how the father's sexual identity, in many of these cases, is not consolidated, and he is interested in sexual gratification with members of the same sex. Fathers' case histories sometimes revealed that they were molested by their fathers as children or adolescents, and this remained a secret between father and son. It may also be the case that the pubertal development of the son awakens homosexual tendencies in the father. Meiselman describes a case where a father developed a very close relationship with his pubertal son, which began with joint weight-lifting sessions and proceeded to the father introducing his son to mutual masturbation.

In some cases, the father–son interaction may not involve a definite sexual act between them. It is rather that the relationship is sexualized, and the son may suffer what Bierker (1989) termed "emotional incest." In such a case, the intense relationship between father and son may represent the father's substitution for a deteriorating relationship with his wife.

In a case we treated recently, a father contacted the clinic seeking help for his 11-year-old boy owing to behavioral problems at school. In the first interview the father complained that his wife did not care about the children, and could be abusive. His major complaint was the mother's incompetence and lack of interest in the family. When describing their life in the past, a "family myth" was told: when the boy was 3 years old, he went with his mother to buy ice cream in the center of the town. After buying the ice cream, the mother suddenly lost the boy. She did not know what to do. She called the father who was at home and he told her not to leave the center of town in case the boy looked for her there. The father went out of the house and met the boy, who had walked three kilometers by himself. The bond between father and son was strong, and together they complained about the mother, who felt excluded and separated from them both. At the fourth session it became apparent how close father and son were, when they revealed that they used to take long baths together.

We were not certain whether this was almost a case of father–son incest, or simply a fond and close relationship between father and son.

Yet it is clear that this father–son relational pattern recalls the first family pattern mentioned in the previous section. As a result of relational imbalance between husband and wife, one of the children may be parentified and become the parent's confidant, and in some cases this may be the precursor of an incestuous relationship.

LONG-TERM EFECTS OF INCEST

Being trapped in an incestuous relationship reflects a dynamic of family over-involvement, combined with a conflict of loyalties. The incest is a betrayal of the mother. Disclosure of the incestuous affair is a betrayal of the father. Adolescence is the stage when the relationships with parents are supposed to be renegotiated. Parents are supposed to respect and support the adolescent's striving for autonomy and self expression (Shulman and Klein, 1982). Incest implies dissolution of generational boundaries between father and adolescent. The adolescent, either by induction or by coercion, must comply with the father's needs and sacrifice him or herself for the sake of family solidarity, leaving no room for the adolescent's own wishes. Thus, psychologically the adolescent is not allowed emancipation from the family. In some cases, a young girl may identify with the parentified role and prematurely settle on an inadequate identity. Moreover, there are cases where the father does not allow the girl to socialize with peers (Gelinas, 1990), and thus individuation is not possible either from the psychological or the physical perspective.

Being caught in such a web of relationships and loyalties does not leave much room for change. It can thus be understood how an incestuous relationship may last for a few years. Even when the affair is revealed it is well known for victims to resist disclosure and be unwilling to testify. Girls can become silent, resist any change, and further embrace the family in which they have been abused. Gelinas (1990) describes a case of a 12-year-old girl who preferred to be jailed and placed in solitary confinement for a week rather than testify against her father. Other girls may try to escape from their situation. Molnar and Cameron (1975) reported on 10 girls who were hospitalized following incestuous affairs. These girls were characterized by depressive-suicidal reactions associated with running away from home. Other runaways may end up in promiscuous sexual behavior, or even prostitution.

Some girls "grow out" of the incestuous affair. Either they become more mature and are able to resist the father's demands, or they may escape into a close relationship with a boyfriend or into marriage, and by this act put an end to the incest. However, this supposedly adaptive runaway may also encounter future problems. Sroufe and Fleeson (1986) suggested a theory on the coherence of close relationships, namely that individuals tend to repeat the patterns of relationships with which they are familiar. It is well known that many women with a history of incest end up as battered wives, and thus the cycle of pathological and violent over-involvement is re-enacted in the new relationship. Yet this re-enactment is found not only on the behavioral level, but also in the psychological inner model of the girl, where relationships are inadequately portrayed and sexual relations with a partner may lead to an increase of anxiety. Wingerson (1992) suggests that difficulties of incest survivors include disturbed object relations. The lack of trust, and increased need for empathy due to delayed mourning experienced by such individuals may be related to the establishment of borderline and narcissistic representations.

Clinical experience has shown that the effects of incest or abuse may be manifested in adolescence or in the later life of victims. The following case of Birgit, a girl aged 13, shows how a continuous abuse experience may be expressed in an extreme form of malfunctioning and maladaptive approach toward male figures.

Birgit was a studious pupil in a junior high school. She was the eldest child in a family of three girls and one boy. Her mother, aged 35, was a housewife and the father, also aged 35, was unemployed. A history of abuse started three years prior to the referral of Birgit to a psychiatric unit. The father tended to blame Birgit for the family's difficulties, for his being unemployed, and made her the family scapegoat. In addition, the father claimed that Birgit was a bad influence on her siblings and insisted that she keep away from them. He did not allow her any contact with them, locked her in a room, tied her to a bed, and hit her so harshly that her fingernails were damaged. Family members were aware of this severe abuse but kept silent. At school the girl's condition was noticed and her parents were summoned, but did not show up. In the meantime, Birgit confided in her aunt and told her that her father had been abusing her for a period of three years. The aunt believed the girl, and turned to a youth court. The court ordered a psychiatric examination which revealed Birgit's serious mental state. She was then hospitalized. In the unit, Birgit exhibited a variety of maladaptive behaviors. She was extremely paranoid about adults, was socially isolated, and from time to time involved in petty delinquent behaviors, and she had no personal hygiene habits. After two years of hospitalization she recovered and was discharged.

During the hospitalization period her family was not very co-operative, and prior to her discharge her parents showed no great interest in her. It was decided to look for a foster home for her. A family that already had one foster child was approached. Both parents in this family were special education teachers who also had two children of their own. Shortly after Birgit was placed in this family, problems arose between her, the foster mother and the two children of the family. Following arguments Birgit would run away from the family, and in some cases was arrested for shoplifting. It was interesting that Birgit developed a close relationship with the foster father. However, this relationship with him was very sexualized; she tended to hug him and in one case she entered his bedroom naked.

Both foster parents asked for a psychological consultation. Two psychologists, a male and a female, interviewed Birgit. She was very shy and refrained from eye contact with the male psychologist. When he left the room, trying to make the encounter more relaxed, Birgit's co-operation increased. The consultation revealed that Birgit was very bright, yet had a negative body image and low self concept, and could not show any empathy for other people. In the projective tests she imagined herself to be the returning daughter accepted by her father. In her drawings males were disproportionately big and their genitals emphasized and very enlarged. For this reason it was assumed probable that the girl had been sexually abused also. In the interview Birgit reiterated her strong wish to go back to her family. She started to send letters, especially addressed to her father, and sent the family flowers from time to time. It was decided to hold a supervised meeting between Birgit and her family. While approaching the parents' home she became very restless, ultimately opening the car door and running away. It can be seen that while Birgit's attitudes toward other people were generally impaired, she showed a clear tendency to turn to males in a flattering and sexualized maladaptive manner, which led to her being removed from the foster family.

In other cases the impact of a sexualized or incestuous relationship with the father may be expressed later in life. In the course of a study on the coherence of close relationships we have interviewed mothers regarding their family history. In one case, a woman, although married with two children of her own, was still strongly attached to her father. He visited her house every day; he was her confidant and she consulted him on every important issue. Of course her husband resented this behavior and this led to conflicts between them. In her family history, this woman described an over-involved relationship with her father since adolescence, characterized by her frequently sitting on his lap. No overt incest was mentioned. At a certain stage of the study, the woman called one of the interviewers and asked for a consultation. She complained that her husband had sexually abused her 3-year-old daughter. A further session revealed beyond any doubt that nothing had happened between her husband and daughter. Our suggestion is that this woman had probably internalized her model of father–daughter relationships on the basis of her personal experience, and she resumed the same model with her new family.

The following case further demonstrates how previous relationships with the father, characterized by dissolution of generational boundaries and sexual overtones, can re-emerge in a young adult's relationship with her boyfriend. Franziska, a 24-year-old nurse, came for treatment for sexual problems with her boyfriend and issues related to her identity. She reported that for the previous eight months she had been unable to have intercourse with him, and for the past several weeks she felt repulsion when he tried to approach her. She could not explain these feelings because she loved her boyfriend dearly and had enjoyed having sex with him in the past. She described him as an independent and charming man who was not too serious about his studies, and preferred to enjoy life, particularly riding his motorcycle. His appearance tended to impress other girls. She also raised some questions about her professional identity, and whether or not to turn to another profession. Working through individual psychoanalysis, it became apparent that her father was also a good-looking man, whose appearance impressed other women. Known as a Don Juan, he had married late, and her mother was much younger and not experienced.

Franziska described how she was very much attracted to her father and used to accompany him on his travels inspecting forests, which was his occupation. Several times during the analysis, she brought up a feeling about an event which she was not sure had taken place in reality. In this event, her father put her on a table in front of him in one of the huts they visited. She remembered feeling his hand on her thigh, turning rigid, looking at a clock on the wall and realizing that the clock stopped at that moment. For years she had been bothered about whether this was reality or imagination, and by not being fully aware of what ensued at that particular encounter between her and her father. It was difficult, both for the patient and for the analyst, to figure out whether an incestuous affair did occur in this case. Yet during treatment Franziska realized how similar her father was to her boyfriend. She was then able to associate the beginning of her sexual symptoms to a meeting between her father and boyfriend. For the purpose of our discussion, we can see what might be the long-standing effects of an imagined or real sexually laden encounter between father and daughter.

Research also supports the long-standing effects of sexual abuse. A study by LaBarbara (1984), conducted on a non-clinical sample of female undergraduate students, evaluated the relationship between perceived paternal seductiveness and daughters' perceptions of themselves and of others. Paternal seductiveness was associated with perceptions of male sexuality as dangerous, and with unease in sexual situations. In addition, sexualized father–daughter relationships were related to women's perceptions of themselves as hostile, arrogant and lacking in warmth and nurturance. Their interest in others was low. LaBarbara contended that paternal seductiveness was related not only to deficits in heterosexual functioning but also to difficulties in broader relational domains such as family and parenting. Cole *et al.* (1992) examined the self-reported parenting experiences of 20 women who were incest victims as children. Their parenting reports were compared to those of 25 women whose fathers were alcoholic but not sexually abusive and to those of 39 women who had no known risk during childhood. Incest survivors reported significantly less support in the parental partnership with their spouses. They were also less confident, and had a lesser sense of control as parents. Thus, as the authors suggest, being entangled in an incestuous relationship adversely affects the individual's later efficacy as a marital partner and a parent. It can then be suggested that some form of developmental arrest has taken place, affecting the adolescent girl's attitude toward herself and toward others. It can be added that in the case of father–son incest, the son's consolidation of his sexual orientation is at risk. Even if the son ends up with a heterosexual orientation, gets married and establishes a family, the pattern of father–son incest may be repeated in the next generation (Meiselman, 1978).

12 Conclusions
Fatherhood: personal and relational perspectives

In this book we have tried to understand the role of fathers in the development, adjustment and life of their adolescent offspring as expressed in society at large. Review of the historical antecedents of fatherhood revealed that in the past the role of the father was related to the economic conditions of the family. Because of his role as family head and breadwinner, a father was excluded from the daily demands of childrearing. Fathers were limited to fulfilling rather instrumental and controlling functions in the family. In addition, the father–son relationship was emphasized in order to enhance the economic link between generations. Psychologically, this led fathers to raise their sons as mirrors of themselves. When Freud developed his theory, at the end of the last century, this clear division between mothers' and fathers' roles in the family was still prevalent, and therefore the father, as an active player in the life of his children, was introduced only after a child reached the age of 3.

During this century, major societal and economic changes allowed, and under some circumstances required, fathers to be more available to their children. Melanie Klein's and Margaret Mahler's theories implicitly reacted to these changes, and incorporated fathers as important figures in the lives of their children as early as infancy or toddlerhood. However, reviews of psychological and sociological research into fathers' behavior, and of the role fathers play in the lives of their children and adolescents, have shown that fathers have not actually made major changes in recent generations. In comparison with mothers, they spend less time, and are less involved, with their children. Even when they are together, whereas mothers' interactions with their children are dominated by caregiving activities, fathers act more as playmates (Russell and Russell, 1987). Yet this distinction was not restricted to younger children, in greater need of adult caregiving. Fathers reported spending a third or half the amount of time that mothers spend with their adolescents (Russell, 1983; Montemayor and Brownlee, 1987). Fathers were described as exhibiting less affection than mothers, and were considered less as targets for disclosure (Youniss and Smollar, 1985). When together with their adolescents, fathers engaged more in playful and outdoor activities than did mothers (Montemayor and Brownlee, 1987; Shulman and Posen, 1992). Moreover, neither male nor female adolescents expected their fathers' behavior to deviate from the traditional paternal role. Even adolescents raised in the 1990s, when asked to portray a good father, stuck to familiar stereotypes (see Chapter 2):

> A father is more preoccupied in work, a mother has more free time for her children and therefore they turn to her. A mother loves her child as a father does but she really does it. A father is more like a friend with whom you can do things together.

Although fathers today can be seen to be more engaged with their children as compared with their own fathers, and capable of performing caregiving activities, many reminders of the historical distinctions between fathers and mothers are still widely found. It is striking that even unemployed fathers were not more engaged with their children although they had ample time (Jahoda, 1982). Moreover, in a study conducted in Sweden (Hwang, 1986), fathers who were primary caregivers of their infants were compared both to traditional fathers and to mothers, on the level of engagement with their infants. In general, mothers were more engaged and displayed more affection toward their infants. However, the surprising results were that fathers who were primary caregivers had much lower levels of engagement and affection than did traditional fathers. Thus, in spite of major historical and sociological changes which have led women into employment outside the home and allowed men to have more free time with their families, fathers and mothers in many cases stick to the traditional models of parenthood developed through generations. The results of the Swedish study may even suggest that fathers are fundamentally unwilling to change their roles and to share in the care of their children. Why have fathers not changed? Why have they not taken the opportunity to redefine their role as parents? Why have fatherhood and motherhood not become more egalitarian even in a society, like Sweden, that legally supports more active participation of fathers in raising their children?

We would like to analyze the psychological reasons and to suggest two explanations for this phenomenon. The first is related to fathers themselves, namely paternal identity, and the second is related to the broader perspective of relations between males and females within the nuclear family. Moreover, as our book suggests, the distinctive role of fathers may serve certain functions in the development and adjustment (or maladjustment) of their children.

PATERNAL IDENTITY

It is interesting to notice that the terms "woman" and "female" are quite often interchangeable with the term "mother." This trend is well pronounced in psychoanalytic writings. The terms "man" or "male" are less perceived as interchangeable with the term "father." Men are related to more as men and less as fathers, and fatherhood is a less emphasized aspect of the male identity.

One plausible explanation for this phenomenon could be that men are less familiar with adequate models of fatherhood. Social changes not only have led to a more egalitarian division of labor in the family but have also increased the rate of divorce. A growing percentage of children grow up not living with their biological father or with any adult male figure at all. Mitcherlich (1972) in a psychoanalytic analysis of German post-war society described it as a "fatherless society." Originally Mitcherlich referred to children whose fathers were killed during the war, and to children who had problems developing a close relationship and identifying with their fathers, owing to the fathers' role during the Third Reich. In this view, an entire society was raised "apart" from the father figure. The father was then perceived as a distant, questionable figure. Mitcherlich suggested that the students' revolt in the 1960s was targeted at the remote and negative father representing the law (Lacan, 1977), and in search of a more benevolent and accepting father. It is not uncommon to hear young men complaining about their own fathers being good grandfathers, expressing tenderness and love to their grandchildren, which these young men missed as children.

Gerson (1989) investigated the meaning of parenthood for young men. Results showed that fatherhood fantasies of 22- to 42-year-old fathers were less developed, less textured, and less reciprocal and intimate than those of the women with whom they were involved. Fathers tended to envision themselves filling traditional roles with regard to future children, mainly the roles of educator or disciplinarian. These men felt distant from the experience of fatherhood, particularly in its relational aspects, and tended to project an intense identification with the fantasied child. Thus, for these young men, the expected child seemed to function as a self object (Kohut, 1977). Their own fathers were perceived as domineering or unavailable, and therefore less often described as positive representations or models for fatherhood.

The less developed identity of fatherhood cannot be attributed only to some level of deficiency in the model portrayed by the former generation of fathers. As discussed in Chapter 2, males have different models of close relationships than do women. Men seek less for intimacy (as described in female terms) and disclosure, but prefer companionship and commitment (Davidson and Duberman, 1982). When men are close to others, they achieve their sense of closeness on the basis of shared activities. For many boys and males participation in sports is a common method of establishing connections with others. According to Chodorow (1978), males are torn between guarding their separateness, and their basic need for closeness and intimacy with others. Games and sports are a "safe" place where one can connect with others while maintaining clear boundaries and distance from them. Ochberg describes a similar phenomenon in the business world, until recently male dominated. In this world you can be both personal and completely detached (Ochberg, 1987: 185). Ochberg further suggests that the public image (whether in games, sports or work) forms a large part of males' private self conception. The *role* may become a *personal role* incorporated into the self consciousness. Fatherhood is thus not entirely contingent on the roles males play outside the family. In order to act as a "father," a man may need to make a clear switch to a different role. "I always make a clear separation out [of work], so that I am still processing it. . . . I try to leave it so I am ready to deal with my wife and kids, and not force them to deal with me" (Ochberg, 1987: 175). Nevertheless, it is not clear whether fathers in general are capable of making this transformation once they are at home. Bailyn (1974) found that men who were highly involved and participatory in family life had a more negative self concept. These men had less confidence in both their creativity and their problem-solving abilities, in comparison to males who were highly committed to their jobs.

Some contemporary media and public messages have tried to portray fathers moving from aggression on the battlefield and in the conference room, toward luxuriating in the warm ambience of the nursery (Gerson, 1989). As the previous chapters have suggested, this is probably not the case. Moreover, we suggest that fathers are probably not equipped and not prepared for such an extreme change. Nevertheless, discussion of this issue would be incomplete if conducted only within the framework of the male's self perception and identity of fatherhood. A man does not enter fatherhood on his own; a woman, a mother, is also a partner in this system, and her relation to her man, the father of her child, will affect his relation to his children.

WOMEN'S ATTITUDES TOWARD CAREGIVING FATHERS

It is not uncommon to hear a young expectant couple announce: "we're pregnant." An increasing number of men (in industrialized countries) are present during childbirth. Research has shown that the majority of time that fathers spend with their young children is in the presence of the mother (see Belsky, 1981). Thus, fatherhood, from the very beginning, can be portrayed as a three-person construct. In psychoanalytic theories the father is in fact presented within a triadic framework. In the earlier stages of life, the various approaches talk about an exclusive relationship between the parent and infant, a "dyadic" relationship, mainly referring to the mother–child dyad. In Freudian theory, the father's role is mainly introduced in the oedipal stage, which is by its very nature systemic. Mahler (1979), in describing the symbiotic phase, does not explicitly deal with the father, who is brought onto center stage only at the rapprochement phase, when the mother–toddler relationship is conflictive.

It is interesting to note that on the one hand fathers and mothers are described as one unit – "we are pregnant" – while on the other hand the father is presented as an intruder in the close mother–child dyad. This dialectic probably reflects the ongoing "tension" between a dyadic and triadic perception of parenthood. Is the father expected to develop a relationship with his child that is equal to and interchangeable with that of the mother or is the father's relationship with the child secondary and distinctive? Our review of fatherhood (see Chapter 1) has shown that this tension is not new. Broude (1988) described the couvade ritual, in which fathers act as if they are full partners when their wife is pregnant or in labor. Broude's examination of the incidence of the ritual across different cultures revealed that the ritual is related to the level of hypermasculinity in those societies. Societies high in hypermasculinity, where male roles are most distinctive, tended less to have a couvade ritual in their culture. In societies where male and female roles are less distinctive, men probably wished to become equal partners in reproduction and used couvade as some form of masculine protest.

Research presented in Chapter 1 showed that fathers are capable of learning the skills required for taking care of their children, and this may represent the modern father's couvade ritual. Recently, efforts have been made to develop intervention and training programs to help fathers of preschool children to be more involved and responsive (McBride, 1990). However, mothers are not always pleased to hand over their traditional roles to their spouses. Russell (1983) found that wives of highly involved fathers expressed dissatisfaction with the quality of their husbands' home and childcare performances. In some of the families this dissatisfaction led to marital friction. Moreover, Baruch and Barnett (1984) found that women were more dissatisfied when their husbands were highly involved than when they were less involved. Follow-up of families where men had been primary caregivers revealed that many of the families returned to more traditional divisions of family roles (Russell, 1983). Increased paternal participation probably does not have positive effects on all women. Women may feel that they are losing a source of power once their traditional role of primary caregiver is taken over by the husband. They may not hand over responsibilities to the father, or may criticize his caregiving capabilities. In one case of family intervention the mother was complaining about the father not helping her with childcare and household chores. The husband agreed with his wife's complaints, and explained:

> My tendency was to be involved with the children and to do more at home. But always, she was criticizing what I did: "The kids do not like the food you make." "Whenever you dress the children they look as if they have been neglected by their mother." So I gave up, let her do it better.

Thus, it is not only the unwillingness of men that may interfere with their adopting an equally responsible role in family life, it is also that women are not necessarily prepared to give up what has been considered their "territory" for so many years. It was interesting to observe that under irregular circumstances, such as following divorce (see Chapter 7), or among chronically ill children (see Chapter 8), the distinction between maternal and paternal roles was reinforced.

FATHERHOOD AS A RELATIONAL CONSTRUCT

In relation to the mother

Up to this point, we have discussed fathers' and mothers' reasons for maintaining their traditional roles in the family. However, fatherhood and motherhood can also be perceived as connected constructs and not just as separate entities. Husband and wife are the basic elements which construct the family system. The systemic definition entails two "elements" standing in some consistent relationship or interactional stance with each other (Steinglass, 1978). Several rules govern the organization and activities of a system. In order to survive, a system has to organize itself – to arrive at a consistent state of relationships between elements, and to be flexible enough to adapt and reorganize according to the changing circumstances (Lewis, 1986). Logically, different forms of organization may be anticipated: the first in which all elements play a similar role and have similar functions, and the second where elements may have different roles. Traditionally, the family was organized in a manner whereby the genders had different but complementary functions and roles. The female role was mainly affiliative-expressive, and its primary function was to achieve and maintain emotional harmony among family members. The male role was more instrumental-adaptive and was concerned with the support and protection of the family and establishing its position in the wider society (Lidz, 1980). More recent approaches questioned the adequacy of this division of female–male roles in a society moving toward equality between the sexes.

However, it seems too simplistic to claim that distinctive gender roles have existed solely as a result of historical factors that attributed differential roles to males and females. From a systems perspective, a system's existence is achieved through an ongoing balancing of morphostasis-stability and morphogenesis-change. The different roles that elements in a system play contribute to the balance and adaptability of a system; the different valence of elements is a source of energy in the system that helps keep the system connected and in action (Buckley, 1967). The different roles played by males and females may then be a factor contributing to the stability and flexibility of a system. Results of a study by Gloger-Tippelt (1986) showed how the different functioning of husband and wife contributed to the adaptation of the family system. In this study Gloger-Tippelt followed 96 couples from the beginning of pregnancy until the child was 2 years old. Mood states, psychological complaints and the nature of activities of husbands and wives were evaluated. Functioning couples were characterized by a synchrony of the two partners. Spouses perfectly matched each other's ups and downs, and alternated between supporting the other and being supported. Thus, adjustment of the system was characterized by different functioning of husband and wife regardless of historical sex-role types.

In summary, we suggest that the distinctive roles that fathers and mothers play contribute to the adaptability and stability of the family system. In addition, the relationship between mother and father cannot be measured adequately using a criterion of fair-weather co-operation, namely whether each parent takes a similar share of responsibilities. It is rather that each parent respects and supports the distinctive actions of the other while understanding his/her contribution to the overall functioning of the system. This pattern of relationship recalls Selman's (1980) description of a higher level of ability to take the perspective of the other, whereby within the relationship the autonomy and distinctiveness of each parent is understood and accepted. It can be understood that the chances of rivalry between father and mother under such circumstances are lower.

Parental capabilities for respecting each other's distinctiveness were found to be related to and to support parents' relationship with their child. Pederson *et al.* (1987) investigated the father–infant interaction among men who had contrasting affective responses during early infancy. Men who reported having experienced periods of blues or dysphoric moods, as compared to men who did not report such feelings, were found in home observations at 3 months to have a more disengaged style of relating to their babies. They were more remote, touched their babies less frequently, and provided less caregiving and affection than did the comparison group of fathers. However, at the age of 12 months these fathers were observed to be engaged in these behaviors at higher rates than the comparison group. These unexpected changes contributed to the relationships that the two groups of fathers had with their wives. In the non-dysphoric mood group fathers and mothers displayed a similar attitude toward the infant, and correlations between mothers' and fathers' behaviors were high. Pederson *et al.* suggested that these parents revealed an additive style of parenting in which the behavior of one parent tended to parallel that of the other. This additive style did not last for long and at the age of 12 months these fathers' engagement with their infants was lower. In the dysphoric mood group, negative correlations between mothers' and fathers' behaviors were found, suggesting that the mother was compensating for the father's lower engagement with the infant. In line with our assumption, when parents display different behaviors toward the child yet respect one another's attitudes, in the long run the system is more stabilized and children get more attention from both parents.

An examination of families with a schizophrenic offspring shows that these families were unable to arrive at a family pattern that allowed and respected the distinctive roles of parents and children. In his classic work, Wynne described how those families strove to maintain an appearance of uniformity which undermined the expression and development of an individual identity among its members (Wynne *et al.*, 1958). Lidz described in more detail five types of fathers of schizophrenics. The first group was composed of men who were in serious conflict with their wives. These men tried to undercut their wives' authority, and were hostile toward them. They developed close relationships with their daughters, at times accompanied by sexual seductiveness. A second group of fathers tended to turn their hostility toward their children rather than their wives. These men were especially hostile toward their sons, whom they perceived as potential rivals. The third group of fathers was characterized as having an exalted concept of themselves. Although some did exhibit true capacities and achievements, these they disregarded as insignificant compared to their grandiose self perceptions. The wives supported their husbands' fantasies of omnipotence while at the same time depriving the children of their fathers' attention. These men were aloof and distant from their children. The fourth group were described as failures in life, and had no prestige within the family. They rarely concerned themselves with their children's care owing to their deep sense of worthlessness. The fifth group of fathers was composed of extremely passive men, who were strongly controlled by their wives. Although they were pleasant and in some cases affectionate, they could not serve as sources of strength for their children, nor as models for identification (Lidz *et al.*, 1957).

Thus, the ability of both parents to establish a family pattern with distinctive roles for mothers and fathers can contribute to the adaptability of the family system, and better serve as a source of support and impetus for development for family members. Such a pattern is particularly important when the children reach adolescence, a period when centrifugal forces move the family toward greater separateness (Combrinck-Graham, 1985). When drawing apart, it is important to be able to maintain confidence that newly emerging pattern of relations will not replace the former foundations of intimacy, but will lead to a different expression of the closeness between family members. It is reasonable to assume that familiarity with such a model – expressed by fathers – and acknowledgment of it – expressed by mothers – can facilitate this evolution during the transitional period of adolescence.

In relation to the child/adolescent

Children also play a role in shaping their relationships with parents (Bell and Harper, 1977; Lewis, 1986; Thomas and Chess, 1977). Studies have shown that infants, through their own characteristics and behavior, moderate parental behavior. Child behaviors such as aggression, passivity, affection and level of responsiveness may trigger certain parental behaviors (Bell and Harper, 1977). For example, measurements, taken on the seventh day of life, of an infant's ability to orient toward the mother and to regulate his/her state predicted the formation of an insecure attachment to his/her mother (Waters *et al.*, 1980). Newborns who were described by nurses as difficult to care for were more likely to develop insecure attachments later (Egeland and Farber, 1984). Infants who revealed more sociability at 3 months showed less avoidant behavior at 1 year (Thomas and Chess, 1977). Child characteristics thus affect the nature of interaction which develops between parent and child, and in turn contribute to parents' inner sense of parenthood.

Two child characteristics, age and sex, were described as influencing paternal behaviors and attitudes (Berman and Pederson, 1987). In Chapters 1 and 2 we have shown that the age of the child contributed to the amount and nature of father involvement. Fathers were found to be more involved with older children, and their interaction was of a playful quality. The older the children, the easier it became for fathers to interact with them. One father described how he enjoyed spending Sunday afternoons with his 12-year-old son. He commented: "The boy is crazy about sports, and I am crazy too, so every Sunday we watch football together. It is a great time for both of us." Men's preference for interaction with older children is also evident in their expectations. Gerson (1989) interviewed expectant fathers and asked them to describe the image of a child that they had in their minds. More than half of them described an image of an oedipal-age child, whereas only 25 percent of the expectant mothers did so. Men imaged significantly fewer infants than did women. Beyond the higher incidence of imagining an older child, men had less of a tendency to imagine children as needy and dependent, and rather emphasized autonomy and self sufficiency. It can thus be understood why fathers feel more at ease with older children and adolescents than do mothers (Steinberg, 1987a). The emerging autonomy of the adolescent is appealing to the father, and coincides with his and the family's penchant for separation during this stage of development (Combrinck-Graham, 1985: see Chapters 2 and 3). Recently a high school teacher reflected that the older the children she teaches the more fathers she sees attending parent–teacher conferences and expressing interest in the lives of their adolescents. Fathers are more interested and, as described in Chapter 2, more sensitive and responsive to the needs of their developing adolescents. Moreover, fathers may feel more at ease enacting their own mode of relatedness, and in this manner they support the adolescent's developmental tasks.

A recently published collection of letters from famous fathers and mothers to their children clearly shows the difference between fathers' and mothers' attitudes toward their adolescents (Scheib and Laub, 1994). The mother of the 19-year-old Karl Marx wrote to him: "Please, wash yourself at least once a week with soap and sponge." Maria Theresa wrote to her 15-year-old daughter, Marie Antoinette: "Please brush your teeth, keep clean, do not neglect your appearance." Letters from fathers sound different; the father of the 19-year-old Walter Rathenau wrote him: "You should not overwork, besides work you should have some fun with your friends, go out, have a drink and be in a good mood." The father of 21-year-old Leopold Mozart wrote him: "Do not compose too quickly. Skip what you do not like. And please do not forget that they should pay you for every piece of work. Do not work when not paid." The father of 20-year-old Frank Wederkind, a poet, wrote his son while he was studying in England:

> Whatever you decide to study, I am sure we will see good results in the future. Now you have reached the age of an adult and your fate is in your hands. Therefore pursue your goals. What you reach will serve as a firm ground. If you wish you can develop a relationship with an English girl, I'll accept her.

It is quite evident that fathers, as reflected in these historical letters, are sensitive and supportive of their adolescents' growing individuality. Nevertheless, we keep in mind that in some cases adolescents may evoke their fathers' own adolescence, leading to over-identification and in some cases (as presented in Chapter 9) to psychopathology in the child.

In Chapters 4 and 5 we elaborated upon the different relationships that fathers establish with their sons and daughters. Many of the differences were attributed to historical and sociological factors. However, this analysis would be incomplete if we overlook the child's own contribution to the distinctive relationship he/she establishes with the father. Fathers' interactions with their children are of a more playful nature. In early and middle childhood, boys as well as girls can perceive their father as an interesting playmate, and vice versa.

Following puberty and the different interests emerging among adolescent males and females, father–daughter and father–son relationships become more distinctive. Brooks-Gunn and Ruble (1982) showed that the majority of girls do not share the experience of pubertal development with their fathers. For example, girls did not tend to tell their fathers when they had menarche. Blos (1962) wrote that the "tomboy" behaviors evident in pre-adolescent girls such as climbing, riding and wild play, which are the last reminders of "male activity," are repressed during adolescence. Identification with the mother and with female passivity increases during adolescence. The mother is the partner for self disclosure, and the father turns into an observer. At best, issues related to school and studies are referred to him. Boys' interests may coincide more with those of fathers. However, owing to males' emphasis on individuality, the son may not expect his father to be very involved in his life. Furthermore, as described in Chapter 4, competition between father and son may be experienced. It is interesting to recall that pathological father–daughter and father–son relationships reflect the distinctive relations that each gender develops with the father. Typical non-optimal father–daughter relations occur when fathers become too involved instead of maintaining some distance, and their relationships with their daughters are sexualized (see Chapters 5 and 11). Non-optimal father–son relationships are more often characterized by increased strife and aggression which in some instances, such as in the myth of Oedipus, may lead, under extreme circumstances, to the death of one party (see Chapters 4 and 10).

In sum, fatherhood is a relational entity which men are expected to negotiate with their wives and with their growing children. In this web of relationships, men negotiate between their inclination toward individuality and their wives' penchant for closeness and intimacy. By expressing their inclination toward individuality, fathers can become both models and catalysts for balance and flexibility within the family. Since adolescents are at a stage where they strive to assert their distinction and individuation, fathers may also become a source of support and guidance for them.

THE CENTRALITY OF THE FATHER IN DEVELOPMENT AND IN PATHOLOGY

Understanding fatherhood as a relational construct enhances our perception of the father's role as central in the development of his children. The centrality of the father figure and a continuous need for the idealized father is evident even in cases where the father is not necessarily positive. As presented in Chapters 6, 10 and 11, even in cases where the father was absent or abusive, children exerted enormous efforts to preserve the ideal image. The negative image of the father may even be reconstructed into a positive and idealized figure. It is then that the father is an integral part of the child's "inner picture of the family" (Cierpka, 1992). In the analysis of the child/ adolescent's relationship with the father, two types of relationships can be considered: dyadic and triadic/systemic. Although, in the majority of cases, the infant is born into a family and not into a dyad, close relationships in infancy and early childhood are generally conceptualized as dyadic. Mahler *et al.* (1975) emphasized the symbiosis between mother and infant; Bowlby (1969) described the mother as the primary attachment figure. It is mainly from the infant's perspective that the primary close relationship is dyadic. The (pre-oedipal) relationship with the father is also described as dyadic (Blos, 1985). In reality, the dyadic perception is a reduction of the complexity of existing relationships; relationships between spouses, between parent and child, and among siblings. This primary structuring of relationships is transformed as development progresses, and the child is expected to develop a more complex model of relationships that includes the father.

The dialectic between a dyadic and a triadic relationship involving child and father parallels the distinction between adaptation and pathology. The positive dyadic close relationship between child and father (see Chapter 4) is characteristic of the pre-oedipal and younger age. In adolescence such a close relation may represent a strong identification with the father and his philosophy of life, and recall an identity status of foreclosure (Marcia, 1966). As we have discussed in Chapters 5 and 11, for daughters a strong dyadic relationship with the father during adolescence is particularly non-optimal. The father in such cases becomes the admired adult male in the life and fantasies of the girl. Balsam (1989) described such cases, in which girls had difficulties establishing meaningful intimate relationships with men. It is interesting that even in cases where the father is absent but his image is idealized, a similar phenomenon may occur. We recently dealt with a case of a young woman whose father left the family when she was 5 years old, and moved to a different country. Her contact with him was not consistent, yet he tended to show up from time to time and get deeply involved with his daughter. The father, who was very successful in his profession, did not establish a new family, so the daughter was the only family he had. During his visits he treated her in a very tender manner, and her admiration for him increased. Our impression was that the life of this young woman was engulfed by the dyadic relationship with her father, which did not allow her to pursue her own life.

When the father is an active partner in the family system, the dyadic relationship with the child/adolescent is confronted and hence co-ordinated with the other relationships in the family. The relationship also has to be balanced with the broader role that the father plays in the family. In such a case, not only does the dyadic relationship contribute to the dissolution of the "infantile" bond between mother and child, but it also serves as an impetus for the father to consolidate a mature relationship with the adolescent. The renegotiation of the family's "connectedness" can thus be facilitated by the father, who initiates and facilitates more balanced forms of closeness. When a father does not fill an active role, and is too detached or weak (as described previously in this chapter), the probability of psychopathology among his offspring is higher. Moreover, in some cases (as presented in Chapter 9) the adolescent's pathology may actually serve the father's needs, by helping the father to assert himself or to bring the family into a more balanced mode.

FATHERHOOD: A LIFE-LONG DIALECTIC

Our contention is that fatherhood is to some extent paradoxical. On the one hand fathers are described as less involved, and on the other their role in the development of children and adolescents is emphasized. There is no doubt that fathers are less engaged with their children than are mothers, and this situation is probably not going to change, at least in the near future. *Time* magazine recently reported that although fathers in Sweden are allowed to take paternity leave, very few took advantage of this opportunity. Subsequently, one town council in southern Sweden decided to legislate that fathers are required to take at least one month of paternity leave.

Fathers are differently engaged with their children than are mothers, and serve as different models. Nevertheless, their distinctive contribution to the development of their children should not be under-estimated. A growing number of studies show the major role that fathers play in the development of their children. They support children's and adolescents' independence, and serve as models for interaction with extra-familial objects. Further research on adolescents and young adults can highlight the contribution of the father to the development of his maturing offspring. When fathers do not pursue their appropriate role, either in relation to the child or in relation to their status in the family, the chances of psychopathology in the family may increase. Our formulations would therefore support the use of intervention strategies like family therapy, that take into consideration the father and his central role in the family.

Bibliography

Abelin, E. (1975) "Some further observations and comments on the earliest role of the father" *International Journal of Psychoanalysis* 56, 293–302.

—— (1980) "Triangulation, the role of the father and the origins of care gender identity during the rapprochement subphase" in E. R. Lax (ed.) *Rapprochement*, New York: Aronson.

Aberle, D. F., Bronfenbrenner, U., Hess, D. R., Miller, R., and Spuhler, J. M. (1963) "The incest taboo and the mating patterns of animals" *American Anthropologist* 65, 253–65.

Adams, D. J. (1982) "A comparison of confidence and degree of contentment in parental role of custodial and non-custodial stepmothers" unpublished doctoral dissertation, Florida State University, Tallahassee, FL.

Ahorns, C. R. and Wallisch, L. (1987) "Parenting in the binuclear family: Relationships between biological and step-parents" in K. Pasley and M. Ihinger-Tallman (eds) *Remarriage and step-parenting: Current research and theory* (128–37), New York: Guilford Press.

Ainsworth, M. D. S., Blehar, M., Waters, E., and Wall, S. (1978) *Patterns of attachment*, Hillsdale, NJ: Erlbaum.

Allen, J. P., Hauser, S. T., Bell, K. L., and O'Connor, T. G. (1994) "Longitudinal assessment of autonomy and relatedness in adolescent–family interactions as predictors of adolescent ego development" *Child Development* 65, 176–94.

Almeida, D. M. (1991) "Competing models linking father involvement, father acceptance, and adolescent self-image" paper presented at the Meeting of the American Psychological Association (August), San Francisco, CA.

Almeida, D. M. and Galambos, N. L. (1991) "Examining father involvement and the quality of father–adolescent relations" *Journal of Research on Adolescence* 1, 155–72.

Alsaker, F. (1992) "Timing of puberty and reactions to pubertal changes" paper presented at conference Youth in the Year 2000, 5–7 November, Schloss Marbach, Germany.

Ambert, A. (1982) "Differences in children's behavior toward custodial mothers and custodial fathers" *Journal of Marriage and the Family* 46, 73–86.

Ammerman, R. T., Loeber, R., Kolko, D. J., and Blackson, T. C. (1994) "Parental dissatisfaction with sons in substance abusing families: Relationship to child and parent dysfunction" *Journal of Child and Adolescent Substance Abuse* 3, 23–37.

Angermeyer, M. C. (1982) "The association between family atmosphere and hospital career of schizophrenic patients" *British Journal of Psychiatry* 141, 1–11.

Aponte, H. J. (1976) "Underorganization in the poor family" in P. J. Guerin (ed.) *Family therapy, theory and practice* (12–27), New York: Gardner Press.

Apter, T. (1990) "Altered views: Fathers' closeness to teenage daughters" in R. Josselson and A. Lieblich (eds) *The narrative study of lives*, Newbury Park, CA: Sage.

Arbinger, R. (1991) "Die motorische Entwicklung" in H. Hetzer, E. Todt, and I. Seiffge-Krenke (eds) *Angewandte Entwicklungspsychologie des Kindes- und Jugendalters* (21–39), Heidelberg: UTB.

Aries, P. (1962) *Centuries of childhood: A social history of family life*, New York: Vintage.

Arlow, J. (1951) "A psychoanalytic study of a religious initiation rite: Bar mitzvah" *Psychoanalytic Study of the Child* 6, 313–74.

Atkins, R. N. (1989) "The fate of father representation in adolescent sons" *Journal of the American Academy of Psychoanalysis* 17, 271–91.

Babcock, B., Freedman, A. E., Norton, E. H. and Ross, S. C. (1975) *Sex Discrimination and the Law: Causes and Remedies* Boston: Little Brown, p.147.

Babcock, R. J. (1979) "The symbolism of the father" *British Journal of Sociology* 30, 206–17.

Badinter, E. (1980) *Die Mutterliebe*, Munich: Piper.

—— (1993) *Die Identität des Mannes*, Munich: Piper.

Bailyn, L. (1974) "Accommodation as career strategy: implications for the realm of work" working paper 728–74, Sloan School of Management, Massachussetts Institute of Technology.

—— (1978) "Accommodation of work to family" in R. Rappaport, R. N. Rappaport, and J. M. Bumstead (eds) *Working Couples*, New York: Harper & Row.

Balsam, R. H. (1989) "The paternal possibility. The father's contribution to the adolescent daughter when the mother is disturbed and a denigrated figure" in S. H. Cath, A. Gurwitt, and L. Gunsberg (eds) *Fathers and their families*, Hillsdale, NJ: The Analytic Press.

Bandura, A. (1971) "Social learning theory of aggression" in J. F. Knutson (ed.) *Control of aggression: Implications from basic research* (201–50), Chicago: Aldine.

—— (1973) *Aggression: A social learning analysis*, Englewood Cliffs, NJ: Prentice Hall.

Baruch, G. K. and Barnett, R. C. (1984) "Consequences of fathers' participation in family work: Parents' role strain and well-being" unpublished manuscript, Wellesley College.

Bary, B. and Ohlson, R. (1985) "The father–daughter dilemma: Incest and counter-incest" *Transactional Analysis Journal* 15, 275–7.

Bateson, G. (1972) *Steps to an ecology of mind*, San Francisco, CA: Chandler.

Becker, G. W., Landes, E. M., and Michael, R. T. (1977) "An economic analysis of marital instability" *Journal of Political Economy* 85, 1141–87.

Becker, R. D. (1979) "Adolescents in the hospital" *Israeli Annals of Psychiatry & Related Disciplines*, 17, 328–52.

Bell, R. U. and Harper, L. V. (1977) *Child effects on children*, Hillsdale, NJ: Erlbaum.

Belsky, J. (1979) "Mother–father–infant interaction: A naturalistic observational study" *Developmental Psychology* 15, 601–7.

—— (1981) "Early human experience: A family perspective" *Developmental Psychology* 17, 3–23.

Belsky, J. and Rovine, M. J. (1988) "Non-maternal care in the first year of life and the security of infant–parent attachment" *Child Development* 59, 157–67.

Belsky, J., Gilstrap, B., and Rovine, M. (1984) "The Pennsylvania infant and family development project. I: Stability and change in mother–infant and father–infant interaction in a family setting at 1–3–9 months" *Child Development* 55, 692–705.

Benson, M. J., Harris, P. B., and Rogers, C. S. (1990) "Identity consequences of attachment to mothers and fathers among late adolescents" paper presented at the Third Biennial Meeting of the Society for Reseach on Adolescence (March), Atlanta, GA.

Berman, P. W. and Pederson, F. A. (1987) "Research on men's transitions to parenthood: An integrative discussion" in P. W. Berman and F. A. Pederson (eds) *Men's transitions to parenthood: Longitudinal studies of early family development*, Hillsdale, NJ: Erlbaum.

Bernard, J. (1956) *Remarriage: A study of marriage*, New York: Russell & Russell (second edn 1971).

—— (1981) "The good provider role, its rise and fall" *American Psychologist* 36, 1–12.

Bernfeld, S. (1923) "Über eine typische Form der männlichen Pubertät" *Imago* 9, 169–88.

Bierker, S. B. (1989) *About sexual abuse*, Springfield, IL: Charles C. Thomas.

Billings, A. G. and Moos, R. H. (1982) "Family environments and adaptation: A clinically applicable typology" *American Journal of Family Therapy* 10, 26–38.

—— (1983) "Comparisons of children of depressed and non-depressed patients: A social-environmental perspective" *Journal of Abnormal Child Psychology* 11, 463–86.

Binger, C. M., Ablin, A. R., Feuerstein, R. C., Kushner, J. H., Zoger, S., and Mikkelson, C. (1969) "Childhood leukemia: Emotional impact on patient and family" *New England Journal of Medicine* 80, 414–18.

Bischof, N. (1985) *Das Rätsel Oedipus. Die biologischen Wurzeln des Urkonfliktes von Autonomie*, Munich: Piper.

Björkqvist, K. and Österman, K. (1992) "Parental influence on children's self-estimated aggressiveness" *Aggressive Behavior* 18, 411–23.

Blatt, S. J. and Blass, R. B. (1990) "Attachment and separateness: A dialectical model of the products and processes of development throughout the life cycle" *The Psychoanalytic Study of the Child* 45, 107–27.

Block, J. H. (1973) "Conceptions of sex role: Some cross-cultural and longitudinal perspectives" *American Psychologist* 2, 512–26.

Blos, P. (1962) *On adolescence: A psychoanalytic interpretation*, New York: The Free Press.

—— (1967) "The second individuation process of adolescence" *The Psychoanalytic Study of the Child* 22, 162–86.

—— (1973) *Adoleszenz*, Stuttgart: Klett.

—— (1974) "The genealogy of the ego ideal" *The Psychoanalytic Study of the Child* 29, 43–88.

—— (1985) *Son and father*, New York: The Free Press.

—— (1991) "The role of the early father in male adolescent development" in S. I. Greenspan and G. H. Pollock (eds) *The course of life*, Vol. IV: *Adolescence*, Madison, WI: International Universities Press.

Blyth, D. A., Simmons, R. G., and Zakin, D. F. (1985) "Satisfaction with body image for early adolescent females: The impact of pubertal timing within different school environments" *Journal of Youth and Adolescence* 14, 207–25.

Boeger, A. and Seiffge-Krenke, I. (1994) "Symptombelastung, Selbstkonzept und Entwicklungsverzögerung bei gesunden und chronisch kranken Jugendlichen" *Zeitschrift für Kinder- und Jugendpsychiatrie* 22, 5–15.

Bohannan, P. and Yahraes, H. (1979) "Stepfathers as parents" in E. Corfman (ed.) *Families today: A research sampler on families and children* (89–101), Washington, DC: US Government Printing Office.

Boose, L. E. (1989) "The father's house and the daughter in it: The structures of western culture's father–daughter relationship" in L. E. Boose and B. S. Flowers (eds) *Daughters and fathers*, Baltimore, MD: The Johns Hopkins University Press.

Boss, P. and Greenberg, J. (1984) "Family boundary ambiguity: A new variable in family stress theory" *Family Process* 23, 535–46.

Bosse, H. (1990) "Violence and care: The appropriation of 'sons' by their 'fathers' in Papua New Guinea" *Group Analysis* 23, 5–16.

Boszormenyi-Nagy, I. (1965) "A theory of relationships: Experience and transaction" in I. Boszormenyi-Nagy and J. L. Framo (eds) *Intensive family therapy: Theoretical and practical aspects*, New York: Harper & Row.

Bowen, M. (1976) *Family therapy in clinical practice*, New York: Aronson.

Bowlby, J. (1969) *Attachment and loss*, Vol. 1: *Attachment*, London: Hogarth.

Bowman, M. E. and Ahrons, C. R. (1985) "Impact of legal custody status on fathers' parenting post divorce" *Journal of Marriage and the Family* 47(2), 481–5.

Bray, J. H. (1987) "Becoming a stepfamily" symposium presented at the Meeting of the American Psychological Association, New York.

Brody, S. and Axelrad, S. (1978) *Mothers, fathers, and children*, New York: International Universities Press.

Bronfenbrenner, U. (1979) "Contexts of child rearing: Problems and prospects" *American Psychologist* 34, 844–50.

Bronstein, P. (1984) "Differences in mothers' and fathers' behaviors toward children: A cross-cultural comparison" *Developmental Psychology* 20, 994–1003.

—— (1988) "Father–child interaction: Implications for gender-role socialization" in P. Bronstein and C. P. Cowan (eds) *Fatherhood today: Men's changing role in the family*, New York: Wiley.

Bronstein, P. and Cowan, C. P. (eds) (1988) *Fatherhood today: Men's changing role in the family*, New York: Wiley.

Brook, J. S., Whiteman, M., Gordon, A. S., and Brook, D. W. (1983) "Paternal correlates of adolescent marijuana use in the context of the mother–son and parental dyads" *Genetic Psychology Monographs* 108, 197–213.

—— (1984) "Identification with paternal attributes and its relationship to the son's personality and drug use" *Developmental Psychology* 20, 1111–19.

—— (1986) "Father–daughter identification and its impact on her personality and drug use" *Developmental Psychology* 22, 743–8.

Brooks-Gunn, J. and Ruble, D. (1980) "Menarche: The interaction of physiological, cultural, and social factors" in A. Dan, E. Graham, and C. Beecher (eds) *The menstrual cycle*, New York: Springer.

—— (1982) "The development of menstrual-related beliefs and behaviors during early adolescence", *Child Development* 53, 1576–7.

Broude, G. J. (1988) "Rethinking the couvade: Cross-cultural evidence" *American Anthropologist* 90, 902–11.

Brown, A. C. (1986) "Factors associated with family functioning in non-counseling and counseling stepfamilies" unpublished dissertation, California Graduate School of Marital and Family Therapy, San Rafael, CA.

Brownfield, D. (1987) "Father–son relationships and violent behavior" *Deviant Behavior* 8, 65–78.

Buckley, W. (1967) *Sociology and modern systems theory*, Englewood Cliffs, NJ: Prentice-Hall.

Bulcroft, R. A. (1991) "The value of physical change in adolescence: Consequences for the parent–adolescent exchange relationship" *Journal of Youth and Adolescence* 20, 89–105.

Burchinal, L. G. (1964) "Characteristics of adolescents from unbroken, broken, and reconstituted families" *Journal of Marriage and the Family* 26, 44–51.

Cain, A. C., Fast, I., and Erickson, M. E. (1964) "Children's disturbed reactions to the death of a sibling" *American Journal of Orthopsychiatry* 34, 741–52.

Caplan, P. J. (1989) *Don't blame mother: Mending the mother–daughter relationship*, New York: Harper & Row.

Caplan, P. J. and Hall-McCorquodale, I. (1985) "Mother-blaming in major clinical journals" *American Journal of Orthopsychiatry* 55, 345–53.

Carrol, M. P. (1984) "The Trickster-Father feigns death and commits incest: Some methodological contributions to the study of myth" *Behavior Science Research* 19, 24–57.

Carter, B. (1989) "Fathers and daughters" in M. Walters, B. Carter, P. Papp, and O. Silverstein (eds) *The invisible web. Gender patterns in family relationships*, New York: Guilford Press.

Chase-Lansdale, P. L. and Owen, M. T. (1987) "Maternal employment in a family context: Effects on infant–mother and infant–father attachments" *Child Development* 58, 1505–12.

Chasseguet-Smirgel, J. (1979a) "A woman's attempt at a perverse solution of its failure" *International Journal of Psycho-Analysis* 69, 149–61.

—— (1979b) (ed.) *Psychoanalyse der weiblichen Sexualität*, Frankfurt a.M.: Suhrkamp.

Chodorow, N. (1978) *The reproduction of mothering: Psychoanalysis and the sociology of gender*, Berkeley, CA: University of California Press.

Christ, H. (1978) *Psychoanalytische Gruppenbehandlung im Jugendgefängnis*, Stuttgart: Enke.

Christiansen, J. R. and Blake, R. H. (1990) "The grooming process in father–daughter incest" in A. L. Horton, B. L. Johnson, L. M. Roundy, and D. Williams (eds) *The incest perpetrator*, Newbury Park, CA: Sage.

Cierpka, M. (1992) "Die Entwicklung des Familiengefühls" *Forum Psychoanalyse* 8, 32–46.

Clark, C. A., Worington, E. L., and Danser, D. B. (1988) "The transmission of religious beliefs and practices from parents to firstborn early adolescent sons" *Journal of Marriage and the Family* 50, 463–72.

Clark, M. S. and Reis, H. T. (1988) "Interpersonal processes in close relationships" *Annual Review of Psychology* 39, 609–72.

Coe, R. N. (1984) *When the grass was taller*, Ann Arbor, MI: Yale University Press.

Cohen, L. H., Burt, C. E., and Bjork, J. P. (1987) "Effects of life events experienced by young adolescents and their parents" *Developmental Psychology* 23, 583–92.

Cohen, O. (1991) "Sex role, coping and well-being of divorced mother and father headed family" unpublished PhD thesis, Bar Ilan University: Ramat Gan.

Cole, P. M., Woogler, C., Power, T. H., and Smith, K. D. (1992) "Parenting difficulties among adult survivors of father–daughter incest" *Child Abuse and Neglect* 16, 239–49.

Coleman, J. C. (1978) "Current contradictions in adolescent theory" *Journal of Youth and Adolescence* 7, 1–11.

—— (1992) "The nature of adolescence" in J. C. Coleman and C. Warren-Adamson (eds) *Youth policy in the 1990s: The way forward*, London: Routledge.

Collins, W. A. (1990) "Parent–child relationships in the transition to adolescence: Continuity and change in interaction, affect and cognition" in R. Montemayor, G. R. Adams, and T. P. Gullota (eds) *From childhood to adolescence: A transitional period?* Newbury, CA: Sage.

Collins, W. A. and Laursen, B. (1992) "Conflict and the transition to adolescence" in C. U. Shantz and W. W. Hartup (eds) *Conflict in child and adolescent development*, New York: Cambridge University Press.

Collins, W. A. and Luebker, C. (1991) "Change in parent–child relationships: Bilateral processes in the transition to adolescence" paper presented at the Meeting of the International Society for the Study of Behavioral Development (July), Minneapolis, MN.

Collins, W. A. and Russell, G. (1991) "Mother–child and father–child relationships in middle childhood and adolescence: A developmental analysis" *Developmental Review* 11, 99–136.

Combrinck-Graham, L. (1985) "A developmental model for family systems" *Family Process* 24, 139–50.

Constantine, L. L. (1987) "Adolescent process and family organization: A model of development as a function of family paradigm" *Journal of Adolescent Research* 2, 349–66.

Cook, J. A. (1984) "Influence of gender on the problems of parents of fatally ill children" *Journal of Psychosocial Oncology* 2, 71–91.

Crohn, H., Sager, C. J., Brown, H., Rodstein, E., and Walker, L. (1982) "A basis for understanding and treating the remarried family" in J. C. Hansen and L. Messinger (eds) *Therapy with remarriage families* (36–52), Rockville, MD: Aspen Publications.

Crosbie-Burnett, M. (1984) "The centrality of the steprelationship: A challenge to family theory and practice" *Family Relations* 33, 459–63.

—— (1985) "Type of custody and involvement with children by father and stepfather" unpublished paper presented at Annual Conference, National Council on Family Relations, November.

Crosbie-Burnett, M., Giles-Sims, J., and Plummer, C. (1986) "Power in stepfamilies: A test of normative-resource theory" unpublished paper presented at Annual Conference, National Council on Family Relations, November.

Dalton, R. D. (1986) "The psychology of fathers and daughters: A feminist approach and methodology" *Women and Therapy* 5, 207–18.

Davidson, L. R. and Duberman, L. (1982) "Friendship: Communication and interactional patterns in same-sex dyads" *Sex Roles* 8, 809–22.

Deb, M. and Gulati, J. K. (1989) "Paternal attitude in relation to academic achievement of adolescent daughter" *Indian Journal of Behavior* 13, 10–15.

Decker, H. S. (1991) *Freud, Dora and Vienna 1900*, New York: The Free Press.

Dickerson, V. C. and Zimmerman, J. (1992) "Families with adolescents: Escaping problem lifestyles" *Family Process* 31, 341–53.

Doane, J. A. (1978) "Family interaction and deviance in disturbed and normal families: A review of research" *Family Process* 17, 357–76.

Doherty, W. J. (1991) "Beyond reactivity and the deficit model of manhood: A commentary on articles by Napier, Pittman, and Gottman" *Journal of Marital and Family Therapy* 17, 29–32.

Dornbusch, S., Carlsmith, J., Bushwall, S., Ritter, P., Leiderman, H., Hastorf, A., and Cross, R. (1985) "Single parents, extended housholds and the control of adolescents," *Child Development* 56, 329–41.

Dravoj, G. (1983) "Self-disclosure behavior in adolescence" unpublished diploma thesis, University of Giessen.

Drill, R. L. (1986) "Young adult children of divorced parents: Depression and the perception of loss" *Journal of Divorce* 10, 169–87.

Dubbert, J. L. (1979) "Shaping the ideal during the masculine century" in J. L. Dubbert (ed.) *A man's place. Masculinity in transition*, Englewood Cliffs, NJ: Prentice-Hall.

Duberman, L. (1975) *The reconstituted family: A study of remarried couples and their children*, Chicago: Nelson-Hall.

Duncan, P. (1971) "Parental attitudes and interactions in delinquency" *Child Development* 42, 1751–65.

Duvall, E. (1977) *Family development*, Philadelphia, PA: Lippincott.

Egeland, B. and Farber, E. A. (1984) "Infant–mother attachment: Factors related to its development and change over time" *Child Development* 55, 753–71.

Eiser, C. (1990) *Chronic childhood disease*, Cambridge, MA: Cambridge University Press.

Eissler, K. R. (1958) "Notes on problems of technique in the psychoanalytic treatment of adolescents" *The Psychoanalytic Study of the Child* 13, 223–54.

—— (1966) "Bemerkungen zur Technik der psychoanalytischen Behandlung Jugendlicher nebst einigen Bemerkungen zur Perversion" *Psyche* 20, 837–72.

Elder, G., Nguyen, T., and Caspi, A. (1985) "Linking family hardship to children's lives" *Child Development* 56, 361–75.

Elkind, D. (1967) "Egocentrism in adolescence" *Child Development* 38, 1025–34.

Emihovich, C. A., Gaier, E. L., and Cronin, N. C. (1984) "Sex-role expectation changes by fathers for their sons" *Sex Roles* 11, 861–8.

Enos, C. and Enos, S. F. (1985) "The men in your life" *Ladies Home Journal* March, 99–101, 180–3.

Erikson, E. H. (1968) *Identity, youth and crisis*, New York: Norton.

Esman, A. H. (1985) "Discussion: Paternal hostility and paternal ambivalence" *The Psychoanalytic Study of the Child* 40.

Fagot, B. I. (1978) "The influence of sex of child on parental reaction to toddler children" *Child Development* 49, 459–65.

Faller, K. C. (1990) "Sexual abuse by paternal caretakers: A comparison of abusers who are biological fathers in intact families, stepfathers, and noncustodial fathers" in A. L. Horton, B. L. Johnson, L. M. Roundy, and D. Williams (eds) *The incest perpetrator*, Newbury Park, CA: Sage.

Farrington, D. F. (1995) "The development of offending and antisocial behaviour from childhood, key findings from the Cambridge Study in Delinquent Development" *Journal of Child Psychology and Psychiatry* 360, 929–64.

Fein, R. A. (1978) "Considerations of men's experience and the birth of a first child" in W. Miller and L. Newman (eds) *The first child and the family formation*, Chapel Hill, NC: Carolina Population Studies.

Feldman, S. S. and Quatman, T. (1988) "Factors influencing age expectations for adolescent autonomy: A study of early adolescents and parents" *Journal of Early Adolescence* 8, 325–43.

Feldman, S. S. and Wood, D. N. (1994) "Parents' expectations for preadolescent sons' behavioral autonomy: A longitudinal study of correlates and outcomes" *Journal of Research on Adolescence* 4, 45–70.

Fend, H. (1990) "Ego strength development and patterns of social relationships" in H. Bosma and S. Jackson (eds) *Coping and self-concept in adolescence*, Berlin: Springer Verlag.

Ferri, E. (1984) *Stepchildren: A national study*, Berkshire, England: NFER-Nelson Publishing.

Feshbach, S. (1980) "Child abuse and the dynamics of human aggression and violence" in J. Gerbner, C. J. Ross, and E. Zigler (eds) *Child abuse: An agenda for action*, New York: Oxford University Press.

Fesler, B. (1985) "Feeling like a stranger in a stepfamily" *Stepping Forward* 8, 1: 6 (Publication of Stepfamily Association California Division).

Fine, M. A., Voydanoff, P., and Donelly, B. W. (1993) "Relations between parental control and warmth and child well-being in stepfamilies" *Journal of Family Psychology* 7, 222–32.

Fine, R. A. (1976) "Men's entrance to parenthood" *Family Coordinator* 25, 341–8.

Finkelhor, D. (1979) *Sexually victimized children*, New York: The Free Press.

Flannery, D. J., Montemayor, R., Eberly, M. B., and Potter, P. (1990) "Adolescent helpfulness toward mothers and fathers" paper presented at the Fourth Biennial Meeting of the Society for Research on Adolescence (March), Washington, DC.

Forehand, R. and Smith, K. A. (1986) "Who depresses whom? A look at the relationship of adolescent mood to maternal and paternal mood" *Child Study Journal* 16, 19–23.

Forehead, R. and Nousiainen, S. (1993) "Maternal and paternal parenting: Critical dimensions in adolescent functioning" *Journal of Family Psychology* 7, 213–21.

Fox, R. (1982) "Les conditions de l'évolution sexuelle" *Communications, Sexualités Accidentales* 35, 2–13.

Freedman, J. L. (1984) "Effects of television on aggressiveness" *Psychological Bulletin* 96, 227–46.

Freedman, R. (1989) *Die Opfer der Venus*, Zurich: Kreuz.

French, A. (1977) *Disturbed children and their families: Innovations in evaluation and treatment*, New York: Human Sciences Press.

Freud, A. (1958) "Adolescence" *The Psychoanalytic Study of the Child* 13, 255–78.

Freud, S. (1905/1952) "Drei Abhandlungen zur Sexualtheorie" in A. Freud, E. Bibring, W. Hoffer, E. Kris, and O. Isakower (eds) *Sigmund Freud, Gesammelte Werke* (Vol. XV: 27–145), London: Imago.

—— (1909/1952) "Der Familienroman der Neurotiker" in A. Freud, E. Bibring, W. Hoffer, E. Kris, and O. Isakower (eds) *Sigmund Freud, Gesammelte Werke* (Vol. VII: 228–31), London: Imago.

—— (1914/1952) "Zur Einführung des Narzissmus" in A. Freud, E. Bibring, W. Hoffer, E. Kris, and O. Isakower (eds) *Sigmund Freud, Gesammelte Werke* (Vol. X: 137–70), London: Imago.

—— (1930/1958) *Civilization and its discontents*, Standard Edition, 21: 59–145, London: Hogarth Press.

—— (1933/1952) "Die Weiblichkeit" in A. Freud, E. Bibring, W. Hoffer, E. Kris, and O. Isakower (eds) *Sigmund Freud, Gesammelte Werke* (Vol. XV: 119–45), London: Imago.

—— (1937/1952) "Konstruktionen in der Analyse" in A. Freud, E. Bibring, W. Hoffer, E. Kris, and O. Isakower (eds) *Sigmund Freud, Gesammelte Werke* (Vol. XVI: 351–92), London: Imago.

—— (1942) *Die Traumdeutung*, Frankfurt a.M.: Fischer.

Friedrich-Cofer, L. and Huston, A. C. (1986) "Television violence and aggression: The debate continues" *Psychological Bulletin* 100, 364–71.

Fullinwider-Bush, N. and Jacobvitz, D. B. (1993) "The transition to young adulthood: Generational boundary dissolution and female identity development" *Family Process* 32, 87–103.

Furniss, T. (1991) *The multiprofessional handbook of sexual abuse*, London: Routledge.

Furstenberg, F. F. (1983) "Marital disruption and childcare" invited talk, Catholic University, Washington, DC.

—— (1987) "The new extended family: The experience of parents and children after remarriage" in K. Pasley and M. Ihinger-Tallman (eds) *Remarriage and step-parenting: Current research and theory* (70–92), New York: Guilford Press.

Furstenberg, F. F. and Nord, C. W. (1985) "Parenting apart: Patterns of childrearing after marital disruption" *Journal of Marriage and the Family* 47, 4: 893–904.

Furstenberg, F. F. and Spanier, G. B. (1984) *Recycling the family: Remarriage after divorce*, Beverly Hills, CA: Sage Publications.

Furstenberg, F. F. Jr, Nord, C. W., Peterson, J. L., and Zill, N. (1983) "The life course of children of divorce: Marital disruption and parental contact" *American Sociological Review* 48, 656–68.

Gaddis, A. and Brooks-Gunn, J. (1985) "The male experience of pubertal change" *Journal of Youth and Adolescence* 14, 61–9.

Gallop, J. (1989) "The father's seduction" in L. E. Boose and B. S. Flowers (eds) *Daughters and fathers*, Baltimore, MD: The Johns Hopkins University Press.

Ganong, L. H. and Coleman, M. (1984) "The effects of remarriage on children: A review of the empirical literature" *Family Relations* 33, 389–408.

Garfinkel, P. E., Garner, D. M., Rose, J., Darby, P. L., Brandes, J. S., O'Hanlon, J., and Walsh, N. (1983) "A comparison of characteristics in the families of patients with anorexia nervosa and normal controls" *Psychological Medicine* 13, 821–8.

Gecas, V. and Schwalbe, M. L. (1986) "Parental behavior and adolescent self-esteem" *Journal of Marriage and the Family* 48, 37–46.

Gelinas, D. J. (1990) "Unexpected resources in treating incest families" in M. H. Karpel (ed.) *Family resources: The hidden partner in family therapy*, New York: Guilford.

Geller, M. and Ford-Somma, L. (1984). *Violent homes, violent children. A study of violence in the families of juvenile offenders* (New Jersey State Department of Corrections, Trenton, Division of Juvenile Services). Report prepared for the National Center on Child Abuse and Neglect, Department of Health and Human Services, Washington, DC.

Gerson, M. J. (1989) "Tomorrow's fathers: The anticipation of fatherhood" in S. H. Cath, A. Gurwitt, and L. Gunsberg (eds) *Fathers and their families*, Hillsdale, NJ: The Analytic Press.

Gilbert, S. M. (1989) "Life's empty pack: Notes toward a literary daughteronomy" in L. E. Boose and B. S. Flowers (eds) *Daughters and fathers*, Baltimore, MD: The Johns Hopkins University Press.

Giles-Sims, J. (1984) "The step-parent role: Expectations, behavior sanctions" *Journal of Family Issues* 5, 116–30.

—— (1987) "Social exchange in remarried families" in K. Pasley and M. Ihinger-Tallman (eds) *Remarriage and step-parenting: Current research and theory* (196–204), New York: Guilford Press.

Gilligan, C. (1982) *In a different voice*, Cambridge, MA: Harvard University Press.

Gilmore, D. D. (1990) "Men and women in southern Spain: 'Domestic power' revisited" *American Anthropologist* 92, 953–70.

Glick, P. C. and Lin, S.-L. (1986) "Recent changes in divorce and remarriage" *Journal of Marriage and the Family* 48, 737–47.

Gloger-Tipplet (1986) "Der Übergang zur Elternschaft. Eine Entwicklungspsychologie Analyse" *Zeitschrift für Entwicklungspsychologie und Pädagogische Psychologie* 17, 53–92.

Goldberg, S., Marcovitch, S., MacGregor, D., and Lojkasek, M. (1986) "Family responses to developmentally delayed preschoolers: Etiology and the father's role" *American Journal of Mental Deficiency* 90, 610–17.

Goldner, V. (1982) "Remarriage family: Structure, system, future" in J. C.

Hansen and L. Messinger (eds) *Therapy with remarriage families* (126–41), Rockville, MD: Aspen Publications.

Goldstein, J. (1986) *Aggression and crimes of violence*, New York: Oxford University Press.

Goodall, J. (1984) "The nature of the mother–child bond and the influence of the family on the social development of free-living chimpanzees" in N. Kobayashi and T. Brazelton (eds) *The growing child in family and society*, Tokyo: Tokyo University Press.

—— (1986) *The chimpanzees of Gombe patterns of behavior*, Cambridge, MA: The Belknap Press of the Harvard University Press.

Greenacre, P. (1966) "Problems of overidealization of the analyst and of analysis" *Psychoanalytic Study of the Child* 21, 193–213.

Greenbaum, C. W. and Landau, R. (1982) "The infant's exposure to talk by familial people: Mothers, fathers and siblings in different environments" in M. Lewis and L. Rosenblum (eds) *The social network of the developing infant*, New York: Plenum.

Greenberg, M. T., Siegel, J. M., and Leitch, C. J. (1983) "The nature and importance of attachment relationships to parents and peers during adolescence" *Journal of Youth and Adolescence* 12, 373–86.

Greenberger, E. and O'Neil, R. (1990) "Parents' concerns about the child's development: Implications for fathers' and mothers' well-being and attitudes toward work" *Journal of Marriage and the Family* 56, 621–35.

Grey, M. J., Genel, M., and Tamborlane, W. V. (1980) "Psychosocial adjustment of latency-aged diabetics: Determinants and relationship to control" *Pediatrics* 65, 69–73.

Grossman, S. K. (1989) "Separate and together: Men's autonomy and affiliation in the transition to parenthood" in P. W. Berman and F. A. Pedersen (eds) *Men's transition to parenthood*, Hillsdale, NJ: Erlbaum.

Grotevant, H. D. and Adams, G. R. (1984) "Development of the objective measure to assess ego identity in adolescence: Validation and replication" *Journal of Youth and Adolescence* 13, 419–38.

Grotevant, H. D. and Cooper, C. R. (1985) "Patterns of interaction in family relationships and the development of identity exploration in adolescence" *Child Development* 56, 415–28.

—— (1986) "Individuation in family relationship: A perspective on individual differences in the development of identity and role taking in adolescence" *Human Development* 29, 82–100.

Groth, A. N. (1982) "The incest offender" in S. Sgroi (ed.) *Handbook of clinical intervention in child sexual abuse*, Lexington, MA: Heath.

Gunsberg, L. (1989) "Issues in fathering: how they are reflected in the psychoanalytic treatment of men" in S. H. Cath, A. Gurwitt, and L. Gunsberg (eds) *Fathers and their families*, Hillsdale, NJ: The Analytic Press.

Gyolay, J. E. (1978) *The dying child*, New York: McGraw-Hill.

Hanson, C. L., Henggeler, S. W., and Burghen, G. A. (1987) "Social competence and parental support as mediators of the link between stress and metabolic control in adolescents with insulin dependent diabetes Mellitus" *Journal of Consulting and Clinical Psychology* 55, 529–33.

Hanson, S. M. (1988) "Divorced fathers with custody" in P. Bronstein and C. P. Cowan (eds) *Fatherhood today: Men's changing role in the family*, New York: Wiley.

Harris, I. D. and Howard, K. I. (1984) "On psychological resemblance: A questionnaire study of high school students" *Psychiatry* 47, 125–34.

Hartstone, E. and Hansen, K. V. (1984) "The violent juvenile offender: An empirical portrait" in R. A. Mathias (ed.) *Violent juvenile offenders. An anthology* (83–112), San Francisco, CA: National Council on Crime and Delinquency.

Hauser, S. T. (1991) *Adolescents and their families*, New York: Free Press.

Hauser, S. T., Book, B. K., Houlinhan, J., Powers, S., Weiss-Perry, B., Follansbee, D., Jacobson, A. M., and Noam, G. (1987) "Sex differences within the family: Studies of adolescent and family interaction" *Journal of Youth and Adolescence* 16, 199–213.

Hauser, S. T., Jacobson, A. M., Noam, G., and Powers, S. (1983) "Ego-development and self-image complexity in early adolescence. Personality studies of psychiatric and diabetic patients" *Archives of General Psychiatry* 40, 325–52.

Hauser, S. T., Jacobson, A. M., Weiss-Perry, B., Vieyra, M. A., Rufo, P., Spetter, L., Wertlieb, D., Wolfsdorf, J., and Herskowitz, R. D. (1988) *Family coping strategies: A new approach to assessment*, Harvard Medical School, Massachusetts Mental Health Center and Joslin Diabetes Center.

Hauser, S. T., Liebman, A., Houlihan, J., Powers, S. Jacobson, A. M., Noam, G., Weiss, B., and Follansbee, D. (1985) "Family contexts of pubertal timing" *Journal of Youth and Adolescence* 14, 317–37.

Hauser, S. T., Powers, S., Noam, G., Jacobson, A. M., Weiss, B., and Follansbee, D. (1984) "Familial context of adolescent ego development" *Child Development* 55, 195–213.

Havinghurst, R. J. (1972) *Developmental tasks and education*, New York: Longman, Green & Co.

Heath, D. H. and Heath, H. E. (1991) *Fulfilling lives: Pathways to maturity and competence*, San Francisco, CA: Jossey-Bass.

Heilbrun, A. B. (1976) "Identification with the father and sex-role development of the daughter" *Family Coordinator* 25, 411–16.

Henggeler, S. W., Edwards, J., and Borduin, C. M. (1987) "The family relations of female juvenile delinquents" *Journal of Abnormal Child Psychology* 15, 199–209.

Herrenkohl, F. C., Herrenkohl, R. C., and Toedter, L. J. (1983) "Perspectives on the intergenerational transmission of abuse" in D. Finkelhor, R. J. Gelles, G. T. Hotaling, and M. A. Straus (eds) *The dark side of families* (305–16), Beverly Hills, CA: Sage.

Herzbrun, M. B. (1993) "Father–adolescent consensus in the Jewish community: A preliminary report" *Journal for the Scientific Study of Religion* 32, 163–8.

Herzog, J. M. (1982a) "On father hunger: The father's role in the modulation of aggressive drive and fantasy" in S. H. Cath, A. Gurwitt, and J. M. Ross (eds) *Father and child*, Boston, MA: Little, Brown.

—— (1982b) "Patterns of expectant fatherhood" in S. H. Cath, A. Gurwitt, and J. M. Ross (eds) *Father and child*, Boston, MA: Little, Brown.

Hess, R. D. and Camera, K. A. (1979) "Post-divorce family relationships as mediating factors in the consequences of divorce for children" *Journal of Social Issues* 35, 79–96.

Hetherington, E. M. (1972) "Effects of father's absence on personality development in adolescent daughters" *Developmental Psychology* 73, 313–26.

—— (1979) "Divorce – a child's perspective" *American Psychologist* 34, 851–8.

—— (1987) "Family relations six years after divorce" in K. Pasley and M. Ihinger-Tallman (eds) *Remarriage and step-parenting: Current research and theory* (185–205), New York: Guilford Press.

Hetherington, E. M. and Clingempeel, W. G. (1992) "Coping with marital transitions" *Monographs of the Society for Research in Child Development*, Chicago: University of Chicago Press.

Hetherington, E. M., Cox, M., and Cox, R. (1976) "Divorced fathers" *Family Coordinator* 25, 415–28.

—— (1982) "Effects of divorce on parents and children" in M. E. Lamb (ed.) *Non-traditional families: Parenting and child development* (233–88), Hillsdale, NJ: Erlbaum.

Hetherington, E. M., Stanley-Hagan, M., and Anderson, E. R. (1989) "Marital transitions: A child's perspective" *American Psychologist* 44, 303–12.

Hewlett, B. (1987) "Intimate fathers: Patterns of paternal holding among Aka pygmies", in M. Lamb (ed.) *The father's role, cross-cultural perspectives*, Hillsdale, NJ: Erlbaum.

Hill, J. P. (1980) *Understanding early adolescence: A framework*, Chapel Hill, NC: Center for Early Adolescence.

Hill, J. P. and Holmbeck, G. N. (1986) "Attachment and autonomy during adolescence" *Annals of Child Development* 3, 145–89.

Hinde, R. A. (1976) "On describing relationships" *Journal of Child Psychology and Psychiatry and Related Disciplines* 17, 1–19.

Hochchild, A. A. (1979) "Emotion work, feeling rules, and social satisfaction" *American Journal of Sociology* 85, 551–75.

Holahan, C. J. and Moos, R. H. (1987) "Risk, resistance, and psychological distress: A longitudinal analysis with adults and children" *Journal of Abnormal Psychology* 96, 3–13.

Holladay, B. (1984) "Challenges of rearing a chronically ill child. Caring and coping" *Nursing Clinics of North America* 19, 361–8.

Holmbeck, G. N. (1992) "Autonomy and psychological adjustment in adolescents with and without spina bifida" paper presented at the Fourth Biennial Meeting of the Society for Research on Adolescence (March), Washington, DC.

Holmbeck, G. N. and Hill, J. P. (1988) "Storm and stress beliefs about adolescence: Prevalence, self-reported antecedents, and effects of an undergraduate course" *Journal of Youth and Adolescence* 17, 285–306.

Humphrey, L. L. (1986) "Structural analysis of parent–child relationships in eating disorders" *Journal of Abnormal Psychology* 95, 395–402.

—— (1989) "Observed family interactions among subtypes of eating disorders using structural analysis of social behavior" *Journal of Consulting and Clinical Psychology* 57, 206–14.

Hunter, F. T. and Youniss, J. (1982) "Changes in functions of three relations in adolescence" *Developmental Psychology* 18, 806–11.

Hwang, C. P. (1986) "Behavior of Swedish primary and secondary caretaking fathers in relation to mother's presence" *Developmental Psychology* 22, 749–51.

Ihinger-Tallman, M. (1987) "Sibling and step-sibling bonding in stepfamilies" in K. Pasley and M. Ihinger-Tallman (eds) *Remarriage and step-parenting: Current research and theory* (54–73), New York: Guilford Press.

Inoff-Germain, G., Arnold, G. S., Nottelmann, E. D., Susman, E. J., Cutler, C. B., and Chrousos, G. P. (1988) "Relations between hormone levels and observational measures of aggressive behavior of young adolescents in family interaction" *Developmental Psychology* 24, 129–39.

Isaacs, M. B. (1982) "Facilitating family restructuring and linkage" in J. C. Hansen and L. Messinger (eds) *Therapy with remarriage families* (29–40), Rockville, MD: Aspen Publications.

Israel, L. (1983) *Die unerhörte Botschaft der Hysterie*, Munich: Reinhardt.

Israels, H. (1989) *Schreber: Father and son*, Madison, WI: International University Press.

Jacklin, C. N., DiPietro, J. A., and Maccoby, E. E. (1984) "Sex-typing behavior and sex-typing pressure in child/parent interaction" *Archives of Sexual Behavior* 13, 413–25.

Jacobson, D. S. (1987) "Family type, visiting patterns, and children's behavior in the stepfamily: A linked family system" in K. Pasley and M. Ihinger-Tallman (eds) *Remarriage and step-parenting: Current research and theory* (74–90), New York: Guilford Press.

Jahoda, M. (1982) *Employment and unemployment*, Cambridge: Cambridge University Press.

James, K. and MacKinnon, L. (1990) "The 'incestuous family' revisited: A critical analysis of family therapy myth" *Journal of Marital and Family Therapy* 16, 71–88.

Johnson, A. M. (1949) "Sanctions for superego lucane of adolescence" in K. R. Eissler (ed.) *Searchlights on delinquency*, New York: International University Press.

Johnson, B. M. and Collins, W. A. (1988) "Perceived maturity as a function of appearance cues in early adolescence: Ratings by unacquainted adults, parents, and teachers" *Journal of Early Adolescence* 8, 357–72.

Johnston, R. E. (1987) "Mother's versus father's role in causing delinquency" *Adolescence* 86, 305–15.

Jouriles, E. N., Barling, J., and O'Leary, K. D. (1987) "Predicting child behavior problems in maritally violent families" *Journal of Abnormal Child Psychology* 15, 165–73.

Kafka, F. (1919/1975) *Brief an den Vater*, Frankfurt a.M.: Fischer.

Kaplan, K., Schwartz, L., and Markus-Kaplan, M. (1984) "Oedipus and Isaac: Sons in Greek and Hebrew families" *Journal of Psychology and Judaism* 8, 157–80.

Kazak, A. E., Reber, N., and Switzer, L. (1988) "Childhood chronic disease and family functioning: A study of phenylketonuria" *Pediatrics* 81, 224–30.

Kestenbaum, C. J. (1983) "Fathers and daughters: The father's contribution to the feminine identification in girls as depicted in fairy tales and myths" *American Journal of Psychoanalysis* 43, 119–28.

Kierkegaard, S. (1847/1954) *Fear and trembling and the sickness unto death*, New York: Doubleday Anchor Books.

Kinsey, A. C., Pomeroy, W. B., Martin, C. E., and Gebhart, R. L. (1953) *Sexual behavior in the human female*, Philadelphia, PA: Saunders.

Klein, M. (1946) *The psychoanalysis of children*, London: Hogarth Press.

—— (1975) *The writings of Melanie Klein, Vol. I*, London: Hogarth.

Kohut, H. (1977) *The restoration of the self*, New York: International Universities Press.

Komarovsky, M. (1967) *Blue-collar marriage*, New York: Random House, Vintage Books.

Kotelchuk, M. (1981) "The infant's relationship to the father: Experimental evidence" in M. E. Lamb (ed.) *The role of the father in child development*, New York: Wiley.

Kraemer, S. (1991) "The origins of fatherhood: An ancient family process" *Family Process* 30, 377–92.

Kratcoski, P. C. (1982) "Child abuse and violence against the family" *Child Welfare* 61, 435–44.

Krol, J. (1983) "Young people's image of father and its influence on their image of God" *Roczniki Filozoficzne Psychologia* 30, 73–103.

Kroupa, S. E. (1988) "Perceived parental acceptance and female juvenile delinquency" *Adolescence* 89, 171–85.

Kruk, E. (1991) "Discontinuity between pre- and post-divorce father–child relationship: New evidence regarding paternal disengagement" *Journal of Divorce and Remarriage* 16, 195–277.

Kumin, I. M. (1978) "Emptiness and its relation to schizoid ego structure" *International Review of Psycho-Analysis* 5, 207–16.

LaBarbara, J. D. (1984) "Seductive father–daughter relationships and sex roles in women" *Sex Roles* 11, 941–51.

Lacan, J. (1977) *Ecrits: A selection*, New York: Norwood.

Lamb, M. E. (1975) "Fathers: Forgotten contributors to child development" *Human Development* 18, 245–66.

—— (1980) "The development of parent–infant attachment in the first years of life" in F. A. Pederson (ed.) *The father–infant relationship*, New York: Prager.

—— (1981) "Fathers and children's development: An integrative overview" in M. E. Lamb (ed.) *The role of the father in child development*, New York: Wiley.

—— (1987) *The father's role: Cross-cultural perspectives*, New York: Wiley.

Lamb, M. E. and Oppenheim, D. (1989) "Fatherhood and father–child relationships: Five years of research" in S. H. Cath, A. Gurwitt, and L. Gunsberg (eds) *Fathers and their families*, Hillsdale, NJ: The Analytic Press.

Lamb, M. E., Owen, M. T., and Chase-Lansdale, E. (1974) "The father–daughter relationship: Past, present, future" in C. B. Kopp and M. Kirkpatrick (eds) *Becoming female*, New York: Plenum.

Lamb, M. E., Hwang, C.·R., Brookstein, F. L., Bromberg, A., Hult, G., and Frodi, M. (1988) "Determinants of social competence in Swedish preschoolers" *Developmental Psychology* 24, 58–70.

Lang, D., Pampenfuhs, R., and Walter, J. (1976) "Delinquent females' perceptions of their fathers" *The Family Coordinator* 25, 146–53.

Langan, P. A. and Innes, C. A. (1985) *The risk of violent crime*, Bureau of Justice Statistics Special Report, NCJ-97119, Washington, DC: US Government Printing Office.

Lansky, M. R. (1989) "The paternal imago" in S. H. Cath, A. Gurwitt, and L. Gunsberg (eds) *Fathers and their families*, Hillsdale, NJ: The Analytic Press.

Laplanche, J. (1975) *Hölderlin oder die Suche nach dem Vater*, Stuttgart: Frommann-Holzboog.

Lapsley, D. K., Harwell, M. R., Olson, L. M., Flannery, D., and Quintana, S. M. (1984) "Moral judgment, personality, and attitude to authority in early and late adolescence" *Journal of Youth and Adolescence* 13, 527–42.

Larson, H. and Richards, M. H. (1991) "Daily companionship in late childhood and early adolescence" *Child Development* 62, 284–300.

Lasser, V. and Snarey, J. (1989) "Ego development and perceptions of parent behavior in adolescent girls: A qualitative study of the transition from high school to college" *Journal of Adolescent Research* 4, 355–80.

Laufer, M. and Laufer, M. E. (1984) *Adolescence and developmental breakdown*, New Haven, CT: Yale University Press.

Laursen, B. and Collins, W. A. (1994) "Interpersonal conflict during adolescence" *Psychological Bulletin* 115, 197–209.

Lavang, C. A. (1988) "Interactional communication patterns in father-daughter incest patterns" *Journal of Psychology and Human Sexuality* 1, 53–68.

Lavee, Y., McCubbin, H. I., and Olson, D. H. (1987) "The effect of stressful life events and transitions on family functioning and well-being" *Journal of Marriage and the Family* 49, 857–73.

Lazar, R. A. (1988) "Vorläufer der Triangulierung" *Forum der Psychoanalyse* 4, 28–39.

LeCroy, C. W. (1988) "Parent–adolescent intimacy: Impact on adolescent functioning" *Adolescence* 23, 137–47.

Lee, C. (1991) "Parenting as a discipleship" *Journal of Theology and Psychology* 19, 268–77.

Lepontois, J. (1975) "Adolescents with sickle-cell anemia deal with life and death" *Social Work in Health Care* 1, 71–80.

Lerner, R. (1985) "Adolescent maturational changes and psychosocial development: A dynamic international perspective" *Journal of Youth and Adolescence* 14, 355–72.

Lévi-Strauss, C. (1970) *The elementary structures of kinship*, London: Social Science Paperbacks.

Lewis, J. M. (1986) "Family structure and stress" *Family Process* 25, 235–47.

Lewis, R. A. (1986) "Men's changing roles in marriage and the family" in R. A. Lewis and M. B. Sussman (eds) *Men's changing roles in the family*, New York: Haworth Press.

Lidz, T. (1968) *The person: His development throughout the life cycle*, New York: Basic Books.

—— (1980) "The family and the development of the individual" in C. K. Hofling and J. M. Lewis (eds) *The family evolution and treatment*, New York: Brunner/Mazel.

Lidz, T., Cornelison, A., Fleck, S., and Terry, D. (1957) "Intrafamilial environment of the schizophrenic patient. I. The father" *Psychiatry* 20, 329–42.

Loeb, L. (1986) "Fathers and sons: Some effects of prolonged custody litigation" *Bulletin of the American Academy of Psychiatry and the Law* 14, 177–83.

Loewald, H. W. (1979) "The waning of the Oedipus complex" *Journal of the American Psychoanalytic Association* 27, 751–6.

Loewen, J. W. (1988) "Visitation fatherhood" in P. Bronstein and C. P. Cowan (eds) *Fatherhood today: Men's changing role in the family* (28–42), New York: Wiley.

Lorenz, K. (1966) *On aggression*, New York: Harcourt, Brace, Jovanovich, Inc.

Lozzof, M. (1974) "Fathers and autonomy in women" in R. Knudsen (ed.) *Women and success*, New York: Morrow.

Lutz, P. (1983) "The stepfamily: An adolescent perspective" *Family Relations* 32, 367–75.

Lytton, H. and Romney, D. M. (1991) "Parents' differential socialization of boys and girls: A meta-analysis" *Psychological Bulletin* 109, 267–96.

Maccoby, E. E. and Jacklin, C. N. (1974) *The psychology of sex differences*, Stanford, CA: Stanford University Press.

McBride, B. A. (1990) "The effects of parent education/play group program on father involvement in child rearing" *Family Relations* 39, 250–6.

McCall, G. J. and Shields, N. (1986) "Social and structural factors in family violence" in M. Lystad (ed.) *Violence in the home: Interdisciplinary perspectives* (98–123), New York: Brunner/Mazel.

McCarthy, I. C. and Byrne, N. O. (1988) "Mis-taken love: Conversations on the problem of incest in an Irish context" *Family Process* 27, 181–99.

McDougall, J. (1987) "Ein Körper für zwei" *Forum Psychoanalyse* 3, 265–87.

McGoldrick, M. and Carter, E. A. (1980) "Forming a remarried family" in E. A. Carter and M. McGoldrick (eds) *The family life cycle: A framework for family therapy* (201–18), New York: Gardner Press.

McGuire, J. (1991) "Sons and daughters" in A. Phoenix, A. Woollet, and E. Lloyd (eds) *Motherhood – Meanings, practices and ideologies*, London: Sage.

Mackey, W. C. (1985) "A cross-cultural perspective on perceptions of paternalistic deficiencies in the US: The myth of the derelict daddy" *Sex Roles* 12, 509–33.

McLanahan, S. S. (1983) "Family structure and stress: A longitudinal comparison of two-parent and female headed families" *Journal of Marriage and the Family* 46, 347–57.

Madsen, W. (1973) *The Mexican-American of South Texas*, New York: Holt, Rinehart & Winston.

Mahler, M. (1979) *Selected writings*, New York: Aronson.

Mahler, M. S., Pine, F., and Bergman, A. (1975) *The psychological birth of the human infant*, New York: Basic Books.

Malinowski, S. (1927) *Sex and repression in the savage society*, London: Routledge & Kegan Paul.

Malson, L., Itard, J., and Mannoni, O. (1972) *Die wilden Kinder*, Frankfurt a.M.: Suhrkamp.

Mandelbaum, A. (1988) "Adolescents and their aging parents" *Bulletin of the Menninger Clinic* 52, 246–58.

Marcia, J. E. (1966) "Development and validation of ego identity status" *Journal of Personality and Social Psychology* 3, 551–8.

Mead, M. (1970) "Aftermath" in P. Bohannon (ed.) *Divorce and after* (21–40), Garden City, NY: Doubleday.

Meiselman, K. C. (1978) *Incest*, San Francisco, CA: Jossey-Bass.

Messinger, L., Walker, K. N., and Freeman, S. J. (1978) "Preparation for remarriage following divorce. The use of group techniques" *American Journal of Orthopsychiatry* 78, 263–72.

Millen, L. and Roll, S. (1977) "Relationships between sons' feelings of being understood by their fathers and measures of sons' psychological functioning" *Journal of Genetic Psychology* 130, 19–25.

Mills, D. M. (1984) "A model for stepfamily development" *Family Relations* 33, 365–72.

Minde, K. (1978) "Coping styles of 34 adolescents with cerebral palsy" *American Journal of Psychiatry* 135, 1344–9.

Minuchin, S. (1974) *Families and family therapy*, Cambridge, MA: Harvard University Press.

—— (1984) *Family Kaleidoscope*, Cambridge, MA: Harvard University Press.

Minuchin, S., Montalvo, B., Guerney, B., Rosman, B., and Schumer, F. (1967) *Families of the slums*, New York: Basic Books.

Minuchin, S., Rosman, B., and Baker, L. (1978) *Psychosomatic families: Anorexia nervosa in context*, Cambridge, MA: Harvard University Press.

Mitchell, J., McCauley, E., Burke, P., Calderon, R., and Schloredt, K. (1989) "Psychopathology in parents of depressed children and adolescents" *Journal of the American Academy of Child and Adolescent Psychiatry* 28, 352–7.

Mitcherlich, A. (1969) *Die vaterlose Gesellschaft* Frankfurt: Suhrkamp.

Molnar, G. and Cameron, P. (1975) "Incest syndromes: Observations in a general hospital psychiatric unit" *Canadian Psychiatric Association Journal* 20, 373–7.

Monreau, C. (1989) "The influence of the father–daughter relation on the self-esteem of the adult female" *Canadian Journal of Counselling* 23, 151–65.

Montemayor, R. (1982) "The relationship between parent–adolescent conflict and the amount of time adolescents spend alone and with parents and peers" *Child Development* 53, 1512–19.

—— (1984) "Maternal employment and adolescents' relations with parents, siblings, and peers" *Journal of Youth and Adolescence* 13, 543–57.

Montemayor, R. and Brownlee, J. R. (1987) "Fathers, mothers and adolescents: Gender based differences in parental roles during adolescence" *Journal of Youth and Adolescence* 16, 281–91.

Montemayor, R., McKenry, P. C., and Julian, T. (1993) "Men in midlife and the quality of father–adolescent communication" *New Directions in Child Development* 62, 59–72.

Moorjani, A. (1994) "Fetishism, gender masquerade, and the mother–father fantasy" in J. H. Smith and A. M. Mahfous (eds) *Psychoanalysis, feminism and the future of gender*, Baltimore, MD: The Johns Hopkins University Press.

Moos, R. H. and Moos, B. S. (1981) *Family Environment Scale Manual*, Palo Alto, CA: Consulting Psychologists Press, Inc.

Moss, H. B., Mezzich, A., Yao, J. K., and Galvr, J. (1995) "Aggressivity among sons of substance-abusing fathers. Association with psychiatric disorder in father and son. Paternal personality, pubertal development and socio-economic status" *American Journal of Drug and Alcohol Abuse* 21, 195–208.

Mott, F. L. (1990) "When is a father really gone? Paternal child contact in father-absent homes" *Demography* 27, 499–517.

Mouzakitis, C. M. (1981) "An inquiry into the problem of child abuse and juvenile delinquency" in R. J. Hunner and Y. E. Walker (eds) *Exploring the relationship between child abuse and delinquency* (220–32), Montclair, NJ: Allenheld, Osmun.

Moyer, K. E. (1968) "Kinds of aggression and their physiological basis" *Commun. Behav. Biol. (Part A)*, 2: 425–35.

Munroe, R. L., Munroe, R. H., and Whiting, J. W. M. (1973) "The couvade: A psychological analysis" *Ethos* 1, 30–74.

Musa, K. and Roach, M. (1973) "Adolescent appearance and self-concept" *Adolescence* 8, 385–94.

Nachmani, G. (1992) "The difficult patient or the difficult dyad? On mourning the death of a parent who has not died" *Contemporary Psychoanalysis* 28, 524–51.

Nadler, J. H. (1976) "The psychological stress of the stepmother" unpublished doctoral dissertation, California School of Professional Psychology, Los Angeles, CA.

Napier, A. (1991) "Heroism, men and marriage" *Journal of Marital and Family Therapy* 17, 9–16.

Neapolitan, J. (1981) "Parental influences on aggressive behavior: A social learning approach" *Adolescence* 16, 831–40.

Negron, C. (1988) "Methods of birth control used in father–daughter incest" paper presented at the Western Social Sciences Association (April), Denver, CO.

Neubauer, P. B. (1989) "Fathers as single parents: object relations beyond mother" in S. H. Cath, A. Gurwitt, and L. Gunsberg (eds) *Fathers and their families*, Hillsdale, NJ: The Analytic Press.

Niethammer, C. (1977) *Daughters of the earth. The lives and legends of American Indian women*, New York: Collier.

Noller, P. (1978) "Sex differences in the socialization of affectionate expression" *Developmental Psychology* 14, 317–19.

—— (1980) "Cross-gender affect in two-child families" *Developmental Psychology* 16, 159–60.

Nydegger, C. N. and Mitteness, L. S. (1991) "Fathers and their adult sons and daughters" *Marriage and the Family Review* 16, 249–56.

Ochberg, R. L. (1987) "The male career code and the ideology of role" in H. Brod (ed.) *The making of masculinities*, London: Allen & Unwin.

O'Leary, K. D., Arias, I., Rosenbaum, A., and Barling, J. (1985) "Premarital physical aggression" unpublished manuscript, State University of New York at Stony Brook.

Oliveri, M. E. and Reiss, D. (1987) "Social networks of family members: Distinctive roles of mothers and fathers" *Sex Roles* 17, 719–36.

Olson, D. H. (1988) "Family types, family stress, and the family satisfaction: A family developmental perspective" in C. J. Falicov (ed.) *Family transitions*, New York: Guilford Press.

Olweus, D. (1980) "Familial and temperamental determinants of aggressive behaviour in adolescent boys: A causal analysis" *Developmental Psychology* 16, 644–60.

Orr, D. P., Wellers, S. C., White, B., and Pless, I. B. (1984) "Psychosocial implication of chronic illness in adolescence" *Journal of Pediatrics* 104, 152–7.

Orvaschel, H., Walsh-Allis, G., and Ye, W. (1988) "Psychopathology in children of parents with recurrent depression" *Journal of Abnormal Child Psychology* 16, 17–28.

Osherson, S. (1993) *Wrestling with love. How men struggle with intimacy*, New York: Fawcett Columbine.

Owens, D. J. and Straus, M. A. (1975) "The social structure of violence in childhood and approval of violence as an adult" *Aggressive Behavior* 1, 193–211.

Palkovitz, R. (1984) "Parental attitudes and fathers' interactions with 5-month-old infants" *Developmental Psychology* 20, 1054–60.

Palmeri, S. (1989) "Papi, or the child is father to man" in S. H. Cath, A. Gurwitt, and L. Gunsberg (eds) *Fathers and their families*, Hillsdale, NJ: The Analytic Press.

Papernow, P. (1980) "A phenomenological study of the developmental stages of becoming a step-parent: A Gestalt and family systems approach" *Dissertation Abstracts International* 41, 8B: 3192–3.

Papp, P. (1989) "The godfather" in M. Walters, B. Carter, P. Papp, and O. Silverstein (eds) *The invisible web – gender pattern in family relationships*, New York: Guilford Press.

Parke, R. D. and Sawin, D. B. (1980) "The family in early infancy: Social interactional and longitudinal analyses" in F. A. Pederson (ed.) *The father–infant relationship*, New York: Prager.

Parke, R. D. and Tinsley, B. R. (1981) "The father's role in infancy: Determinants of involvement in caregiving and play" in M. E. Lamb (ed.) *The role of the father in child development*, New York: Wiley.

Parke, R. D., McDonald, K. P., Burks, V. M., Carson, J., Bharnagri, N., Barth, J. M., and Beitel, A. (1989) "Family and peer systems: In search of linkages" in K. Kreppner and R. M. Lerner (eds) *Family system and life span development*, Hillsdale, NJ: Erlbaum.

Parker, H. and Parker, S. (1986) "Father–daughter sexual abuse: An emerging perspective" *American Journal of Orthopsychiatry* 56, 531–49.

Parsons, T. (1954) "The incest taboo in relation to social structure and socialization of the child" *British Journal of Sociology* 5, 101–17.

Parsons, T. and Bales, R. F. (1955) *Family, socialization and interaction process*, Glencoe, IL: Free Press.

Pasley, K. (1987) "Family boundary ambiguity: Perception of adult remarried family members" in K. Pasley and M. Ihinger-Tallman (eds) *Remarriage and step-parenting: Current research and theory* (228–40), New York: Guilford Press.

Pederson, F. A. (1980) "Research issues related to fathers and infants" in F. A. Pederson (ed.) *The father–infant relationship*, New York: Prager.

Pederson, F. A., Zaslow, M. J., Cain, R. L., Suwalsky, J. T. D., and Rabinovich, B. (1987) "Father–infant interaction among men who had contrasting affective responses during early infancy" in P. W. Berman and F. A. Pederson (eds) *Men's transition to parenthood*, Hillsdale, NJ: Erlbaum.

Peterson, J. L. and Zill, N. (1986) "Marital disruption, parent–child relationships, and behavior problems in children" *Journal of Marriage and the Family* 48, 245–307.

Phares, V. (1992) "Where's Poppa?: The relative lack of attention to the role of fathers in child and adolescent psychopathology" *American Psychologist* 47, 656–64.

Phares, V. and Compas, B. E. (1992) "The role of fathers in child and adolescent psychopathology: Make room for daddy" *Psychological Bulletin* 111, 387–412.

Pleck, J. H. (1983) "Husbands' paid work and family roles: Current culture issues" in H. Lopata and J. H. Pleck (eds) *Research in the interweave of social roles: Vol. 3, Jobs and families*, Greenwich, CT: JAI Press.

Poluda-Korte, E. (1992) "Identität im Fluss. Zur Psychoanalyse weiblicher Adoleszenz im Spiegel des Mentruationserlebens" in K. Flaake and V. King (eds) *Weibliche Adoleszenz* (147–65), Frankfurt a.m.: Campus.

Power, T. G. and Shanks, J. A. (1988) "Parents as socializers: Maternal and paternal views" *Journal of Youth and Adolescence* 18, 203–20.

Rauste-von-Right, M. (1989) "Body image satisfaction in adolescent girls and boys: A longitudinal study" *Journal of Youth and Adolescence* 18, 71–83.

Reiss, D. (1981) *The family's construction of reality*, Cambridge, MA: Harvard University Press.

Richardson, R. A., Galambos, N. L., Schulenberg, J. E., and Peterson, A. C. (1984) "Young adolescents' perceptions of the family environment" *Journal of Early Adolescence* 4, 131–53.

Richardson, W. J. (1983) "Lacan and the subject of psychoanalysis" in J. H. Smith and W. Kerrigan (eds) *Psychiatry and the humanities*. Vol. VI, *Interpreting Lacan*, New Haven, CT: Yale University Press.

Riege, M. G. (1972) "Parental affection and juvenile delinquency in girls" *British Journal of Criminology* 12, 55–73.

Ritchie, K. (1981) "Research note: Interactions in the families of epileptic children" *Journal of Child Psychology and Psychiatry and Allied Disciplines* 22, 65–71.

Ritvo, S. (1975) "Female psychology and development in adolescence" paper presented at the Meeting of the American Psychoanalytic Association (May), Beverly Hills, CA.

Roberts, C. L. and Zuengler, K. L. (1985) "The parental transition and beyond" in S. Hanson and F. W. Bozett (eds) *Dimensions of fatherhood*. Beverly Hills, CA: Sage.

Roberts, G., Block, J. H., and Block, J. (1984) "Continuity and change in parents' child rearing practices" *Child Development* 55, 586–97.

Roll, S. and Abel, T. (1988) "Variations in the secondary themes of the oedipal legend" *Journal of the American Academy of Psychoanalysis* 16, 537–47.

Rosenthal, K. M. and Keshet, H. F. (1980) *Fathers without partners*, Totowa, NJ: Rowman & Allanheld.

Ross, J. M. (1982) "Oedipus revisited: Laius and the 'Laius complex'" *The Psychoanalytic Study of the Child* 37, 169–200.

—— (1985) "The darker side of fatherhood: Clinical and developmental ramifications of the 'Laius motif'" *The Psychoanalytic Study of the Child* 40, 117–44.

Rubin, J. Z., Provenzano, F. J., and Luria, Z. (1974) "The eye of the beholder: Parents' views on sex of newborns" *American Journal of Orthopsychiatry* 44, 512–19.

Russell, D. E. H. (1984) *Sexual exploitation: Rape, child sexual abuse, and sexual harassment*, Beverly Hills, CA: Sage Publications.

Russell, G. (1978) "The father's role and its relation to masculinity, family and androgyny" *Child Development* 49, 1174–81.

—— (1983) *The changing role of fathers*, Brisbane: University of Brisbane Press.

Russell, G. and Russell, A. (1987) "Mother–child and father–child relationships in middle childhood" *Child Development* 58, 1573–85.

Rutter, M. (1981) *Maternal Deprivation Reassessed*, New York: Penguin.

Sager, C. J., Brown, H. S., Crohn, H., Engel, T., Rodstein, E., and Walker, L. (1983) *Treating the remarried family*, New York: Brunner/Mazel.

Sagi, A. (1982) "Antecedents and consequences of various degrees of parental involvement in childrearing: the Israeli project" in M. Lamb (ed.) *Nontraditional families: Parenting and child development*, Hillsdale, NJ: Erlbaum.

Salt, R. E. (1991) "Affectionate touch between fathers and preadolescent sons" *Journal of Marriage and the Family* 53, 545–55.

Sandler, J. (1987) *From safety to superego*, New York: Guilford Press.

Santrock, J. W., Warshak, R. A., and Elliott, G. L. (1982). "Social development and parent–child interaction in father-custody and stepmother families" in M. E. Lamb (ed.) *Nontraditional families: Parenting and child development*, Hillsdale, NJ: Erlbaum.

Sarigiani, P. A. (1987) "Perceived closeness in relationship to father: Links to adjustment and body image in adolescent girls" paper presented at the Biennial Meeting of the Society for Research in Child Development (April), Baltimore, MD.

Schatzman, M. (1973) *Die Angst vor dem Vater. Langzeitwirkungen einer Erziehungsmethode. Der Fall Schreiber*, Hamburg: Rowohlt.

Scheib, A. and Laub, G. (1994) *Dein wahrhaft sorgfaeltiger Vater – Briefe an Kinder*, Cologne: Middelhauve.

Schiefelbein, S. (1979) "Children with cancer: New hope for survival" *Saturday Review* 14, 11–16.

Schiff, H. S. (1972) *The bereaved parent*, New York: Crown.

Schorsch, A. (1979) *Images of childhood*, New York: Mayflower Books Inc.

Schulman, G. L. (1972) "Myths that intrude on the adaptation of the stepfamily" *Social Casework* 49, 131–9.

Schulz, A. (1991) "Das Körperbild weiblicher Jugendlicher und seine Auswirkungen auf Erleben und Verhalten" unpublished diploma thesis, University of Bonn.

Scott, R. L. and Flowers, J. V. (1988) "Betrayal by the mother as a factor contributing to psychological disturbance in victims of father–daughter incest: An MMPI analysis" *Journal of Social and Clinical Psychology* 6, 147–54.

Seginer, R. (1985) "Family learning environment: the subjective view of adolescent males and females" *Journal of Youth and Adolescence* 14, 121–31.

Seiffge-Krenke, I. (1986) *Psychoanalytische Therapie Jugendlicher*, Stuttgart: Kohlhammer.

—— (1990) "Developmental process in self-contempt and copying behavior" in H. Bosma and S. Jackson (eds) *Self-Concept and Copying in Adolescence*, New York: Springer.

—— (1994) *Gesundheitspsychologie des Jugendalters*, Göttingen: Hogrefe.

—— (1995) *Stress, Coping and Relationships*, Hillsdale, NJ: Erlbaum.

Seiffge-Krenke, I. and Brath, K. (1990) "Krankheitsverarbeitung bei Kindern und Jugendlichen" in I. Seiffge-Krenke (ed.) *Jahrbuch für Medizinische Psychologie* (Vol. IV: 3–24), Berlin: Springer.

Seiffge-Krenke, I., Boeger, A., Schmidt, C., Kollmar, F., Floss, A., and Roth, M. (1996) *Chronisch kranke Jugendliche und ihre Familien – Belastung, Bewältigung und psychosoziale Konsequenzen*, Stuttgart: Kohlhammer.

Selman, R. L. (1980) *The growth of interpersonal understanding: Developmental and clinial analyses*, San Diego, CA: Academic Press.

Shinn, M. (1978) "Father absence and children's cognitive development" *Child Development* 43, 455–69.

Shopper, M. (1969) "Toiletry revisited: An integration of developing concepts and the father's role in toilet training" in S. H. Cath, A. Gurwitt, and L. Gunsberg (eds) *Fathers and their families*, Hillsdale, NJ: The Analytic Press.

Shulman, S. (1990) "Körperlich behinderte und chronisch kranke Kinder: Familiäres Coping und Anpassung. Eine systemische Perspektive" in I. Seiffge-Krenke (ed.) *Jahrbuch der Medizinischen Psychologie*, Vol. IV: *Krankheitsverarbeitung bei Kindern und Jugendlichen* (173–85), Berlin: Springer Verlag.

Shulman, S. and Klein, M. M. (1982) "The family and adolescence: A conceptual and experimental approach" *Journal of Adolescence* 5, 219–34.

—— (1983) "Psychological differentiation, self-concept, and object relations of adolescents as a function of family consensual types" *Journal of Nervous and Mental Disease* 171, 734–41.

Shulman, S. and Posen, Y. (1992) "The distinctive role of the father in adolescent separation-individuation" paper presented at the Fourth Biennial Meeting of the Society for Research on Adolescence (March), Washington, DC.

Shulman, S., Becker, A., and Sroufe, L. A. (1992) "Child–mother, child–adult and child–child relationships in a cooperative nursery school as related to mother's history and child's attachment" final research report submitted to the US–Israel Binational Science Foundation, Jerusalem.

Shulman, S., Collins, W. A., and Dital, M. (1993) "Parent–child relationships and peer-perceived competence during middle childhood and preadolescence in Israel" *Journal of Early Adolescence* 31, 204–18.

Siegal, M. (1987) "Are sons and daughters treated more differently by fathers than by mothers?" *Developmental Review* 7, 183–209.

Siegelman, M. (1965) "Evaluations of Bronfenbrenner's questionnaire for children concerning parental behavior" *Child Development* 36, 163–74.

Silbereisen, R. and Noack, P. (1990) "Adolescents' orientations for development" in H. Bosma and S. Jackson (eds) *Coping and self-concept in adolescence*, Berlin: Springer Verlag.

Silverberg, S. B. and Steinberg, L. (1990) "Psychological well-being with early adolescent children" *Developmental Psychology* 26, 658–66.

Simmons, R. G. and Blyth, D. A. (1987) *Moving into adolescence: The impact of pubertal change and school context*, New York: Aldine de Gruyter.

Sinnema, G. (1986) "The development of independence in chronically ill adolescents" *International Journal of Adolescent Medicine and Health* 2, 1–14.

Sirles, E. A., Smith, J. A., and Kusama, H. (1989) "Psychiatric status of intrafamilial sexual abuse victims" *Journal of the American Academy of Child and Adolescent Psychiatry* 28, 225–9.

Smetana, J. G. (1989) "Adolescents' and parents' reasoning about actual family conflicts" *Child Development* 60, 1052–67.

Smith, J. H. (1994) "Equality and difference" in J. H. Smith and A. M. Mahfous (eds) *Psychoanalysis, feminism and the future of gender*, Baltimore, MD: Johns Hopkins University Press.

Smith, P. K. and Bulton, M. (1990) "Rough and tumble play, aggression and dominance: Perception and behavior in children's encounters" *Human Development* 33, 271–82.

Smith, T. E. (1989) "Mother–father differences in parental influence on school grades and educational goals" *Sociological Inquiry* 59, 88–98.

Snarey, J. (1993) *How fathers care for the next generation*, Cambridge, MA: Harvard University Press.

Spiegelman, A. and Spiegelman, G. (1991) "The relationships between parental divorce and the child's body boundary definiteness" *Journal of Personality Assessment* 56, 96–105.

Spitz, R. A. (1957) *Nein und Ja. Die Ursprünge der menschlichen Kommunikation*, Stuttgart: Klett.

Spruiell, V. (1975) "Narcissistic transformations in adolescence" *Journal of Psychoanalytic Psychotherapy* 4, 518–36.

Sroufe, L. A. and Fleeson, J. (1986) "Attachment and the construction of relationships" in W. W. Hartup and Z. Rubin (eds) *Relationships and development*, Hillsdale, NJ: Erlbaum.

Sroufe, L. A. and Rutter, M. (1984) "The domain of developmental psychopathology" *Child Development* 54, 173–89.

Sroufe, L. A., Bennet, C., Eglund, M., Urban, J., and Shulman, S. (1993) "The significance of gender boundaries in preadolescence: Contemporary correlates and antecedants of boundary violation and maintenance" *Child Development* 64, 455–66.

Staller, R. J. (1975) *Perversion. Die erotische Form von Hass*, Hamburg: Rowohlt.

Steinberg, L. (1981) "Transformations in family relations at puberty" *Developmental Psychology* 17, 833–40.

—— (1987a) "Impact of puberty on family relations: Effects of pubertal status and pubertal timing" *Developmental Psychology* 23, 451–60.

—— (1987b) "Single parents, step-parents, and the susceptibility of adolescents to antisocial pressure" *Child Development* 38, 269–75.

—— (1988) "Reciprocal relations between parent–child distance and pubertal maturation" *Developmental Psychology* 24, 122–8.

Steinberg, L. and Silverberg, S. (1986) "The vicissitudes of autonomy in early adolescence" *Child Development* 57, 841–51.

Steinberg, L., Mounts, N., Lamborn, S. and Dornbusch, S. (1991) "Authoritative parenting and adolescent adjustment across various ecological niches" *Journal of Research on Adolescence* 1, 19–36.

Steinglass, P. (1978) "The conceptualization of marriage from a system theory perspective" in T. J. Paulino and B. S. McGrady (eds) *Marriage and marital therapy*, New York: Brunner/Mazel.

Stern, P. N. (1978) "Stepfather families: Integration around child discipline" *Issues in Mental Health Nursing* 1(2), 50–6.

Stierlin, H. (1974) *Separating parents and adolescents*, New York: Quadrangle, The New York Times Book Co.

Stocker, C. M. and McHale, S. M. (1992) "The nature of family correlates of preadolescents' perceptions of their sibling relationships" *Journal of Social and Personal Relationships* 9, 179–95.

Straus, M. A. (1979) "Measuring intrafamily conflict and violence: The conflict tactics (CT) scales" *Journal of Marriage and the Family* 41, 75–88.

Straus, M. A., Gelles, R. J., and Steinmetz, S. K. (1980) *Behind closed doors: Violence in the American family*, Garden City, NY: Anchor.

Strozier, C. B. and Cath, S. H. (1989) "Lincoln and the fathers: reflections on idealization" in S. H. Cath, A. Gurwitt, and L. Gunsberg (eds) *Fathers and their families*, Hillsdale, NJ: The Analytic Press.

Suomi, S. J. (1990) "Primate models of hormonal-behavioral changes in adolescence" paper presented at the Third Biennial Meeting of the Society for Research on Adolescence (March), Atlanta, GA.

Tatar, R. E., Blackson, T. C., Martin, C. S., and Loeber, R. (1993) "Characteristics and correlates of child discipline practices in substance abuse and normal families" *American Journal of Addictions* 2, 18–25.

Tessman, L. H. (1982) "A note of father's contribution to his daughter's way of loving and working" in S. Cath, A. R. Gurwitt, and J. Ross (eds) *Father and child: Developmental and clinical perspectives*, Boston: Little, Brown.

—— (1989) "Fathers and daughters, early tones, later echoes" in S. H. Cath, A. Gurwitt, and L. Gunsberg (eds) *Fathers and their families*, Hillsdale, NJ: The Analytic Press.

Thies, J. M. (1977) "Beyond divorce: The impact of remarriage on children" *Journal of Clinical Child Psychology* 6, 59–61.

Thomas, A. and Chess, S. (1977) *Temperament and development*, New York: Brunner/Mazel.

Tinbergen, N. and Iersel, J. J. A. Van (1947) "Displacement reactions in the three-spined stickleback". *Behaviour* 1, 56–63.

Tobin-Richards, M. H., Boxer, A. M., and Petersen, A. C. (1983) "The psychological significance of pubertal change: Sex differences and social significance" in J. Brooks-Gunn and A. C. Peterson (eds) *Girls at puberty: Biological and psychosocial perspectives*, New York: Plenum.

Truscott, D. (1992) "Intergenerational transmission of violent behavior in adolescent males" *Aggressive Behavior* 18, 327–35.

Trute, B. and Hauch, C. (1988) "Building on family strength: A study of families with positive adjustment to the birth of a developmentally delayed child" *Journal of Marital and Family Therapy* 14, 185–93.

Uddenberg, N., Engelsson, I., and Nettelbladt, P. (1979) "Experience of father and later relations to men: A systemic study of women's relations to their father, their partner, and their son" *Acta Psychiatrica Scandinavica* 59, 87–96.

Udry, J. R. and Billy, J. O. (1987) "Initiation of coitus in early adolescence" *American Sociological Review* 52, 841–55.

US Bureau of the Census (1985) *Household and family characteristics: March 1984* (Current Population Report, series P-20, No. 398), Washington, DC: US Government Printing Office.

Visher, E. B. and Visher, J. S. (1979) *Stepfamilies: A guide to working with stepparents and stepchildren*, New York: Brunner/Mazel (also in paperback under the title *Stepfamilies: Myths and realities*, Secaucus, NJ: Citadel Press).

—— (1988) *Old loyalties, new ties*, New York: Brunner/Mazel.

Vogt, J. (1984) "Interaction between adult males and infants in prosimian and New World monkeys" in T. Taub (ed.) *Primate paternalism*, New York: Van Nostrand Reinhold.

Vuchinich, S. (1987) "Starting and stopping spontaneous family conflicts" *Journal of Marriage and the Family* 49, 591–601.

Wallerstein, J. S. and Blakeslee, S. (1989) *Men, women and children a decade after divorce*, New York: Tickner & Fields.

Wallerstein, J. S. and Kelly, J. B. (1980) *Surviving the break up: How children and parents cope with divorce*, New York: Basic Books.

Walters, M. (1989) "The different faces of close" in M. Walters, B. Cater, P. Papp, and O. Silverstein (eds) *The invisible web. Gender patterns in family relationships*, New York: Guilford Press.

Waterman, A. (1985) "Identity in adolescence: Processes and contents" *New Directions for Child Development* 18, 12–21.

Waters, E., Vaughn, B. E., and Egeland, B. (1980) "Individual differences in infant–mother attachment relationships at age one: Antecedents in neonatal behavior in an urban economically disadvantaged sample" *Child Development* 51, 203–16.

Watzlawick, P., Weakland, J. H., and Fisch, R. (1974) *Lösungen*, Bern: Huber.

Weinberger, D. A. (1994) "Relations between parents' distress and self-restraint and adolescents' adjustment" paper presented at the Fifth Biennial Meeting of the Society for Research on Adolescence (February), San Diego, CA.

Weitzman, M. (1984) "School and peer relations" *Pediatric Clinics of North America* 31, 59–69.

Wellisch, E. (1954) *Isaac and Oedipus: Study in the biblical psychology of the sacrifice of Isaac – the Akedah*, London: Routledge & Kegan Paul.

Wenzel, S. (1990) "Jungensexualität – Mädchensexualität. Gibt es das?" in N. Kluge (ed.) *Jugendsexualität: ein Tagungsbericht* (79–87), Frankfurt a.M.: Dipa.

White, L. A. (1948) "The definition and prohibition of incest" *American Anthropologist* 50, 416–35.

White, L. K. and Booth, A. (1985) "The quality of stability of remarriages: The role of stepchildren" *American Sociological Review* 50, 689–98.

Whitten, P. (1986) "Infants and adult males" in B. Smuts (ed.) *Primate societies*, Chicago: University Press of Chicago.

Wick, S. C. (1981) "Child abuse as causation of juvenile delinquency in central Texas" in R. J. Hunner and Y. E. Walker (eds) *Exploring the relationship between child abuse and delinquency* (233–9), Montclair, NJ: Allanheld, Osmun.

Widom, C. S. (1989) "Does violence beget violence? A critical examination of the literature" *Psychological Bulletin* 1, 3–28.

Wieland, C. (1991) "Beauty and the beast: The father's unconscious and the riddle of femininity" *British Journal of Psychotherapy* 8, 131–43.

Willbern, D. (1989) "Filia Oedipi: Father and daughter in Freudian theory" in L. E. Boose and B. S. Flowers (eds) *Daughters and fathers*, Baltimore, MD: The Johns Hopkins University Press.

Wilson, J. Q. and Herrnstein, R. J. (1985) *Crime and human nature*, New York: Simon & Schuster.

Wingerson, N. (1992) "Psychic loss in adult survivors of father–daughter incest" *Archives of Psychiatric Nursing* 4, 239–44.

Winnicott, D. W. (1965) *The maturational process and the facilitating environment: Studies in the theory of emotional development*, New York: International Universities Press.

——— (1969) "The use of an object" *International Journal of Psycho-Analysis* 50, 711–16.

Wolfe, D. A. (1985) "Child-abusive parents: An empirical review and analysis" *Psychological Bulletin* 97, 462–82.

Wynne, L. C., Rycoff, I. M., Day, J., and Hirsch, S. I. (1958) "Pseudomutuality in the family relations of schizophrenics" *Psychiatry* 21, 205–20.

Yogman, M. (1982) "Observations on the father–infant relationships" in S. H. Cath, A. Gurwitt, and J. M. Ross (eds) *Father and child*, Boston, MA: Little Brown.

Youngsblade, L. M. and Belsky, J. (1995) "From family to friend: Predicting positive dyadic interaction with a close friend at five years of age from early parent–child relations" in S. Shulman (ed.) *Close relationships and socio-emotional development*, Norwood, NJ: Ablex.

Youniss, J. and Ketterlinus, R. D. (1987) "Communication and connectedness in mother– and father–adolescent relationships" *Journal of Youth and Adolescence* 16, 265–80.

Youniss, J. and Smollar, S. (1985) *Adolescent relations with mothers, fathers, and friends*, Chicago: University of Chicago Press.

Zimen, E. (1971) *Wölfe und Königspudel – Vergleichende Verhaltensbeobachtungen*, Munich: Piper.

Index